Business Cultures in Central and Eastern Europe

Business Cultures in Central and Eastern Europe

Edited by
Milford Bateman

Series editor
Collin Randlesome

Butterworth-Heinemann
Linacre House, Jordan Hill, Oxford OX2 8DP
A division of Reed Educational and Professional Publishing Ltd

 A member of the Reed Elsevier plc group

OXFORD BOSTON JOHANNESBURG
MELBOURNE NEW DELHI SINGAPORE

First published 1997

British Library Cataloguing in Publication Data
Bateman, Milford
  Business cultures in central and eastern Europe
  1. Business enterprises – Europe, Central   2. Business enterprises – Europe,
  Eastern   3. Business enterprises – Political aspects – Europe   4. Business
  enterprises – Government policy – Europe
  I. Title
  338.6'094

ISBN 0 7506 2480 9

Composition by Genesis Typesetting, Rochester, Kent
Printed and bound in Great Britain by Biddles Ltd, Guildford and King's Lynn

Contents

Contributors

Milford Bateman is Senior Research Fellow and Head of the Local Economic Development in Transition Economies Unit in the Russian and East European Research Centre, University of Wolverhampton. His work is mainly concerned with small enterprise policy and local economic development issues in Eastern Europe, particularly with regard to the Yugoslav successor states. He is an active consultant on small enterprise policy issues in Eastern Europe, where he has undertaken major assignments for leading international agencies, such as the International Committee of the Red Cross and ODA, and for East European governments, including those in Croatia, Macedonia and Kazakhstan.

Will Bartlett studied economics at Queens' College Cambridge. He is Reader in Social Economics at the School for Policy Studies, University of Bristol, and Co-ordinator of the Balkan Studies Research Programme for the Centre for Mediterranean Studies, University of Bristol. His research interests include problems of economic transition in south-east Europe and he has carried out research projects for the ESRC East-West Research Programme. His publications include articles on the economic problems of former Yugoslavia and the economics of small business development in Slovenia, Macedonia and Bulgaria.

George Blazyca is Professor and Associate Head of Department in the Department of Economics and Management at the University of Paisley, Scotland. His special interest is Polish economic and business development, on which subject he writes regularly for a number of leading UK based research and consultancy organizations.

Marta Bruno is currently a Research Fellow in the Russian and East European Research Centre at the University of Wolverhampton. She is completing her PhD thesis at the Department of Geography, University of Cambridge. Her research focuses on gender issues and the labour market in Russia with particular attention to Russian women working in the service sector in Moscow. She is also conducting research on gender and rural development in Russia and Central Asia.

Martin Dangerfield is Senior Lecturer in Contemporary European Studies (Economics) in the School of Languages and European Studies, University of Wolverhampton. His main research interests are the contemporary Czech economy and the external dimension of the transformation of East and Central European states. He is also actively involved in the EU's TEMPUS (PHARE) programme as a leader of Joint European Projects, working mainly with partner universities in the Czech Republic and Bulgaria.

Vincent Edwards is Head of Research at the Business School, Buckinghamshire College of Higher Education (a college of Brunel University) and teaches strategic management. He has taught on management development courses in Hungary and has conducted research on managers in eastern Germany, Hungary and Slovakia and on the trading relationships between British small and medium-sized enterprises and Central and Eastern Europe and Russia.

Martin Taylor studied social anthropology at Jesus College, Cambridge. He has worked for the Kazakhstan–UK Centre at the University of Middlesex since 1993, where he undertakes research into political, economic and social developments in Kazakhstan, in particular in the field of inter-ethnic relations and nationalism. He has also worked on various ODA (Know How Fund) sponsored health care reform projects in Kazakhstan.

Acknowledgements

This book was nearly twelve months in the making, longer than I had anticipated, thanks to two sports injuries – a broken leg (tennis) and a torn muscle (skiing) – which necessitated hospitalization and a long period of physiotherapy. The injuries were particularly annoying since they represented my first tennis match after nearly a five-year break, and my first ever attempt at skiing. My apologies to all contributors for having substantially to update their original contributions as a result of my misfortune.

My particular thanks to Neil Malcolm, the Head of the Russian and East European Research Centre (REERC) at the University of Wolverhampton. He made constructive suggestions throughout the writing of the book and, at the end of the writing period, took time out of a very busy schedule to read and comment on several of the chapters. My colleagues in REERC, particularly Marta Bruno and Silke Machold, and in the School of Languages and European Studies, especially Tom Dickins, were supportive on many occasions, offering comments, conversation, hospital visits, assistance with transport and so forth. Jill Woodall was a model of efficiency in dealing with the numerous problems and special requests that arose in putting the book together. Thanks also to Collin Randlesome for the idea for the book and for his encouragement, and to the team at Butterworth-Heinemann for their assistance and patience.

Milford Bateman

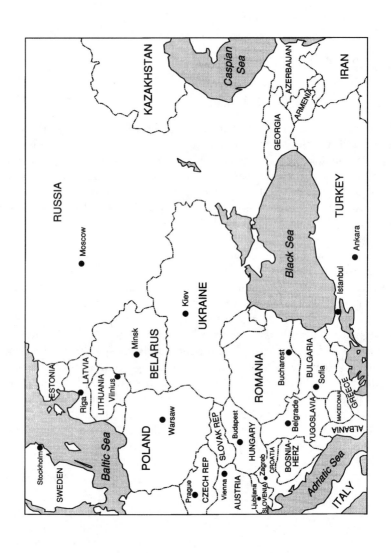

Introduction: the transition towards the market economy

Milford Bateman

Introduction

Since the collapse of the Berlin Wall in 1989, Eastern Europe has undergone the most momentous changes imaginable. A chain of events began in that year which very quickly saw the abandonment of communism, the end of the Cold War, the re-unification of Germany, and the end of the Soviet Union, Yugoslavia and Czechoslovakia. Democratic elections throughout Eastern Europe brought to power a range of governments which had to prepare themselves for the challenge of dismantling the complex administrative, governmental and planning systems associated with communist rule. Moreover, there was also the need to begin to restructure their now post-communist economies upon the principles of the market economy, with the emphasis upon private ownership, entrepreneurship and greater contact with the rest of the world. A new term came into use to describe a post-communist state on the journey towards political democracy and the market economy – a 'transition economy'.

Undeniably, the people of Eastern Europe have benefited greatly from the introduction of political democracy and individual freedom. The new freedoms have led to many economic improvements. The supply of goods and services has increased, where before there was relatively little but cheap and shoddy products on offer, as new opportunities have emerged for everyone to amass wealth through their own hard work and invention and willingness to respond to market signals. Privatization has encouraged a sense of responsibility with capital assets, such as flats and houses, which are now being repaired by their new owners, and greater motivation in the factory under new owners and their appointed managers.

In other respects, however, the change appears to have been far less beneficial. As the East European economies struggle to cast aside their old economic systems, they have simultaneously exposed a great many of their citizens to hitherto unknown problems: joblessness, economic insecurity, fear for the future and despair. The social and industrial infrastructure in many countries has all but collapsed, crime has soared, social tensions have escalated and poverty has spread. Inequality has soared to heights which would have seemed impossible just a few years ago, with a new and ostentatious business elite becoming established in most of the transition economies, in cruel parallel to a growing underclass of working poor. The early hopes of rapid economic progress, and a consequent improvement in general living standards after a few years of the reform, appear not to have been fulfilled. And of those people who have been caught up in the various regional conflicts sparked off by the collapse of communism, very few of them count themselves among the better off.

Several years have now passed since the transition commenced, and it is possible to begin to assess these early, conflicting, and often painful, experiences. In this volume we present studies of several key transition economies. Each is intended to provide a concise account of the principal features of the transition process in one country or region, to outline the main elements of the fledgling market economies which have emerged, and to assess the progress made so far. The studies will also indicate the extent to which progress has been made in the vital process of developing an advanced business culture. Alongside natural endowments, rates of investment, levels of general education and so on, it is generally accepted that the business culture of a society plays a crucial role in determining economic progress and prosperity.[1] Those economies and regions which have flourished in the late twentieth century have in common a business culture which can be broadly described as 'entrepreneurial' – in other words, attuned to the needs of a changing market economy, and receptive to changing demands, innovations, products, opportunities and technologies. This does not just mean that enterprises themselves must be 'entrepreneurial', but also that the surrounding institutional, legal, financial and technical environment must be supportive of entrepreneurship. There must also be a perpective which values both entrepreneurship today, as well as longer term business planning for tomorrow. This implies a creative role for the state in providing a business infrastructure predisposed towards longer run success.

The business culture which developed under the old communist systems can be termed 'bureaucratic-administrative'. It reflected the belief that management of an enterprise was a technical/adminstrative function which could best be undertaken by teams of people, or by a bureaucracy. It may well have had a positive role to play early on in the construction of some communist economies, where the process of industrialization and planning for war required the central allocation of resources to several key industrial sectors, but it became an increasingly anachronistic feature as the economies concerned reached maturity and

---

[1] A business culture is defined as the shared beliefs, attitudes and values held by the population. See, for example, Randlesome, C. (1990) *Business Cultures in Europe*. Butterworth-Heinemann, Oxford.

as the world economy began to change more rapidly. The bureaucratic-administrative business culture neither understood the importance of entrepreneurship, innovation and personal invention, nor did it favour the state supporting industry and enterprise in a constructive, efficiency-enhancing, but necessarily limited, way. As we shall see, the challenge facing those responsible for reform today is to facilitate the transformation of the existing business culture into a modern, entrepreneurial and far-sighted one, in line with their hopes and aspirations for the economy as a whole.

The collapse of communism and central planning

Origins of the collapse

If there was one key political event which precipitated the collapse it was that which took place only some four and a half years before the fall of the Berlin Wall, in March 1985, with the elevation of Mikhail Gorbachev to the leadership of the Soviet Union. Gorbachev embarked on an ambitious reform programme – *perestroika* – which was designed to save the Soviet Union from the decline which stretched back to the 1960s and which was accelerating alarmingly. Gorbachev realized that *perestroika* was necessary to restore popular support for the Soviet regime. As Sakwa (1990) makes clear, *perestroika* was not meant to replace communism, but only to dispatch the most inefficient and inhumane aspects associated with the Krushchev/Brezhnev era to the historical dustbin, just as Krushchev and Brezhnev had in their time abandoned the terror tactics of the Stalin era. As far as the rest of Eastern Europe was concerned, however, Gorbachev differed from the previous generation of Soviet leaders on one critical count: he no longer believed that it was militarily or politically feasible, or indeed desirable, to maintain communism in Eastern Europe if it had to be done so by force. Once this fact was recognized by the populations of Eastern Europe, it was only a matter of time before the Soviet Union would be challenged by those wanting to bring Soviet domination and indeed communism to an end.

This turn of events in Moscow was preceeded by the cumulative failures of an economic and political system first established in the Soviet Union, later to be forcibly adopted under Soviet pressure in its Eastern European satellite states. It was this inheritance, combined with growing resentment at Moscow's domination, that generated the necessary popular pressure which exploded in several countries in 1989 to sweep everything away so quickly. Though the former Soviet Union began the experiment with central planning in 1917 after the coming to power of the Bolsheviks, it was initially seen as a temporary expedient; a necessary policy to win a bitter, and what could have otherwise been a protracted, civil war. By 1921 the planning system was being dismantled and replaced by the New Economic Policy (NEP), which reintroduced substantial private sector activity and a rudimentary market economy. However, this period was to be short-lived. A retreat from the market was signalled in 1928, by Stalin and those around him, who thought that rapid industrialization could only be brought about by strict state control of the main economic levers, particularly investment activity. The private sector was substantially curbed and a comprehensive planning system reintroduced; thenceforth central planning became frozen into the Soviet model of communism. After the Second World War, the Soviet Union, thanks to the Red Army, was able to impose communism upon most of the newly liberated states of Eastern Europe. Each of the East European economies developed its own version of a communist economy, reflecting its own particular economic, political and historical traditions.

It is sometimes overlooked that the experiment with central planning started out quite promisingly for the Soviet Union. It was, after all, able to emerge victorious from a civil war, reconstruct a war-ravaged economy in its aftermath and then rapidly industrialize in the 1930s and early 1940s. It waged a difficult, but ultimately successful war, against the invading Nazis in 1941–45. Shortly after the end of the Second World War, it began to create a massive industrial and military capacity as part of the Cold War, and by the 1950s the Soviet Union was a military super-power. The newly communist countries of Eastern Europe also experienced rapid growth after the war, associated with a burst of reconstruction and industrialization and the efficient movement of agricultural workers into industry. Throughout the Soviet bloc, the 1950s saw industrial production rapidly increasing and living standards reaching new heights. For a time, it seemed as though the principles of central planning might well hold out the promise of real economic progress for humanity, and communism as a model of industrial development was held in high esteem in many of the developing and under-developed countries of the world.

However, this initial success proved to be short-lived. From the early 1960s, but especially in the 1970s, progress began to falter. Increasingly frequent attempts were made to reform the system, but they failed to tackle its essential limitations in comparison with the western market economy model. Moreover, Soviet control over a number of the Eastern European states was slackening. The Yugoslavs had become estranged from Moscow as early as 1948, and left the Soviet bloc. Other challenges to Soviet hegemony and communism, including the Hungarian Revolution of 1956 and the 1968 Prague Spring in Czechoslovakia, failed because of Soviet military intervention. A whole host of partial reforms were put in place in all the Eastern European economies, including in the Soviet Union itself, though they were to have only a marginal impact upon the efficiency of the planning system. By the mid-1970s and during the 1980s, many of the East European economies chose to incur substantial foreign loan commitments in a last desperate effort to requip their by now hopelessly outdated industries. Latterly, it was the the Soviet Union's deliveries of cheap oil and gas which were mainly instrumental in propping up the increasingly enfeebled Eastern European economies. The severe damage to the western economies after the mid-1970s' oil price hikes provided a painful lesson to the Soviets: they had to keep the cheap oil and gas flowing, no matter the opportunity cost to themselves, otherwise the whole Eastern bloc would collapse very quickly. Finally, the increase in mass communication in the 1980s brought home to the populations of Eastern Europe their relative and, what was even worse, increasing relative impoverishment compared to the western democracies.

Economic failures of central planning

There were many economic factors which helped to precipitate the eventual collapse of communism, and many of these will be touched upon in the individual country studies. What follows is a very brief summary.

The first problem of comprehensive planning is that, by definition, it is inflexible, bureaucratic and slow. The various one- and five-year plans which became the mainstay of the majority of the communist countries were extremely complex and detailed. One immediate problem was the difficulty in actually putting them together, in reconciling them mathematically and technically. In practice, the planners could never have hoped to achieve a satisfactory outcome, no matter how much time or computing power was spent on plan preparation. They were unable to collect perfect information or to cater for change in the planning system. Plans were thus redundant almost as soon as they had been produced. 'Unplannable' factors, such as bad harvests, labour unrest, technological advances, and so on, were naturally not incorporated into the plans, though they could have enormous impact on the results. One widespread consequence of the system was that if certain inputs were not of the required standard it was extremely difficult to get replacements; sufficient reserve capacity may not have been incorporated into the original plans, and even if it had been, it was difficult to get hold of it quickly because of paperwork and communications problems. In the Soviet Union this often intractable problem gave rise to the *tolkach*, an unofficial mediator willing to put customers and suppliers together for a fee.[2] Many enterprise managers throughout Eastern Europe, when asked what they most required for effective management, often replied with one word – 'telephones', a reference to the fact that the bulk of their time was spent phoning round other factories and contacts looking for some input needed in order to keep their factory going!

---

[2] For a further explantion of this, as well as an excellent introduction to the economics of the former Soviet Union, see Nove (1987).

Second, plans were formulated according to political priorities, rather than by objective economic criteria. Enterprises were given instructions about what to produce, when and from where they were to receive inputs, and when and where they were to send their outputs. Enterprise managers were effectively administrators and no more. The result of this feature of the system was what came to be known as 'political factories' – industries and enterprises being set up in areas where politicians indicated, but where there was no real economic justification for such a project. Perhaps the most important political priority was the desire to maintain full employment, probably the main feature of the old system which could be held to denote an advantage over the rival capitalist system. Full employment was a consequence of the system of 'extensive development'. This system implied the fullest possible utilization of labour in industry, because it was abundant and cheap, and economizing on capital, because it was scarce. The end result was the substantial over-manning observed in Eastern European industries in comparison to their western counterparts. While this feature may have conferred important social benefits (which appear all the more valuable in retrospect), it led to low productivity and a culture of 'work avoidance'.

Third, slowness and complexity gave rise to a further problem, the very large-scale in-house production of inputs. Enterprises routinely sought to bypass the planning system by gradually taking over the responsibility for the production of inputs, spare parts and replacements. This practice, including so-called 'secondary machine building' (Dmitrieva, 1996), was a very inefficient shortcut because it discouraged specialization and investment in the production of inputs, with the result that the bulk of inputs going in to the production of final goods were of very poor quality, design and specification. Moreover, enterprises naturally began to expand as they produced more and more of their own requirements, and this exacerbated a number of diseconomies of scale already undermining many enterprises.

A fourth problem was described by the Hungarian economist Janos Kornai (1980) using the concept of the 'soft budget constraint'. Kornai concluded that the very lax financial environment within which enterprises operated encouraged poor economic performance. Enterprise managers were appointees of the political authorities, and as such tended to be supported in their activities as a way of ensuring that both communism and communists were seen to be doing a good job. It was important for the legitimacy of the communist system that its representatives appeared to perform well and be efficient. As a result, enterprises were in general not allowed to close or make job cuts: this could be interpreted as evidence that the system was not working as it should. The authorities therefore increasingly had to provide financial support to avoid any such eventuality. Enterprise managers thus lost the incentive to manage efficiently, because they could always demand financial support and pass it off as being necessary on account of systemic malfunction. The result was growing financial dependence on the state and general lack of concern for the costs of production. This had become particularly obvious by the late 1980s.

Fifth, the communist systems enforced isolation from the international community for political reasons. This isolation, which prevailed throughout most of the post-war period, ultimately proved extremely damaging to economic success. Enterprises were shielded behind trade and information barriers. This meant that they were able to avoid encountering foreign competition. Moreover, there was a lack of access to new technologies, partly as a result of a western embargo and partly because of the cost of the technology. The absence of both these factors was extremely debilitating for Eastern European industry: they could have stimulated improvements to production processes, product development policy and all-round quality. Instead, enterprises generally floundered upon a very weak domestic technology base. This was especially evident in the case of consumer goods industries.

A sixth feature, which was especially characteristic of the Soviet Union, but to a degree was a factor in several other communist countries, was the diversion of the bulk of investment resources to the military–industrial complex. For the Soviet Union, Gregory and Stuart (1990, page 408) quote a number of sources of the percentage share of GNP swallowed up by the military, ranging from 12.5 to 15 per cent, compared to figures for the USA of around 5 to 6 per cent. There are a number of measurement problems regarding these comparisons – for example, how to measure 'quality' (American submarines were much better than Soviet ones) – but it is clear that the burden of defence weighed heavily on the Soviet economy. In the other communist economies the burden was created by their own defence spending and also by the sub-contracting they undertook for the Soviet Union. This investment capital was taken from possible alternative uses, such as consumer goods industries, with obvious results.

Finally, given that private ownership was largely anathema to the communist regimes of Eastern Europe, it is not surprising that there was absent the pressure for innovation and technical change conventionally seen as one of the more important dynamic aspects of entrepreneurship. Schumpeter's 'creative destruction' was almost entirely absent in Eastern Europe: instead the industrial structure increasingly ossified, becoming more and more uncompetitive. Part of the problem related to the prevailing bureaucratic-administrative culture, which discouraged change and innovation because of the problems it brought down upon enterprise managers. Possibly more than any other feature of communism, this in-built resistance to change contributed to the decline of the economy in the 1970s and 1980s, just as the western economies were increasingly incorporating technical advances and innovations, and rapidly upgrading production processes in a wide variety of their industries.

Transforming the business culture

It should be clear that one of the most important longer term changes awaited in Eastern Europe is a decline in importance of the bureaucratic–administrative business culture, and its eventual displacement by a flourishing entrepreneurial one. The country studies to follow will each indicate the progress made in developing a market economy and in creating a business culture which favourably underpins business enterprise. At this point, we can briefly note those key factors which are generally considered the essential prerequisites for an entrepreneurial business culture to take root in the transition economies. Four areas are considered to be of prime importance in the first instance.

Private ownership is overwhelmingly seen as the primary factor which will underpin an entrepreneurial business culture in post-communist Eastern Europe. In most of the early writing on the reform process, such as that undertaken by Kornai (1990), the main stress is on the introduction of private ownership. In addition, all the major international financial bodies, such as the IMF and EBRD, as well as governments in the western countries, supported the transformation of ownership as the first step towards a market economy. What was perhaps more at issue was what mechanisms should be used to promote private ownership, whether the focus should be on the privatization of existing state assets or on developing completely new private enterprises ('green-field developments'). Goldman (1994) considered that 'green-fieldization' should be uppermost in the minds of the reformers, especially in Russia, whereas others consider the privatization and dismantling of the state enterprise sector to be the first priority (Blanchard *et al.*, 1991).

Second, a legal framework would have to be created which sustained, but also effectively disciplined, the emerging private business enterprise system. There must, for example, be contract enforcement, including a system for legal redress in the event of non-performance. Legislation should provide for a wide variety of enterprise structures which would reflect the varying requirements of prospective entrepreneurs. The legal framework should also include an effective anti-monopoly policy and the possibility of bankruptcy, in order to ensure as much of the textbook variety of competition between enterprises as possible. Quite apart from conventional dynamic efficiency reasons, such a policy is highly desirable for social reasons. It was envisaged by many that there would remain a high degree of hostility and ignorance towards business enterprise as a result of likely price rises, individual enrichment and perceived profiteering. Even before the reforms, for example in the Soviet Union, the *kooperativ* sector (the first move towards private business), was plagued by association with high prices and local monopolization (Jones and Moskoff, 1991). In general, antipathy towards business enterprise remains quite widespread throughout Eastern Europe. It is a feature which will only dissipate once private ownership has become widespread and real competition exists between private businesses.

Third, the financial system would need to be transformed in order to eradicate financial indiscipline and to enable it to provide genuine support for business. The first priority would be for the old 'soft budget constraints' to be hardened and for enterprises, especially large state-owned or newly-privatized enterprises, to be given the clear signal that they would have to restructure or face bankruptcy. The flow of credit should be diverted to those enterprises showing the most chances of success. This would also involve reform to the banking system. The banks should cease to act *de facto* as state structures simply allocating funds as they were told, often at the behest of the largest state enterprises, and should become genuinely independent organizations, dependent for success on their ability to encourage savings and to lend on to the most profitable projects. In time, an equity market would also need to be established.

Fourth, education and training would be important to bring Eastern European managers and workers closer to the standards of their counterparts in the west. Plans for business schools were one aspect of the retraining programme, together with much more emphasis on business and entrepreneurship in the education system in general. Existing managers with mainly technical training would have to receive a major upgrading of their managerial skills, especially in strategic planning, marketing, quality control and financial management. A greater part of the aid programmes planned for the Eastern European economies were accordingly in the area of education and training, including the establishment of exchange programmes with western universities and other institutions providing training and management expertise.

Conclusion

It is clear that the construction of successful market economies in each of the East European economies will not be accomplished easily: it will, instead, be an exceedingly long and onerous task. The failures associated with communism have left a bitter legacy of industrial neglect, inefficiency and decline. We have outlined some of the general systemic failures which led to economic collapse prior to 1989 and have also pointed to a few of the basic requirements of a reform programme. Such points are a useful guide to facilitating change in Eastern Europe, but they do not represent an easy solution to the many problems currently being encountered, nor have they been able to address the many unforeseen problems of transition. More country-specific problems will be dealt with in the following chapters, including those arising in systems which were substantially different from the Soviet model, as in the former Yugoslavia and Hungary.

A serious obstacle for policy-makers in the transition economies arises from the fact that there were no ready-made theories, and no practical precedents to enlighten them in their attempts to manage the transition process effectively: there has been no previous transition from communism to capitalism. Lessons (positive and negative) can, of course, be learned from other periods of great change and reconstruction, such as post-war Germany and Japan, the rise of the East Asian economies, or the reconstitution of the British economy under the Thatcher Government. It is a vexed question, however, how applicable such experiences are to the transition economies. This is one of the issues addressed by a new branch of applied economics – 'transition economics' – the study of the transformation of a communist system into a market economy.

Business cultures in Eastern Europe are still at an early stage of transition. The existing bureaucratic–administrative business culture fears and is unwilling to contemplate change, and is suspicious of reform and of reformers. This way of thinking, however, is incompatible with survival in the rapidly changing world economy, into which the Eastern European economies are nevertheless seeking to become further integrated. A particular question to be considered in the country studies which follow must therefore be how successful the ex-communist states have been in facilitating the development of the new more entrepreneurial business culture which is essential to the overall success of reform.

References and suggestions for further reading

Blanchard, O., Dornbusch, R., Krugman, P., Layard, R. and Summers, L. (1991) *Reform in Eastern Europe*. MIT Press, Cambridge.

Dmitrieva, O. (1996) *Regional Development: the USSR and After*. UCL Press, London.

Goldman, M. (1994) *Lost Opportunity: Why Economic Reforms in Russia Have Not Worked*. W. W. Norton and Company, New York.

Gregory, P. R. and Stuart, R. C. (1990) *Soviet Economic Structure and Performance* (4th edn). Harper Collins, New York.

Jones, A. and Moskoff, W. (1991) *The Rebirth of Entrepreneurship in the Soviet Union*. Indiana University Press, Bloomington.

Kornai, J. (1980) *The Economics of Shortage*. Amsterdam.

Kornai, J. (1990) *The Road to a Free Economy*. W. W. Norton and Company, New York.

Nove, A. (1987) *The Soviet Economic System* (3rd edn), Allen and Unwin, London.

Sakwa, R. (1990) *Gorbachev and his Reforms, 1985–1990*. Philip Allan, London.

1 The business culture in the Czech Republic

Martin Dangerfield

Introduction

After some five years of reform efforts, many view the Czech Republic (CR) as one of the most successful of the post-communist economies, a 'leader in political stability and economic growth' which, in 1994, 'maintained and solidified its reputation as the first former Soviet bloc nation to be well on the road towards a functioning market economy and a politically stable democracy' (Pehe, 1995, page 29). It is a fact that several of the CR's economic indicators compare favourably with member states of the European Union (EU) let alone the other transition economies against which they should be properly judged. The Czech government has achieved a balanced budget, for example, and, at around 2.9 per cent in mid-1995, the unemployment rate is phenomenally low by any European standard. Economic growth returned after 1993 and was forecast to accelerate from 2.6 per cent in 1994 to around 5 per cent in 1995. The private sector now accounts for some 65 per cent of GDP, generating nearly half of total employment, and no other transition economy is considered to have achieved such a level of de-regulation of economic activity. On the external front, trade with the OECD area (particularly the EU states) has grown substantially; there has been significant progress towards a fully convertible koruna, and Czech firms have begun engaging in foreign direct investment. In November 1995 the country was confirmed as the first post-socialist member of the OECD and full EU membership cannot be too far off. In the political arena, former communists have not re-emerged as a significant political force and popular support for the reform programme remained solid throughout the first half of the 1990s.

As in other former socialist bloc countries, drastic overhaul of the business environment is at the heart of the transformatory endeavour in the CR and, as a result, a new business culture is gradually emerging. A thriving and dynamic business community, operating in the framework of a market economy, is seen not only as the vital prerequisite for economic, social and ecological improvement but also the only reliable basis for lasting political stability and consolidating democracy. The process of establishing a radically different environment for business began, of course, in the setting of the former Czechoslovakia. The following section draws attention to aspects of this heritage together with other important parts of the overall background against which a post-communist business culture is forming.

First we should consider the economic legacy in post-communist Czechoslovakia, which can be interpreted as a mixed one when compared with other transition economies. On the plus side the population's living standards were relatively favourable and a burdensome foreign debt and chronic shortage had largely been avoided. Though its technological level had steadily fallen behind global standards there was still 'extraordinary breadth and scale of Czechoslovak industry: its per capita production in many important products and in aggregate ranked it among the relatively most advanced industrialized producers in the world' (Komarek, 1993, page 59). In addition the country possessed a solid infrastructure of rail and road transport and a well-placed geographical position straddling major north–south and east–west routes in Europe. Disadvantages included the excessive energy and raw material intensity of production compounded by dependency on imports of most major energy and raw material items. Manufacturing industry was also heavily oriented to the ex-Soviet market. There had been virtually no serious experimentation with reforms, leaving the country with no small-scale private sector already in place and state enterprise personnel without even limited experience of market conditions. Finally, the level of industrial activity in the socialist setting had generated massive ecological damage.

Second, the break-up of the federal state, as of 1 January 1993, delayed economic recovery and complicated reform processes in both the CR and Slovakia. The main effects seemed to be a big drop in bilateral trade (a principal cause of the 0.9 per cent fall in Czech GDP in 1993) which was without doubt a setback for Czech producers, the distraction of policy-makers' attention as they focused on managing the dissolution into two separate states, and a delay in implementing the first round of voucher privatization. However, the general impression is that the costs to the CR have only been short-term and more than compensated for by the opportunity to discard the 'baggage' of the economically weaker and less liberally oriented part of the former federal State.

Third, despite the overall turbulence and drama of the post-communist political scene, there has been strong continuity as far as economic management and implementation of reform measures are concerned. The same team has occupied the key economic posts throughout, and Czech economic policies have been a smooth progression of those set in motion between 1990 and 1992. Therefore, in contrast to the other Visegrad[1]

[1] The 'Visegrad' group includes the Czech Republic, Hungary, Poland and Slovakia.

neighbours, the crucial phase of reform was able to progress in a stable political climate. Indeed, surveys taken in 1994 showed that the Czech Republic was the only post-communist state where the new economic system had the approval of the majority of the population (Rose, 1994). Even though the June 1996 general election deprived the coalition that had ruled since the beginning of 1993 of its overall majority (see Business and Government), the population nevertheless remain firmly in favour of the direction *economic* reform policies has taken.

Business and government

Following the 'Velvet Revolution', the 'Government of National Unity' was sworn in on 10 December 1989. Soon after, on 29 December, the country elected a new president, Vaclav Havel. Parliamentary elections held in June 1990 resulted in a resounding win for the Civic Forum (CF) and its Slovak counterpart Public Against Violence (PAV). CF and PAV, holding 170 of 300 seats in the Federal Assembly, formed a coalition government, together with a mixture of Slovak Christian Democrats and independents. A group of academic economists who had developed their economic philosophies while working together at the Institute of Prognosis of the Czechoslovak Academy of Sciences (the main centre of reformist thought in the 1980s) quickly established their positions as the custodians of economic reform. The former head of that institute, the social democratic-leaning Valtr Komarek, was jettisoned from the economic administration after the June 1990 elections, clearing the way for a fast-track transformation programme aspiring to a right of centre model of market capitalism in the US/UK tradition. The eminence of the radical perspective was reflected in the selective implementation of the blueprint for transformation, the 'Scenario for economic reform', approved by the federal assembly on 17 September 1990.

Thereafter the course of political developments was dominated by events which culminated in the division of the federal state. As Batt (1991, page 99) wrote: 'After the elections, it became clear that the federal issue had to take precedence over everything else, and particularly over economic transformation, since the division of the economic powers and resources was at the heart of both issues.' Slovak nationalist politicians protested that the speed of reform was ill-suited to Slovakia and that federal policies, formulated in Prague, were ignoring this. These views had some basis. According to OECD economists (OECD, 1994, pages 44–6) Slovakia suffered from three major disadvantages. First, its industries had been more dependent on former Soviet markets. Second, Bratislava was (and still is) very much less of a magnet for tourists and foreign capital than Prague. Third, Slovakia is not in receipt of the many economic advantages which close proximity to both Germany and

Austria has offered the Czechs. Given the gulf between parties elected by Czech and Slovak voters in the 1992 election (right-of-centre parties in favour of pressing on with fast track economic reforms and left-inclining nationalist parties wanting less extreme policies respectively) the choice facing the Czech and Slovak prime ministers boiled down to this: either the constituent parts of the Federation go their own way or prepare for a parliament disabled by political deadlock. The agreement to separate was confirmed after a meeting between Vaclav Klaus and Vladimir Meciar in Brno during September 1992. The common currency was abandoned on 8 February 1993, sealing the 'Velvet Divorce'.

The political structure of the Czech Republic is defined by the 1993 constitution (ratified 16 December 1992, in operation as of 1 January 1993). This superseded the 1968 federal constitution which itself had been subject to an extensive amendment at the end of 1991. The form of state is a parliamentary republic with branches of government as follows: the president, elected for a five-year term by the legislature, and head of state; an executive branch made up of prime minister and cabinet; a legislative branch being the bicameral National Council (Narodni rada) consisting of an 81-member upper house or Senate (due to be elected for the first time on 15 and 16 November 1996) and a 200-member lower house or Chamber of Deputies elected on the basis of proportional representation; a judicial branch made up of the Supreme Court, Supreme Administrative Court and Constitutional Court. The country is sub-divided into eight administrative regions, of which Prague is one, in turn further divided into seventy-three districts. All citizens aged eighteen or over are eligible to vote.

Results of the 1992 and 1996 elections to the Czech National Council are shown in Table 1.1. The 1992 election took place, of course, in the federal context, so those deputies inherited the mantle of state government after Czechoslovakia divided. This first post-communist Czech government, headed by Prime Minister, Vaclav Klaus, was based on a centre-right coalition including the dominant Civic Democratic Party (CDP), Civic Democratic Alliance (CDA), and Christian Democratic Union-Czechoslovak People's Party (KDU-CSL). The June 1996 general election initially produced political deadlock as the ruling coalition narrowly failed to secure a parliamentary majority and the revitalized Czech Social Democratic Party (CSSD), led by Milos Zeman, emerged as the new power broker in Czech politics.

It can be argued that political stability has the virtue of being something beyond a public good in a transforming country. Strong and popular government reduces the likelihood of policy vacuums and inconsistencies which cause confusion within the business community and generate hesitancy in both domestic and foreign investors. There were no real signs that the strong social consensus in favour of the transformation strategy was under threat until the end of 1994. Unlike much of the rest of East and indeed Central Europe, therefore, former

Table 1.1 *Results of the 1992 and 1996 general elections (Czech National Council)*

Party	Number of seats won in 1992 election	Number of seats won in 1996 election	Change in % of votes received, 1996/1992
Civic Democratic Party/Christian Democrat	72	68	–0.1
Social Democratic Party	22	61	+19.9
Civic Democratic Alliance	16	13	+0.5
Communist Party	10	22	–3.8
Christian Democratic Union-People's Party	24	18	+1.8
Czech Republican Party	5	18	+2.0
Others	28	0	–20.3

Source: The Economist, 8 June 1996, p. 45

communists and indeed leftist parties in general, had not re-emerged as a political force of any consequence. In this context, Vaclav Klaus declared that his country remained an 'island of stability and liberalism in Central Europe following the election of former communists in Hungary'.

Attention therefore became focused on why neo-liberal reform ideology seemed to be a political success in the Czech Republic, whereas it had been rejected in several other post-communist states. The lack of any serious prolonged attempts to change the economic system during the communist period was one obvious advantage, as it meant the population were without any ingrained fatigue of, and lack of faith in, economic reforms. Also, the importance of the country's political culture, specifically the pre-communist traditions of democracy and consensus politics, is often referred to. But in the view of some the major reason was that behind the facade of uncompromising liberalism (the objective, according to self-confessed 'Friedmanite' Vaclav Klaus has been to create 'a market economy without any adjectives') the government's political tactics have been based on blending certain elements of economic liberalism with a far less publicized strategy of interventionism designed to mitigate the negative effects of reform.

Fisher (1994b, p. 31), for example, wrote: 'the reforms can hardly be seen as "Thatcherite", as they have been labelled by Klaus. In fact, the strong hand of government has produced carefully controlled economic reforms that have ensured social well-being and thus contributed to a peaceful political scene. The Czech leadership's success in presenting its vision to the population has also been important: this has contributed to the social consensus for continued reforms that has been lacking in many other countries in the midst of transition.' Orenstein (1994, p. 4) argued that '(f)ive types of policies have enabled the Czech government to maintain popular allegiance to the economic reform. Broadly speaking, these policies are: (1) unemployment control policies; (2) corporatist labour market policies; (3) social safety net policies; (4) reasonably fair and equitable privatization; (5) ideology and attiduinal shaping.' In the same vein, *The Economist* (22 October 1994, p. 26) observed that the Czech government was prone to 'interfere much more in business affairs than it cares to admit, notably by supporting bail-outs for large companies in trouble and by discouraging the calling-in of debts.'

The extent to which Czech government 'interventionism' was instrumental in maintaining the social peace associated with the Czech transition is open to debate, as it is possible to point to some strong neo-liberalist credentials of the Czech government too. What is clear, however, is that the mid 1990s more or less marked the end of the period of consensus as opposition to government policies manifested itself in several ways. A massive anti-government demonstration took place during spring 1995 in Wenceslas Square, organized by leftist groupings. Also, some serious public sector unrest came into the open in 1995 and dragged on into 1996, involving doctors and health workers, teachers and rail workers all disgruntled by public sector pay levels, working conditions and effects of privatization initiatives on their services. Furthermore, officials of the national trade union movement were becoming increasingly impatient with the government's increasingly evident desire to downgrade their input to social and economic policies and the government's apparent reluctance to satisfactorily protect certain disadvantaged social groups, particularly pensioners.

As well as these expressions of dissatisfaction with the government's style and substance, other ammunition for the opposition parties' electoral campaigns included the ruling coalition's failure to establish the Senate and foot-dragging as far as decentralization of the state administrative apparatus is concerned. There was also the question of proved and alleged scandals involving high-level political figures. These issues crystallized into a broader debate over how to create a 'civic society' and highlighted not only differences between the political parties but also the divergent philosophies of the CDP leadership and the president. Finally, the run in to the June 1996 general election took place in the context of some warning signs about economic performance, in particular a trade deficit which had accelerated from $0.4 billion for 1994 to $4 billion for 1995. In June 1995 the *Financial Times* quoted the Trade and Industry Minister as follows; 'Mr Dloughy fears that the Czech economy is losing its competitive edge. "Productivity and microeconomic competitiveness are the main problems," he says' (Financial Times Survey, 2 June 1995, p. 1). Thus the question of whether the Czech Republic is in need of an industrial policy was also an important item on the agenda.

Despite the above, the failure of the ODS/ODA/KDU-CSL alliance to receive a clear mandate to stay in office took most observers by surprise and raises the question of whether the Czech business culture must now prepare for an alternative political climate. As *The Economist* (8 June 1996, p. 45) informs us the 'Czechs did not vote against reform. The coalition actually increased its combined share of the vote from 42 per cent in 1992 to 4 per cent in 1996'. The Social Democrats thrived because they managed to attract most of the votes that last time went to a cluster of fragmented left-wing parties and benefited from the intricacies of the electoral rules and from the ruling coalition's complacency. At the time of writing it was expected that ongoing negotiations would result in Klaus continuing as Prime Minister and heading a minority government. However in 'return for their support of a minority government, the Social Democrats are demanding the post of parliamentary chairman, self-government for the regions, more local government and separation of the government's social-welfare funds from the state budget' (*The Economist*, 8 June 1996, p. 45). If the Social Democrats are faithful to their manifesto, the government will also come under pressure to become more proactive in the sphere of industrial policy.

Whatever its final complexion the next Czech government's main task will be to build on the reforms already introduced so as to ensure that the economy remains on a sound growth path without further endangering the degree of public allegiance to transformation policies. In order to arrive at a clear strategy to resolve the range of economic and social policy dilemmas facing the country the role of the state and other social partners in the economy will have to be clarified. There is no love lost between Mr Klaus and Mr Zeman and whether they are able to work together effectively remains to be seen. The prospect of further elections in the near future should therefore not be ruled out at this stage. To add to the scale of the political task ahead, these domestic challenges must be tackled in the context of the country's attempt to negotiate its path towards full membership of the European Union.

Business and economic reform

The introduction of the package of measures designed to deliver 'shock therapy' to Czech businesses was delayed until more than one year after the political revolution. Nevertheless it is important to note that in 1990 important progress was made in laying some of the foundations for a market economy in Czechoslovakia. As early as January 1990 the interim government introduced a two-tier banking system and unemployment compensation provision. By the end of April the Planning Commission and the Prices Board had been abolished, as had the state monopoly of foreign trade. Other legislation introduced at the same time included a new law on private enterprise – described by Sobell (1990, page 12) as 'certainly one of the most important pieces of economic legislation that the postcommunist government could have formulated ... the new law ensures conditions for the operation of private enterprises in Czechoslovakia essentially comparable to those for western companies' – permitted anyone to set up a private business without limits on number of employees. New legislation on the formation and operation of joint stock companies was also introduced, again approximating western practices, and amendments to the 1988 law on joint ventures greatly enhanced conditions for potential inward investors.

The platform put in place during 1990 needed to be accompanied by a major set of reforms which could unleash market mechanisms and generate competitive pressures. In line with the 'Scenario for Economic Reform' – officially described as 'a rational project for solving the complex problems of the country's economy' (Martin, 1990, page 5) – 85 per cent of retail and wholesale prices were freed from state control on 1 January 1991 and the koruna became convertible for current account purposes. The package also included a 20 per cent import surcharge, tax-based measures to restrict the growth of wages and reinforcement of the social safety net. On the macroeconomic front, the government became committed to a strict anti-inflationary stance, which would override all other macroeconomic goals, based on standard monetarist tenets, i.e. restrictive government budgets and tight monetary policy. Important reforms in the external environment also came into effect on 1 January, namely the suspension of the traditional system for trade and payments between CMEA states in favour of settlement in convertible currencies and application of world market prices.

The relatively balanced and stable state of the inherited economy led to the consequences of the January 1991 steps being labelled a 'minimum bang' (Koves, 1992, page 30). The initial effects on the Czech Republic were nevertheless severe. Inflation rocketed to around 57 per cent in 1991, GDP plummeted by over 14 per cent and industrial production by more than 22 per cent. Unemployment appeared, although at 4.1 per cent it was comparatively mild. The overall effects on the population were hard. Svejnar (1992, page 39) reported that, for Czechoslovakia as a whole, real earnings declined by 26 per cent in 1991, personal consumption by 33 per cent and social consumption by 10 per cent. He also noted that investment, again in Czechoslovakia as a whole, fell by around 20 per cent in 1991 as enterprises cut back in the face of low demand, restrictive monetary policies and uncertainty generated by impending privatization. Recession was more severe in Slovakia, where unemployment reached 11.8 per cent in 1991.

Yet some developments in the first year of the transition were clearly positive. The number of officially registered private companies grew from 124,555 on 1 January 1991 to 891,872 by 1 January 1992, and the number of joint stock companies grew from 658 to 2541 over the same period. What was of possibly more importance than sheer numbers was the structure of new private enterprise development, especially in terms of small and medium sized enterprises. Benacek and Zemplinerova (1995) point out that a high proportion of new private firms have been established in the manufacturing sector, around 10.6 per cent of total manufacturing output in fact. This means that smaller-scale private firms have begun to contribute to indigenous industrial development and are supporting the efficiency improvements sought after by the larger Czech firms through providing a potentially more efficient local sourcing alternative to imports and in-house production learning from Japanese-style total quality management (TQM) techniques.

In addition, though the real wages of the population had been seriously eroded, import liberalization and the growth of the new private sector offered vastly greater choice and quality of consumer goods and services. Though trade with ex-CMEA partners declined strongly, some foreign trade developments were encouraging, most notably exports to OECD states which, already up by 20 per cent in 1990, grew by a further 35 per cent in 1991. The rise in unemployment was far less than the recorded decline in economic activity and the unemployed were generously supported and helped by active labour market policies. Finally, the decline in economic activity was probably in any case overexaggerated by official data, mainly because of the latter's inability to account for the contribution of the new private and informal sectors (see Dyba and Svejnar, 1994, page 10).

After the launch of 'shock therapy', among the main tasks of the Czechoslovak and subsequently Czech government were the need to prevent the negative trends set in motion, particularly inflation, from spiralling out of control, and to ensure that the population were cushioned from the most painful consequences of the measures. In addition, as Minister for Economy Karel Dyba (Dyba and Svejnar, 1994, page 7) has explained: 'The first few years of the transformation have also been the period of building the legal and institutional base for a functioning market economy. This was a tremendous task which is still in the process of being completed. It has required the revamping of a large number of existing laws, drafting and approval of many new laws and statutes, and issuing countless numbers of decrees.'

Some of the main results of legal and institutional aspects of the Czech reform policies are as follows. The private sector is currently generating some two-thirds of GDP and around half of employment. As far as price liberalization and trade are concerned, price controls now apply only to rents, public utilities and public services and there is almost complete de-regulation of exports and imports with a highly liberal import regime (5.7 per cent average tariff) operating. A customs-based system of collecting foreign trade data has been put in place, as has a comprehensive tax system which introduced VAT and rationalized corporation and income tax rates. In addition the Czech National Bank has been endowed with normal central bank powers including setting of interest rates, which have been completely liberalized since April 1992, and supervision of the numerous privately-owned commercial banks who offer the typical range of banking services. After an interval of over fifty years, the Prague Stock Exchange resumed operations on 6 April 1993.

Privatization

If the Czech transformation is indeed more advanced than other fast-adjusting ex-socialist states and is in any way unique then this is because of the privatization experience. Right from the outset the Czech reform team were absolutely convinced that any transformation efforts would be futile unless rapid privatization was built in, since they believed that 'the absence of effective ownership rights was at the heart of the old system's inefficiencies. Right from the start , the consensus in Czechoslovakia was that privatization was necessary' (Takla, 1994, page 155). As a result the 'scenario' incorporated what looked at the time like a highly ambitious timetable for transferring state enterprises to private hands via a mixture of methods and 'extensive privatization became the cornerstone of Czechoslovak and Czech economic transformation from 1990 onward. Apart from East Germany, the Czech Republic has by mid-1994 carried out the most extensive privatization program among the transitional economies' (Dyba and Svejnar, 1994, page 6).

The restitution law passed in October 1990 allowed for property expropriated by the communist regime after 25 February 1948 to be returned to its original owners. By the end of 1992 assets valued at between Kcs 70 and 100 bn had been involved in this process. The Small-Scale Privatization law, passed in November 1990, allowed for shops, hotels, restaurants, small-scale production plants, etc., to be auctioned off or sold to existing lease-holders. Small-scale privatization was terminated at the end of 1993, by which time over 22,000 small businesses, worth in excess of Kcs 30 bn, had been transferred. The Large-Scale Privatization law passed in February 1991, covered some 4000 large enterprises including industrial enterprises, states farms, financial institutions, insurance companies and foreign trade organizations.

Large-scale privatization has so far been administered in two waves, one launched in the federal context in May 1992 and completed in May 1993. In the CR 1900 enterprises were included, with a book value of around Kcs 650 bn. The second round, completed in autumn 1994 involved a further 2000 enterprises, with a book value of Kcs 550 bn. A third wave was scheduled to begin in 1996, to include hospitals and other 'social institutions'. Four methods were used to transfer ownership, including: public tender, direct sales, unpaid transfers (restricted to municipalities, banks or savings banks) and voucher privatization which enabled citizens to receive shares in exchange for coupons purchased for a nominal fee. The Ministry for the Administration of National Property and its Privatization had the basic function of analysing privatization proposals and approving those considered to be the best, and the National Property Fund was charged with carrying out the actual transfers and administering state property entrusted to it. Voucher privatization involved 988 companies in the first wave and 861 in the second. Shares worth Kcs 212 bn and Kcs 155 bn respectively were distributed to the population, either directly or indirectly through the numerous investment funds which now operate.

The Czech government claims that privatization policies have placed 80 per cent of the economy in private ownership. Now that the pivotal aspect of the Czech government's reform strategy has therefore been implemented, where does the reform programme go next? In May 1995 Vaclav Klaus, appearing at a panel discussion on transformation in Eastern Europe declared that he 'would have nothing to say: in the Czech Republic the transformation was finished.' By contrast Jeffrey Sachs, sitting on the same panel, argued that radical action is still needed in order to scale back a still vastly oversized state sector – 'the true legacy that remains from the communist period' (*Central European Business Weekly*, June 2–8 1995, page 3). More neutral assessments stress that the transformation cannot be considered complete until capital and labour markets are functioning correctly and bankruptcies can occur in a routine way. Moreover, there remain doubts over the contribution and activities of some of the investment funds set up to take advantage of the sell-off programme and which obtained assets 'on the cheap'. Some of these assets have ended up in the hands of speculators who may adopt 'slash and burn' policies in order to extract maximum value out of their shareholdings in the short term. One fund – Harvard Capital and Consulting – bought up large stakes in the Czech economy only for part of these shareholdings (worth around $200 million) to pass somewhat surreptitiously into the hands of an American corporate financial group, Stratton Investments, without the markets, stock exchange bodies or virtually anyone else knowing what was happening or being in a position to do anything about it (*Central European* 1996, page 3). The result could be a restructuring phase without regard for the longer term viability of an enterprise, only its immediate share price.

Finally, some important reservations have been expressed over the true extent of privatization. Not only does the government have big stakes in many partially privatized companies, in the form of the shareholding held by the National Property Fund, but also has retained significant indirect involvement. According to Jan Vaneous, President of Planecon, the result may be more a case of 'pseudo' privatization: 'The government has typically a 40 per cent stake in all the major banks. Major banks control the funds, and the funds are the single biggest shareholders in the economy.' (*Central European Business Weekly*, June 16–22 1995, page 2)

The changing legal structure

The legal dimensions of the transforming business culture have so far developed ambivalently. On the one hand the Czech Republic is regarded as being relatively advanced in establishing the essential components of the formal legal framework for a functioning market economy; on the other, a deep-seated disregard for the law is thought to permeate many business activities. Opinion polls carried out in early 1995 indicated that most Czech citizens believed that corruption is widespread at every level of economic and political life (Kettle, 1995) and that a staggering 97 per cent of Czech managers were convinced that their firms were affected by 'dubious business practices' (*Economist*, 11 February 1995, page 47). Statistics put together by the Ministry of Justice seem to add weight to this impression. The total of recorded offences almost doubled between 1990 and 1993 in the Czech Republic, with the majority of this growth having been in the category 'theft, embezzlement, fraud' (from 3919 cases in 1990 to 15,946 in 1993).

Doubts that a business culture is emerging which does not take the law seriously and that enforcement procedures are failing have also been fuelled by a number of high-level scandals which have called into question the ethics and morality of political leaders. Irregularities surrounding party finances have been widely reported, and on several occasions Czech politicians have been accused of taking advantage of largely ineffective laws on conflict of interests. The most spectacular case of abuse of public office involved the former head of the Centre for Coupon Privatization, Jaroslav Lizner, who was arrested on 31 October 1994 and charged with bribery in connection with manipulation of share dealings. Lizner, the highest ranking public official ever to be accused of corruption, was eventually given a seven-year jail sentence and fined Kc 1 million.

The true extent of corruption and other malpractice is of course extremely difficult to assess, especially as judgement is clouded by some important cultural factors. Kettle (1995, page 39) has pointed that the 'distinction between outright corruption and bad practice is not always clear in a country where people love to see a conspiracy behind any apparently simple event'. Also, experiences of other East and Central European transition economies suggest that scandals are inevitable in the transitionary period, and in the Czech Republic they do not represent a general threat to development of democracy and rule of law since, as the *Economist* (11 February, 1995, page 47) argued, they 'probably reflect the country's bursting entrepreneurialism, as much as a breakdown in law and order. What is really unusual in the Czech Republic is that its scandals are financial ones; they are not about murder and mayhem as happens farther East.'

The Czech Commercial Code, which superseded the 1991 Czechoslovak version in 1993, provides the basic legal framework for business and allows for the following business forms: joint-stock company; limited liability; limited partnership; unlimited partnership; co-operative; silent partnership; branch offices of foreign companies. Czech companies are obliged to apply to be entered on the Commercial Register, a public list kept by the relevant district or regional court. The petition for entry onto the Commercial Register must be accompanied by key documents including, for example, leases or contracts for business premises, confirmation the initial capital is on deposit at a bank, local authority approval for the company's location, trade certificate and so on.

The most common business forms are the joint stock companies (*akciove spolecnosti*) and limited liability companies. Limited liability companies may be founded by a single person and must comply with a minimum starting capital requirement, currently 100,000 Kcs. The Code's regulations for joint stock companies are extensive. They cover rules of foundation, acceptable company structures (for example companies with fifty or more employees must ensure that at least one third of the board of supervisors are elected by employees), regulations concerning preference shares, issue of shares to employees (limited to 5 per cent of the value of the capital stock), and issue of bonds (limited to half the value of capital stock), and rules about the roles of foreign nationals.

Under Czech law foreigners can operate businesses according to the same conditions as Czech nationals. Foreign investors are generally not offered any special foreign incentives or other preferential treatment, though the environmental sphere offers one of the few advantages since the Czech National Property Fund will take over liability for past environmental damage in the case of firms where 40 per cent or more of capital is foreign owned. Foreigners with business operations abroad can operate as long as they own an enterprise or branch office in the Czech Republic. In the case of the latter, planned business activities must be fully listed in the petition for entry in the Commercial Register and the company is restricted to those activities. To be eligible to head or act on behalf of a foreign owned company, a foreigner must possess a valid residency permit. Approval for foreign investment is required from the Ministry of Finance only for the defence and or banking/finance sectors or if companies involved are part of the large-scale privatization programme. The latter condition has to be interpreted as one way in which the Czech government can restrict or carefully control foreign involvement in the most profitable sectors (e.g. brewing).

Effective competition and bankruptcy laws are regarded as crucial features of a market economy and are therefore important yardsticks for assessing transformation progress. A 1991 federal competition law was amended in November 1993 in order to achieve further consistency with EU practice by broadening the definition of restrictive practice and raising financial penalties. In its October 1994 *Transition Report* the EBRD described the law as 'rudimentary and ineffectively enforced' (EBRD, 1994, page 22). Though some well-publicized actions against allegedly-colluding coffee companies, (including Douwe Egberts and Tchibo), potato growers and the Pharmaceutical Association in 1994 seemed to indicate an increasingly energetic and assertive Ministry of Economic Competition, they were also interpreted as high-profile easy targets and when the minister, Stanislav Belehradek, proposed easing car import duties to challenge VW/Skoda's dominance of the domestic market '(f)ellow ministers shot the idea down at once' (*Business Central Europe*, November 1994, page 53).

Though the 1991 Bankruptcy and Composition Act was intended to become operational in October of that year, it was deferred twice (until October 1992 and again until April 1993 since when it has applied in both the CR and Slovakia). The various 'special provisions' incorporated in the act in March 1994 which protected insolvent state enterprises, private farmers (until December 1994) and the official intention to delay possible liquidations until after coupon privatization, meant that closure or reorganization of non-viable enterprises effectively could not get underway until after the end of 1994. The Trade and Industry Minister says that '(o)ver 3,000 state owned enterprises are waiting for liquidation. In the meantime they are sucking up subsidies and keeping people inefficiently unemployed.' (*Financial Times*, FT Survey, 2 June 1995, page II).

Business and the economy

The overall profile of the Czech economy reveals a well-developed, diverse and reasonably trade-oriented structure based on a range of industries, an agricultural sector capable of meeting the country's food requirements and a fast-growing services sector. Its principal natural resources are bituminous coal and lignite, uranium, glass sands and kaolin. Crude oil, gas and iron ore supplies must be imported. The transport and communications infrastructure is extensive, if in need of substantial upgrading, with 55,912 km of roads and motorways, 9441 km of railway line, 303 km of navigable waterways and six airports. Agricultural output concentrates on cereals (wheat and barley), sugar-beet, potatoes, hops, grapes, rape-seed and flax. In addition livestock raising (pigs, cattle, poultry) and dairy farming are important. The Czech Republic possesses a host of tourist attractions including cities of historical importance, numerous spa towns with thermal and mineral springs and areas of natural beauty such as the previously closed Sumava

Table 1.2 *Structure of GDP of the Czech Republic in 1994*

Percentage of total GDP generated by individual sectors

Agriculture, forestry, water	3.8
Industry	39.5
Construction	4.8
Transport/communications	5.5
Services and others	32.0
VAT	14.4
Total	100.0

Source: EIU, *Country Report for Czech Republic/Slovakia*, EIU, London, various issues 1994, 1995.

(Bohemian Forest) region. The most important sector, however, remains industry, which is a reflection both of the importance of the CR's pre-communist industrial tradition and its relative efficiency under communism. Presently, the major industries are engineering (industrial machinery, transport equipment), chemicals, metallurgy, food processing, rubber, textiles and glass. Table 1.2 illustrates the extent to which industry is a major feature of the CR.

Over-capacity in heavy industry and aged over-sized plants built to supply now defunct CMEA markets are among the main problems, along with the legacy of low innovation which has degraded the technological level of most branches of the economy. Since 1990 deep structural changes have been occurring in the Czech economy. Table 1.3 illustrates the trends in employment according to sector and provides a clear indication of the scale of decline of not only industrial activity but also mining and quarrying, agriculture and forestry. At the same time the tertiary sector has been growing significantly. In 1994, for example, services grew four times faster than both industrial output and GDP. This reflects not only the relative neglect of services in the communist era but also the country's tourism boom which has provided strong stimulus to the development of the private sector in this sphere. In 1994 both the number of tourists and the amount they spent, at 90.5 million and US$ 2 bn respectively, increased by 26 per cent over 1993. However, at the regional level effects of adjustments are being distributed unevenly, with the Prague area significantly favoured.

Foreign participation in the economy has expanded substantially since the reforms began. CzechInvest data shows that FDI to the value of US$3.47 bn flowed into the country between January 1990 and March 1995, with German (36.4%), US (20.4%) and French (12.3%) firms having the biggest involvement. Most inward investment has gone to the

Table 1.3 *Employment trends in the Czech Republic, 1990–1994*

Number of people employed by branch (thousands)	1990	1991	1992	1993	Index, 1993/1990
Agriculture, hunting, forestry	631	508	425	331	52
Mining and quarrying	186	169	124	111	60
Manufacturing	1760	1705	1582	1511	84
Electricity, gas, water supply	79	75	92	88	111
Construction	403	404	408	453	112
Wholesale and retail trade, repairs of motor vehicles, motorcycles and personal and household goods	524	484	543	609	116
Hotels, restaurants	90	88	101	112	124
Education	317	324	326	324	102
Financial services	28	37	51	65	232

Source: Statisticka Rocenka Ceske Republiky, 1994.

automotive industry (22.5%), consumer goods and tobacco (19.9%), construction (13.8%), banks and insurance (12%) and the food industry (9.2%). Volkswagen's involvement in Skoda Automobilova has been the most high-profile inward investment. Its 70 per cent shareholding was acquired in 1991 at a cost of US$ 972 million and by the year 2000 the total investment will be in the region of $US 3.7 billion. Yet an even bigger deal, involving SPT Telecom, was announced in June 1995. A foreign consortium, including PTT Telecom Netherlands, Swiss Telecom and US AT&T, will pay US$ 1.45 billion for a 27 per cent stake in the Czech phone company, representing the biggest single investment to date anywhere in Central Europe (*Central European Business Weekly*, 30 June–13 July 1995, page 1).

Turning to the macroeconomic environment, by 1994 there were signs that the negative developments of the early phase of the transformation had largely been reversed. Inflation had been brought down to 9.7 per cent by the end of the year, part of an overall highly successful stabilization effort throughout the transformation period. Real GDP grew by 2.6 per cent, and domestic demand was on the increase with growth of 6.8 per cent and 8 per cent for investment and consumption respectively. In this connection, retail sales were up 5.5 per cent and the construction sector recorded a 6.7 per cent increase in activity. Exports grew by 6.7 per cent, including 17.2 per cent and 17.7 per cent increases to the OECD area and EU respectively.

Macroeconomic policy debates during 1995 focused increasingly on the question of when the government should abandon the fixed exchange rate policy. The government has been unsure about such a move because of the advantage an under-valued currency has given to Czech exporters and because of the accelerating trade deficit being caused by a widening gap in the rate of growth of imports and exports respectively. Whilst tourism receipts and capital inflows in particular mean that the Czech balance of payments remains secure for the time being, and machinery and equipment purchases were a significant proportion of growing imports in 1995, trade policy considerations are highly important because of the implications for Czech exporters and unemployment. At the same time, with 'sticky' inflation of around 10 per cent already causing concern, officials at the Czech National Bank (CNB) have argued that the strength of speculative short-term capital inflows in 1995 ($3 billion to the end of May) were continuing to undermine anti-inflation policy by boosting the domestic money supply beyond the extent to which the central bank could absorb them through treasury bill sales. The macroeconomic policy dilemma is further complicated because faltering export growth and surging import demand could cause eventual depreciation of the koruna. As the CNB governor has said, 'We don't know where the long-term market exchange rate equilibrium is' (*Central European Business Weekly*, 9–15 June 1995, page 1).

Foreign trade

Though Czech businesses were somewhat less dependent than Slovak ones (OECD data (OECD, 1994, page 45) for 1992 show that the ex-USSR accounted for 9 per cent of Czech and 17 per cent of Slovak exports) the serious decline in Czech industrial output between 1990 and 1993 was partially attributable to a permanent loss of orders to the former CMEA area. Given that for Czechoslovakia as a whole the growth of exports to the OECD area between 1989 and 1992 was sufficient to compensate for the decline in CMEA trade, the macro-economic consequences of the latter have not proven serious and exports have continued to grow healthily in 1993 and 1994. On the negative side the reduced share of machinery and equipment in exports and expansion of raw material and semi-manufactures has been interpreted as a negative phenomenon in that it suggests degradation of the trade structure. However, we should recognize that this phenomenon largely reflects termination of non-viable sales to the ex-CMEA market. Table 1.4 illustrates the shift in trade away from the ex-CMEA towards the EU.

The main stimuli to the export performance of Czech businesses have been as follows: a very competitive exchange rate; improved market access to West European markets; strong demand in western markets for certain goods available for export during 1990 and 1991; active

Table 1.4   *Macroeconomic indicators and foreign trade breakdown for the Czech Republic, 1990 to 1994*

	1990	1991	1992	1993	1994	1995
GDP	−1.4	−14.2	−7.1	−0.9	2.6	4.8
Industrial output	−3.5	−22.3	−10.6	−5.3	2.3	9.2
Inflation	10.8	56.7	11.1	20.8	9.7	9.0a
Unemployment (%)	0.8	4.1	2.6	3.5	3.4	2.9
Budget deficit	−	−2.1	−0.2	0.1	1.0	0.0
Trade balance	−0.6	−0.5	−1.8	0.3	−0.4	−3.8
Gross debt	8.4	9.8	9.5	8.7	9.2	13.0b
Exports	5.9	8.3	11.5	12.9	14.3	17.1
of which (% share)						
EU	31.4	43.3	52.8	42.7	45.9	55.1
EFTA	9.6	9.0	10.6	8.5	10.2	1.8
ex-USSR	25.1	17.5	8.9	7.2	5.1	6.0
CEFTA	−	−	−	26.0	23.3	23.7
Imports	6.5	8.8	13.3	12.6	14.7	20.9
of which (% share):						
EU	31.9	39.8	47.3	41.5	45.1	56.4
EFTA	12.2	13.3	13.7	12.1	13.1	2.5
ex-USSR	24.3	23.4	18.1	12.1	12.0	10.4
CEFTA	−	−	−	22.1	19.2	17.5

Notes
a Year on year figure as of January 1996
b As of May 1995
Figures in normal type for Czechoslovakia, figures in bold type are for the Czech Republic.
Budget deficit data refers to budget deficit/surplus as % of GDP.
Data for trade balance, debt, total exports and total imports all in $US billions.

Sources: Statisticka Rocenka Ceske Republiky, 1994; Latest Statistical Information: External Trade, various issues; EBRD (1994), Transition Report – 1994, EBRD, London; EIU (1995) Country Report for Czech Republic/Slovakia, 1st Quarter, EIU, London; The Czech Republic in the International Economy, Centre for Foreign Economic Relations, Prague.

pursuit of new sales outlets in Western Europe; and moderate wage growth. The Czech government has so far, much to the disappointment of Czech firms, been slow to respond to calls for a coherent set of export promotion policies on grounds that it is best to leave things to market forces. Some assistance has been materializing gradually, however, including a databank on foreign markets held at the Ministry of Trade and Industry and establishment of the Czech Export Bank, scheduled to begin operating in 1995 (see EIU, 1, 1995, page 21). In addition, the 'Endowment for the Promotion of Czech Products' (a

Ministry of Trade and Industry/Industrial Association initiative founded in October 1993) aims to both support exporters and domestic producers being damaged by liberal import policies. The 'Endowment' aims to help Czech producers overcome traditional problems in the areas of public relations, product/packaging design, and advertising. It is also trying to convince the population that many Czech products (particularly those that carry the 'Czech Made' trademark awarded to selected products by the CR Quality Award Association) are better value purchases than the imported ones automatically assumed to be superior.

International trade agreements are, of course, instrumental in enabling the CR to maintain and profit from open-door trade policies. The trade chapter of the European Agreement (EA), in force since March 1992, provides for the establishment of free trade with EU states within ten years. These agreements are theoretically advantageous to the CR because of asymmetrical tariff removal timetables but attention is often drawn to restricted access for sectors of particular importance for all the EA countries, including steel, chemicals, textiles and agricultural products. The most important export commodities in trade with the EU during 1994 were manufactured goods classified by materials (34%), machinery and transport equipment (23.7%), miscellaneous manufactures (16.9%) and chemicals (9.8%). Over half of Czech exports to the EU go to Germany.

The Central European Free Trade Agreement (CEFTA), effective from 1 April 1993, commits the CR, Hungary, Poland and Slovakia to establishing free mutual trade by 1 January 1998. All CEFTA members also have free trade agreements with Slovenia, which became the fifth member on 1 January 1996, after which Bulgarian and Romanian accession should follow. The most important export commodities in Czech trade with CEFTA states during 1994 were manufactured goods classified by materials (26.8%), machinery and transport equipment (25.3%), chemicals (16.2%), fuels and lubricants (11.3%) and miscellaneous manufactures (9.1%). Whilst exports to Hungary (+25%) and Poland (+49%) grew very dynamically in 1994, exports to Slovakia fell 19 per cent, affecting mainly exports of consumer goods, foodstuffs, food products and machinery and equipment.

According to Czech specialists, the ongoing decline in Czech–Slovak trade reflects 'persisting consequences of the establishment of the two countries . . . coupled with certain restrictions which were, on the Slovak side, of an anti-import nature with respect to the CR . . ., slackened demand at the markets of both countries (due to continued low demand for capital goods), by the weakening of co-operative linkages and by increased foreign competition' (CFER, May 1995, page 67). Whilst the Czech government's July 1995 decision to cancel the ECU-denominated clearing agreement with Slovakia is not expected to disadvantage Czech producers further, the timing of the move to full currency convertibility and the impact on the exchange rate of the koruna is likely to have significant implications for businesses' immediate prospects in foreign (and domestic) markets.

Business and finance

The Czech National Bank (CNB), founded on 1 January 1993 out of the remnants of the former Czechoslovak State Bank (CSB), is legally autonomous and empowered to carry out all normal central bank functions. The impressive degree of financial and monetary stability in the CR is testament to the highly professional skills of the CNB's founding president and current chief, Josef Tosovsky (who had been head of the CSB since December 1989 – another important element of continuity in economic policy-making) and close co-operation between bank officials and government ministers. It is usual for the governor of the CNB to sit in on cabinet meetings. The typical conflict between cautious central banker and ministers pressing for fiscal and monetary excess (as in Russia and Poland, for example) is thought to have been avoided because Tosovsky, Klaus and Finance Minister Ivan Kocarnik share the same philosophy on monetary and fiscal issues.

Around sixty commercial banks operate in the CR at present, most of which offer a range of products including foreign exchange operations, trade promotion, stock market services as well as the standard loan and transaction facilities. Over half of banks have foreign involvement. Because of the dominance of the 'big-four' Czech banks – Investicni Banka, Komercni Banka, Ceskoslovenska Obchodni Banka and Ceska Sporitelna, who between them accounted for 78 per cent of all deposits and 73 per cent of all loans in 1994 – the Czech banking system has been described as 'deeply dysfunctioning' (*Financial Times*, FT Survey, 2 June 1995, page IV). There are suspicions that a cartel arrangement is enabling each bank to maintain monopolies over their specific markets. For small banks interested in corporate business, lending opportunities shunned by the big four have often been the only option, increasing the likelihood of unwise lending decisions. Other problems include absence of a medium-sized banking tier, charges that investment funds owned by Investicni, Komercni and Sporitelna have been preventing executives of the leading enterprises they control taking advantage of more competitive sources of finance and, because of lack of competition the investments in new technology, premises and staff have not generated a major improvement in service.

Following the collapse of three banks in 1994 – AB Banka, Kreditini a Prumyslova Banka and Banka Bohemia – the CNB suspended the granting of new licences, tightened supervision and enhanced its powers of intervention. It also raised the minimum capital requirement to Kcs 500 million as part of its policy of encouraging smaller banks to merge into larger units. Also, anti-monopoly legislation in force since February 1995 restricts the shares of Sporitelna and Komercni to 30 per cent of the deposit and loan markets respectively (*Transition*, Jan–Feb 1995, page 9). While there is optimism that these measures will help correct many existing problems in the banking system, the big four's reluctance to initiate bankruptcy proceedings against companies heavily indebted to them remains a cause for concern, especially since they now actually have large shareholdings in many such companies. This conflict of interest must be resolved if the Czech banking sector is to fulfil the crucial role of switching capital from the stagnant or non-viable sectors of the economy to the dynamic ones.

Securities are traded on both the now three-tier Prague Stock Exchange (PSE) and through the 'RM-S' system, an over-the-counter dealing arrangement through which individuals and companies can buy and sell shares at some 350 share shops throughout the country. The Czech stock market is the biggest in Central Europe in terms of the number of companies floated (over 1600) and its capitalization, close to 30 per cent of Czech GDP. However a mixture of a flooded market, insufficient transparency, outdated securities law (failure to honour deals is common), high brokerage and transaction fees, and capital gains tax disadvantages has resulted in low turnover and a generally illiquid market. Consequently the securities market fails in its most important tasks: 'the stock exchange has been of little use to companies trying to raise investment capital through public offerings ... while the (investment) funds hold claim to pre-existing capital, they lack the resources to inject new money for capital-intensive restructuring' (Harrison, 1995, page 28). In June 1995, share prices slumped to around a third of their late 1993 peak, though many commentators were optimistic that new securities laws being prepared for probable introduction in 1996 would have positive effects. Among the proposals being considered was a controversial ban on off-market trading, stricter penalties for insider dealing and linking the move to a three-tier PSE with much tighter information disclosure requirements for top-tier companies.

Taxation

A comprehensive tax overhaul was introduced on 1 January 1993, the most important features of which were as follows. Basic VAT rates are 22 per cent for goods and 5 per cent for services. Some goods are currently subject to a 5 per cent rate (books, medicines) while some services attract the 22 per cent rate (hotels, restaurants tourism). Businesses with turnover in excess of $US27,300 in three successive months must register for VAT. Exports are exempt. Consumption tax of varied amounts is levied on both domestically produced and imported hydrocarbon fuels and lubrications, spirits and liquors, beer, wine and tobacco. The basic rate of corporate tax, irrespective of whether the company is Czech or foreign-owned, is 41 per cent (lowered in 1996 to 39 per cent) with a range of deductible (e.g. social security contributions, environment-related expenditures) and non-deductible (e.g. entertainment, directors' fees) items. Some incomes, mainly related to environment-improving activities such as operation of wind-power plants or facilities for production of bio-degradable products, are tax-exempt.

Personal income tax rates are progressive, ranging from 15 per cent to 44 per cent (lowered in 1996 to 40 per cent). Incomes in excess of Kcs 1.08 million per annum attract the highest rate. Individuals residing in the CR for 183 days or more in a calendar year must pay tax on total income. Personal allowances for 1995 were 24,000 Kcs for each taxpayer plus 12,000 Kcs for each child and 12,000 Kcs for the taxpayer's spouses not earning more than 24,000 Kcs per annum. Social security contributions are tax-deductible, as are certain other items such as gifts to support humanitarian or environmental activities. Other important taxes levied are road tax on private and business users, immovable property tax on land and buildings and inheritance, gift and immovable property transfer tax.

Business, the labour market and trade unions

Looking at the basic demographic data first, the Czech population, at 10,362,740, was at its post-war peak in 1990. After a slight fall in 1991 (−0.52 per cent) the number of inhabitants has been static with only very modest increases, between 0.001 and 0.1 per cent, recorded for 1992, 1993 and 1994. The effects of improving infant mortality and life expectancy rates over this period appear to have been offset by population outflows (a net migration of 6995 people between 1990 and 1992). The proportion of females has been consistently higher (51.5 per cent of total) over the whole of the post-war period. At the end of 1993, 50.3 per cent of the population were classed as economically active, of which 5.2 per cent (272,719 in total) were of 'post-productive age' (55 and over for women, 60 and over for men). Recent trends have been positive as far as growth of working age population is concerned, but, as elsewhere in the former socialist area, the labour force participation rate has dropped sharply since 1989.

The basic labour market patterns have been significantly disrupted over the past few years, as would be expected. As Table 1.3 demonstrated, manufacturing industry, mining and quarrying and agriculture/hunting/forestry were by 1993 employing considerably fewer workers than in 1990, while employment in construction and more

Table 1.5 *Regional comparison of unemployment and vacancies in the Czech Republic (as of end October 1994)*

	Unemployment %	Vacancies	Persons on unemployment benefit	No. of blue collar workers registered for job vacancies
Czech Republic	3.08	79 480	76 812	104 098
Prague	0.30	15 316	1098	764
Central Bohemia	2.76	8955	8589	9384
South Bohemia	2.10	6519	4476	4847
West Bohemia	2.13	8045	4367	6133
North Bohemia	4.26	7525	10 515	16 853
East Bohemia	2.43	11 892	8297	9048
South Moravia	3.10	10 513	16 517	20 054
North Moravia	5.51	10 715	22 953	37 015

Source: Monthly Statistics of the Czech Republic, No. 1, 1995.

notably services had expanded rapidly. Employment in financial ser-vices has grown particularly impressively, up 132 per cent over the same period. The rate of unemployment peaked at 4.1 per cent in 1991and has been on a general downward trend since, though there was a slight move upwards in 1993 following loss of sales to Slovakia. The regional breakdown of unemployment is illustrated in Table 1.5 and shows the striking contrast between Prague, with just 0.3 per cent unemployment, and other parts of the country. North Moravia has the highest rate, though 5.5 per cent indicates only relatively mild unem-ployment as yet. Female unemployment is 1.75 times that of males at the national level and higher in every region. In terms of educational profiles, graduates and those who attended full secondary schools have been least prone to unemployment, while the age profile of the jobless shows younger people have been most seriously affected. Unemploy-ment amongst the 15–19 year-olds is four times greater than the national average and twice as high among 20–24 year-olds.

The unemployment figures cited in Table 1.5 are based on data from the unemployment register which is, of course, only one of several measures. Yet survey unemployment, even when augmented to include 'discouraged' workers, has not been significantly higher and has been steadily converging with registered unemployment since the beginning of 1993. A major OECD survey of the Czech labour market (OECD, 1995) has attributed the 'Czech unemployment miracle' to three major factors. First, there has been a more significant decline in labour force participation, in part brought about by policy measures designed to 'push' those losing jobs out of the labour force (including more liberal access to early retirement and disability pensions together with forced retirement of working pensioners). Second, there has been an effective degree of wage moderation and, consequently, slower recovery of real wage falls than in Hungary and Poland. Interestingly, the Czech government's wage control policies (until the termination of this policy in July 1995, for firms employing 25 or more, annual wage increases more than inflation plus 5 per cent attracted punitive taxes for enterprises) are not thought to be a significant cause of this. Third, the inherited structure of employment and particularly the relatively low share of agricultural employment.

Bankruptcy prevention and exchange rate policy may have also served to protect employment and the rapid expansion of new private sector businesses, especially in the Prague area, has made an important contribution. In addition, amendments to unemployment benefit entitlements have lowered incentives to register as unemployed. The original provisions of the Unemployment Compensation Scheme introduced in January 1990, which entitled most laid off workers to 90 per cent of their previous earning for the first six months of joblessness, were interpreted as dangerously generous and amended in August 1990 and again in January 1992. The entitlement period is now six months and claimants can receive 60 per cent of previous earnings for the first three months and 50 per cent thereafter.

The Czech government's labour market programmes also include the 'Active Employment Policy' (AEP) which has involved significant numbers of those made, or about to be made redundant. Administered by 76 district labour offices and 160 auxiliary branch offices, it consists of numerous job creation programmes, including 'the creation of "socially purposeful jobs" (SPJs) which includes subsidizing both the self employed (SE) and long term jobs with existing employees, "publicly useful jobs" (PUJs), jobs for new graduates and retraining' (Svejnar and Terrell, 1994, page 6). Had the people involved in AEP programmes at the end 1992 (14,4273 in total) been registered unemployed, the unemployment rate would have been 5.8 per cent instead of 3.0 per cent and at end 1993 (95,523 people on AEP programmes) 5.7 per cent instead of 3.8 per cent. Also AEP appears to have had an important effect in that it has 'played an important role in increasing the turnover of the unemployment pool, thereby preventing a rapid spread of long-term unemployment, as experienced in other transition countries, and contributing to wage moderation via increased competition for jobs' (OECD, 1995, page 27).

AEP cost Kcs 1718 million in 1992 (2.2 per cent of GDP) and Kcs 749 million in 1993 (1 per cent of GDP) with funds typically oriented towards SPJs and SE which together accounted for around 90 per cent of the expenditures in those years. The OECD has recommended the introduction of further active labour market programmes not only because of the range of existing problems, including regional, gender and age-group imbalances, and the growth of long-term unemployment, but also because low average unemployment may not be sustainable, as post-privatization rationalization and restructuring will involve further labour shedding.

Though average earnings have more or less doubled in nominal terms since 1990, it is noticeable that the pay for industrial and construction workers is nowadays about 60 per cent of that of staff in banks and financial institutions, which is almost an exact reversal of the situation under communism. There are also considerable discrepancies between salaries offered by foreign and Czech-owned companies. Again in 1993, a computer operator, for example, could expect to receive between 3500 and 5000 Kcs per month in a state-owned firm and between 5800 and 8000 Kcs in a foreign-owned firm, while a junior technician could expect to receive between 3750 and 5400 Kcs and 10,000 and 13,000 Kcs respectively.

In the communist period money wages and salaries were only part of workers' remuneration. Enterprises were required by law to provide a wide range of non-wage benefits which had four main categories, these being: health care and catering; pre-school facilities for children; recreation including sporting, cultural and educational activities, hobby facilities and holidays; and housing assistance. These legal requirements were removed during 1991 (the private sector was exempted from the outset), and in early 1993 the Czech government shifted overall responsibility for social protection to the newly established National Insurance Company. The latter comprises four separate funds for the provision of pensions, health insurance, disability insurance and unemployment benefits. The funds are covered by taxes levied on employees, who contribute 13.25 per cent of their earnings, and employers who must pay 35.25 per cent of their gross wage and salary bill. The obligatory employer contributions are low by some transforming country standards (e.g. 52.5 per cent and 48 per cent in Hungary and Poland respectively) but high by western standards.

Despite enterprises having been relieved of legal social responsibilities, and the new social insurance levies they must pay, non-wage benefits continue to make up an important part of Czech workers' overall remuneration. The study by Filer, Svejnar and Schneider (1994) showed that enterprises offer various fringe benefits including paid vacations over and above those stipulated in the labour code, sick pay above the legally mandatory amount, food subsidies, contributions to employee housing, payments for 'obstacles to work' (e.g. compensation for a bus delay which causes a missed shift), and private health insurance (which is expected to become increasingly frequent). Provision differs across sectors of the economy and according to type of firm. Small firms and private firms in general offer least non-wage benefits but higher wages; foreign firms provide the highest wages and non-wage benefits; mining, followed by financial/insurance companies have the highest level of indirect labour costs. Filer, Svejnar and Schneider expect the importance of fringe benefits to continue growing for a number of reasons. They are useful for attracting and holding onto labour in generally tight labour market conditions, they do not involve extra social insurance payments or income tax and are a way of circumventing the wage restraint policy.

The main national labour organization is the Czech and Moravian Chamber of Trade Unions (CK KOS) to which 36 trade unions, with 2.5 million members, are affiliated. The CK KOS was formed after the dissolution of the Czech and Slovak Confederation of Trade Unions (CS KOS) on 20 November 1993. The affiliate unions were formed on the basis of strike committees organized in enterprises on 17 November 1989 (which made an important contribution to the political revolution by initiating the general strike of 27 November) and there was no continuity with the communist-era Revolutionary Trade Union Movement (ROH): 'the origin of new Czechoslovak Trade Unions was a spontaneous ceasing of existence of the ROH structures and creation of new trade union structures without any intervention from the top' (CSKOS, 1992, page 2).

For the first phase of the transformation at least, industrial relations have been based on consultation and partnership rather than confrontation. The legal framework for collective bargaining put in place by the 1990–1992 Czechoslovak government has been interpreted as 'strong and relatively pro-labour' (Orenstein, 1994, page 14). Trade unions also have a formal input to government policy, via the Council of Social and Economic Accord, founded in October 1990, which brings together government, employers' associations and trade union representatives each month to discuss labour market and social policy issues. Vaclav Klaus even addressed the first congress of the CK KOS. The main ingredient of labour peace has been a trade-off in which the CK KOS has supported the reform strategy, and generally gone along with policies such as wage restraint, in return for employment protection policies. This, together with the view that trade unions are in fact incapable of successful industrial action anyway (according to CzechInvest, surveys of enterprise managers suggest that employees show little interest in negotiating collective agreements at plant level), has led to the general impression that the Czech business culture features 'passive' trade unions.

Yet there is some evidence that trade unions may in fact be moving in the direction of a less co-operative stance in the future. The wage restraint tax had been a constant source of tension between the unions and the government since its re-introduction on 1 July 1993 (it had been suspended on 1 January of that year) and it was claimed that the government had reneged on an agreement made in the tripartite Council. Union leaders publicly added this to other grievances they held, including delay of minimum wage legislation, and 'began hinting at a possible change of "style" of trade union activity' (EIU, 4, 1993, page 14). More recently, there was a fifteen-minute 'warning strike' organized on 21 December 1994 as a protest against pension reform plans (EIU, 1, 1995, page 14) which was supported by 450,000 workers, heavy union involvement in the massive anti-government demonstration in Wenceslas Square in spring 1995 and the serious public sector disputes of summer 1995 referred to already. On the basis of resolutions passed by the CK KOS Congress, the most pressing issues for organized labour include: claims that employer violations of labour-law regulations are increasing; government plans to ban trade union activity in the civil service; the 'ideologically motivated' proposed privatization of public services; declining real value of old-age pensions; discrimination against female employees; outdated labour health and safety code and industrial accidents increasing both in number and severity.

Business, education and training

Businesses operating in the CR have access to a highly skilled and well-educated workforce. The 1992 literacy level was 98.9 per cent and the higher education system generates a higher percentage of science and engineering graduates than any other country. This reflects a long history of high educational standards. Czech schools existed as far back as the tenth century and Prague is home to Central Europe's oldest academic institution, Charles University (Univerzita Karlova), founded in 1348 by Charles IV. Czech educational principles and innovations (for example the pedagogic ideas of the famous seventeenth-century theologian and educational reformer Jan Komensky) have been widely influential. Indeed, 'the democratic character and balanced curriculum of Czech schools from the end of the Austro–Hungarian empire until the start of the Second World War was a model for educational systems throughout the world' (*Financial Times*, 11 January 1993, page 11).

The Czech school system consists of the primary or basic school, which is compulsory for all children from the age of six to fifteen, and a variety of secondary schools, which usually require a further four years of study. The secondary apprentice training centre prepares its students for trades (e.g. electrical engineering, printing, wood-working, forestry), grammar schools provide general education and mainly prepare students for higher education. Secondary vocational schools prepare students for business, technical, economic, educational, health care, socio-legal, administrative, artistic and cultural activities. Special schools exist for students with chronic learning difficulties due to mental or physical illness, handicaps and so on.

State higher education institutions, of which there are twenty-three at present, include universities, technical universities, schools of economics, agriculture, forestry, education and veterinary medicine and academies of art. The right to establish, abolish and reorganize them rests with the Czech National Council. Higher education programmes last between three and six years, depending on the type of study, and the academic year is in most cases divided into two fifteen-week semesters. A bachelor's degree (Bc) is awarded after successful completion of three years' study. A further two or three years of specialized study, including final examinations and completion and defence of a thesis, leads to the award of one of the following degrees: Magister: social sciences and humanities (Mgr); Engineer: technical, economic and agricultural study (Ing); Doctor of Universal Medicine (MUDr); Doctor of Veterinary Medicine (MVDr). Postgraduate study, lasting for three years, leads to the academic degree of Doctor after successful defence of a thesis.

The number of full-time students enrolled at higher education institutions has risen from 112,980 in 1990/91 to 127,317 in 1993/94, when study patterns were as follows: 7430 students enrolled on natural sciences courses (of which 3299 were studying physics and mathematics); 38,799 students on technology courses (including 11,156 for metallurgy, mechanical engineering and metal working, 8488 for electrical engineering and 8051 for construction, geodesy and cartography); 7133 students studying agriculture and forestry; 11510 on medicine and pharmacy programmes; 58,106 on social sciences and services courses (including 16,813 taking economics – up 26 per cent from 1992/93 – 6202 taking law and 21,533 trainee teachers); and 3192 students studying art science.

Despite high general educational levels and well organized educational institutions, the CR did not have domestic capability to meet the human resource development requirements involved in successful transition. The Czech government's 'active' labour market programmes have included retraining in order to get unemployed people back to work as soon as possible but this has usually covered less than 3 per cent of the unemployed and therefore is not a huge training provision and does not, of course, meet the retraining needs of those already employed. Many skills and qualifications, especially those that correspond with instruments of the market economy (management, sales and marketing, accounting, public relations, legal practice, etc.), were simply not included in educational and training programmes and have had to be developed from scratch. Western organizations have been assisting the process of both equipping the present generation with new skills and qualifications and developing indigenous capacity for training future generations.

Technical assistance programmes, including the EU's PHARE programme and various bilateral schemes (e.g. the UK government's 'Know-How' scheme) have included substantial training and retraining efforts. The higher education system, still engaged in the inevitable overhaul and renewal necessitated by the end of the communist regime, benefits from educational exchange programmes including TEMPUS, USAID and Fulbright programmes. TEMPUS (operational in the CR since 1990) Joint European Projects, for example, facilitate east–west and west–east staff and student mobility, curriculum development, university restructuring and staff updating/retraining and channel funds for provision of materials and equipment for Czech institutions. Some 88 per cent of Czech higher education institutions have participated in TEMPUS projects to date. In the academic year 1994/95 5.5 million ECU was allocated to fifteen new TEMPUS projects for the CR covering agricultural economics, 'instruments of the market economy', public relations and marketing, European law (mercantile/commercial and consumer), medical sciences and environmental sciences.

Inward investors are also playing an important role. According to CzechInvest more than 70 per cent of foreign companies active in the country are operating training programmes, focusing mainly on language learning (especially English), technical training, and financial and management skills. The range of training methods include: on-the-job training, combined with formal training in most cases; overseas training classes or longer term internships, usually for key staff and where company-specific technical or operational training is necessary; formal corporate classes held in the CR, customized for the local environment by an instructor seconded from a European branch of the company; use of Czech universities or technical institutes for literacy, mathematics, and appropriate engineering and science training; use of management centres offering a range of programmes, from MBA to company-specific ones; sub-contracting training programmes to private companies is also used, mainly where companies do not have their own resources to carry out specific training in Czech and adapt corporate programmes to the in-country requirements; public workshops which can cover anything from secretarial skills to business strategy; assistance with tuition costs of classes taken outside working hours.

Business and the environment

In a candid assessment of the degree of pollution at the end of the 1980s, the Czech Ministry of Environment described the situation as follows: '(t)he environment in some of our regions can be described as disastrous. The atmosphere, water and food are polluted; the quality of the soil has deteriorated; most of the forests are seriously affected; the landscape is devastated in many places and has lost its ecological stability; and living nature suffers. According to European standards, the Czech Republic is one of the greatest exporters of pollution transported by the atmosphere, rivers and other ways to neighbouring and more distant countries ... A warning signal is the retardation in the lengthening of the average life expectancy, where we hold one of the last positions in Europe' (*World Environmental Business Handbook*, page 63).

In their overview of the ecological catastrophe, Cerna and Tosovska (1994) note that in 1988 annual emissions of sulphur dioxide, at 26 tons per square kilometre, were less than the DDR (46.1) but higher than elsewhere in Europe including the UK (15.6), Hungary (15.3), Poland (13.8), FRG (7.7) and Austria (1.7). Emissions in the Prague and North Bohemia regions were especially horrific, exceeding 100 tons. The main problem has been reliance on power stations burning the worst quality brown coal. Some 60 per cent of all waterways are heavily polluted and 23 per cent of major river lengths fall into the worst pollution category, unable to sustain fish. Water damage is attributed to uncontrolled industrial and municipal discharges, excessive use of fertilizers and other agrochemicals, oil-based contamination due to Soviet troop presence and numerous accidental spillages. Cerna and Tososvka also point out that waste management had been seriously neglected and unhygienic and noxious substances deposited in uncontrolled dumps 'that meant danger for proximate settlements'.

Data on changes in various water and atmospheric discharges between 1989 and 1993 indicates some progress in pollution control. Reduced sulphur dioxide emissions clearly reflect reduced demand for electricity as a result of decline in industrial production and increased power charges, together with effects of the range of energy savings programmes which themselves led to 1.4 per cent less emissions between 1991 and 1993 (Cerna and Tosovska, page 43). A major breakthrough in air quality is expected when the Temelin nuclear facility comes on stream in 1997 (itself, of course, an environmental liability in the opinion of many, and having soured relations with Austria) and remaining coal-fired power stations become equipped with desulphurization and denitrification equipment. The requirement for cars produced in the CR to meet EC emission standards should eventually help stabilize carbon monoxide emissions, which have increased 350 per cent since 1989.

Important environmental legislation was passed by the Czech National Council in 1991, including the Act on Environmental Impact Assessment designed to ensure that development projects satisfy environmental criteria, and Waste Management and Clean Air Acts which clarified rights and obligations of individuals, companies and state bodies. The intention is to make environmental laws and standards compatible with EU practices. Institutional measures included increases in the effectiveness of administering new regulations by further empowering the various local and national inspectorates for water and atmospheric protection and waste management. In addition, the State Investment Fund to finance environmental programmes, and the Energy Agency, commissioned to promote energy saving programmes and alternative energy, were created in 1991 and 1993 respectively. Foreign technical assistance funds (from the World Bank, for example, and the EU's PHARE programme) have targeted specific environment projects.

The Czech government's environmental strategy combines legal and institutional measures together with faith that broader reform steps and effects (privatization, price liberalization, permanent contraction of heavily polluting industry) will also produce environmentally favourable results and some environmental-specific economic measures. The latter subject Czech firms to a mixture of payments (varying with the amount and harmfulness of pollutants) for legal use of natural resources, waste discharges and air emissions and fines for illegal use and discharges. Czech firms are also responsible for rectifying past environmental damage caused, though they are entitled to take advantage of 'stimulating economic instruments' (financed from the state budget and income from paying polluters) including partial deferment of pollution charges, low interest loans, grants, tax incentives and customs duty exemptions for environmentally positive activities.

Environmental difficulties represent one of the most formidable challenges facing the CR, especially as trade-offs with short-term economic considerations are often involved (e.g. the employment effects of shifting from coal-fired power generation). The environmental protection legislation and institutional developments are obviously positive steps though at present the country can only afford a fraction of what it will cost to meet target standards. Though market pricing of power and water, for example, can encourage more economic use of resources, Cerna and Tosovska's view that the specific economic instruments need to be much strengthened (air emission charges are less than 1 per cent of operating costs for most firms, for example) if they are to have real impact seems justified.

Conclusion

The Czech Republic stands out as having embarked on the transition to the market economy with the benefit of relatively stable economic conditions prior to the collapse of communism. Partly as a result of this, it has achieved much in the short period since the hard-line Czechoslovak Communist administration was pushed aside in 1989, and then from 1 January 1993 onwards when the Czech Republic became an independent entity and was able to dissassociate itself from more severe restructuring problems located in the Slovak Republic. It has become the beneficiary of the significant amounts of incoming foreign investment as well as the substantial financial resources and economic stimulus generated by tourism. It stands at the threshold of renewed growth and a secure economic place at the heart of Europe.

Czechs are fond of noting that the former Czechoslovakia was the economic equal of Austria before the Second World War, an indication of the relatively strong industrial and commercial progress made in the inter-war period. It is clear that the emerging business culture in the Czech Republic reflects this strong industrial and technical tradition. The burgeoning private small-scale business sector, quite unlike that in many of the other transition economies, is especially well represented in the manufacturing sphere. What is even more impressive here is that that this progress has been made upon a foundation of almost no private small-scale businesses and entrepreneurship prior to 1989, these features of the market economy being anathema to the hard-line Communist party in Czechoslovakia and consequently resisted for most of the period since they came to power.

A great number of problems must be faced, especially relating to import growth and the resulting trade deficit. It is a worrying feature that foreign imports are increasingly taking the bulk of Czech demand for manufactured and technically sophisticated goods, in a country which has a rich history of manufacturing and a still significant manufacturing sector. However, the emerging business culture may provide the most propitious environment within which Czech entrepreneurs can increasingly move back into these and other markets for manufactured goods. As the larger enterprises are being restructured we are seeing further entrepreneurial activity as the individual units are spun off into small-scale suppliers of manufactured inputs to the large enterprises which gave birth to them. Many larger enterprises, such as Volkswagen-Skoda, are already successfully integrating new small-scale private suppliers of manufactured components into their operations. This is all further evidence that the business culture in the Czech Republic reflects its roots in industry and technical services more so than in other transition economies, and to good effect. Given such features, there is reason to be particularly optimistic about the future development of the business culture in the Czech Republic and thus the economic prospects for the country as a whole.

Acknowledgements

I would to thank staff at CzechInvest, Prague for supplying me with some of the detailed information I needed to complete this chapter, particularly concerning regional economic structures and company law. Thanks also to Libuse Jilemnicka of the Faculty of Civil Engineering, Czech Technical University, Prague, for arranging for me to receive the CERGE-EI Working Papers on a regular basis and delivering certain other important materials when she visited the UK in May 1995.

References and suggestions for further reading

Batt, J. (1991) *East Central Europe from Reform to Transformation.* Chatham House Papers, RIIA, London.

Benacek, V. and Zemplinerova, A. (1995) Problems and Environment of Small Businesses in the Czech Republic. *Small Business Economics*, Vol. 7, No. 6, pp. 437–450.

Bonte-Friedheim, R. (1995) Emerging Capital Markets in Central Europe. *Transition*, 14 April, pp. 29.

Business Central Europe, Economist Publications, London.

CEFR, *The Czech Republic in the International Economy* (quarterly), CEFR, Prague, various issues.

Central European (1996), Vol. 6, No. 1, p. 3.

Cerna, A. and Tosovsky, E. (1994) Economic Transformation and the Environment. *CERGE-EI Working Paper Series*, No. 57, April, CERGE-EI/Charles University, Prague.

CSKOS (1992) *Czech and Slovak Confederation of Trade Unions.* CSKOS, Prague, May.

CzechInvest Information Series, Czech Agency for Foreign Investment, Prague, various issues 1994 and 1995.

Commission of the European Communities (1993) *Directory of Higher Education Institutions in Central and Eastern Europe.* Luxembourg, Commission of the European Communities.

Dangerfield, M. (1995) The Economic Opening of East and Central Europe: Continuity and Change in Foreign Economic Relations. *Journal of European Integration*, Vol. XIX, No.1.

Dyba, K. and Svejnar, J. (1994) An Overview of Recent Economic Developments in the Czech Republic. *CERGE-EI Working Paper Series*, No. 61, April, CERGE-EI/Charles University, Prague.

EBRD (1994) *Transition Report – 1994.* European Bank for Reconstruction Development, London.

EIU, *Country Report for Czech Republic/Slovakia.* Economist Intelligence Unit, London, various issues 1993, 1994, 1995.

Filer, R., Svejnar, J. and Schneider, O. (1994) Wage and Non-wage Labour Cost in the Czech Republic: the Impact of Fringe Benefits. *CERGE-EI Working Paper Series*, No. 77, November, CERGE-EI/Charles University, Prague.

Financial Times Survey (1993) The Czech Republic. *Financial Times*, 11 January.

Financial Times Survey (1993) The Czech Republic. *Financial Times*, 24 March.

Financial Times Survey (1995) Czech Republic: Finance, Industry and Investment. *Financial Times*, 2 June.

Fisher, S. (1994a) Czech–Slovak Relations Two Years after the Elections. *RFE/RL Research Report*, Vol. 3, No. 27, 8 July, pp. 31–38.

Fisher, S. (1994b) 'Czech Economy Presents Mixed Picture', *RFE/RL Research Report*, Vol. 3, No. 29, 22 July, pp. 9–17.

Harrison, J. (1995) A Rough Year for Central European Stock Markets. *Transition*, 14 April, pp. 20–25

Jeffries, I. (1993) *The Socialist Economies and Transition to the Market: A Guide*. Routledge, London.

Kettle, S. (1995) Of Money and Morality. *Transition*, 15 March 1995, pp. 37–39.

Komarek, V. (1993) Czech and Slovak Republic: a new approach, in Portes, R. (ed.) *Economic Transformation in Central Europe: A Progress Report*. CEPR, London, pp. 59–106.

Koves, A. (1992) *Central and East European Economies in Transition: The External Dimension*. Westview, Oxford.

Latest Statistical Information: External Trade, Cesky Statisticky Urad, Prague.

Martin, P. (1990) 'Scenario for Economic Reform' Adopted. *RFE/RI Report on Eastern Europe*, 19 October, pp. 5–8.

Monthly Statistics of the Czech Republic. Cesky Statisticky Urad, Prague.

OECD (1994) *The Czech and Slovak Republics 1994*. OECD Economic Surveys, OECD, Paris.

OECD (1995) *Review of the Labour Market in the Czech Republic*. OECD, Paris.

Orenstein, M (1994) The Political Success of Neo-Liberalism in the Czech Republic. *CERGE-EI Working Paper Series*, No. 68, June, CERGE-EI/Charles University, Prague.

Pehe, J. (1994) The Czech Republic: A Successful Transition. *RFE/RL Research Report*, Vol. 3, No. 1, pp. 70–75.

Pehe, J. (1995) A Leader in Political Stability and Economic Growth. *Transition*, Vol. 1, No. 1, 30 January, pp. 29–33.

Rose, R. (1994) What post-socialist people have in mind. *Transition*, Vol. 5, No. 6, pp. 10–12.

Sobell, V. (1990) Czechoslovakia Almost Ready for Economic Transformation. *RFE/RI Report on Eastern Europe*, 8 June, pp. 5–8.

Statisticka Rocenka Ceske Republiky, Cesky Statisticky Urad, Prague, 1992, 1993, 1994.

Svejnar, J. (1993), Czech and Slovak Federal Republic: A Solid Foundation, in Portes, R. (ed.) *Economic Transformation in Central Europe: A Progress Report*. CEPR, London, pp. 21–57.

Svejnar, J. and Terrell, K. (1994) Explaining Unemployment Dynamics in the Czech Republic. *CERGE-ECI Working Paper Series*, No. 60, April, CERGE-EI/Charles University, Prague.

Takla, L. (1994) The relationship between privatization and the reform of the banking sector: the case of the Czech Republic and Slovakia, in Estrin, S., *Privatisation in East and Central Europe*.

TEMPUS Compendium Academic Year 1994/95 (1994) European Commission, Brussels.

World Environmental Business Handbook, 1994.

2 The business culture in Hungary

Vincent Edwards

Introduction

For a long time Hungary was widely regarded as the most successful of the transition economies in Eastern Europe. It was seen as different from the other economies, including its Visegrad neigbours, Poland and former Czechoslovakia, because of its much earlier start in attempting to restructure its economy towards the market and in decentralizing economic power. Measures implemented in the 1960s and 1980s went some way toward eliminating many of the most glaring faults of Soviet-style central planning and led to the reintroduction of significant autonomy and managerial responsibility within the state sector. Contact with western enterprises increased in many fields, including technology. The economy was also opened up to entrepreneurship and private initiative well before the collapse of communism, particularly with a series of liberalizing measures in the 1980s which promoted significant private entrepreneurship.

The second factor which set Hungary apart arose in the first couple of years of the transition. In this period Hungary managed to retain an atmosphere of economic and political stability which was the envy of its two Visegrad reforming neighbours, both of which had large economic and political problems to solve in those early years (see Chapters 1 and 3). One of the rewards of this stability was substantial foreign investment, a feature which has been of critical importance in many respects to economic success. The key to this stability was held to be the adoption by the first non-communist government of an avowedly 'gradualist' economic reform strategy, in preference to the more rapid 'shock therapy' approach being implemented in Poland. The intention of the Hungarian government was to retain the more positive elements of the old system – Hungary had one of the highest living standards in the Eastern bloc – as well as to maintain broad political support for the introduction of the market economy.

With hindsight, however, Hungary can only be decribed as having taken the 'gradualist' path to economic reform in the sense that its current reform programme is in many ways simply an extension of reforms begun in the latter part of the communist period. This is because, in spite of its 'gradualist' credentials, Hungary actually underwent a significant, though largely unannounced, degree of shock therapy from 1990 onwards. For example, immediate import liberalization measures resulted in many domestic producers losing significant market share before they had the time to restructure and improve efficiency. Hungary also implemented one of the region's strictest bankruptcy regimes in practice (as opposed to in theory) with the result that many enterprises actually did go bankrupt or, under the threat of bankruptcy, underwent extensive restructuring. There was as a result, therefore, a very rapid rise in unemployment in the first years of transition (from 80,000 to over 400,000 in 1991 alone). Land privatization in 1992–93 was a further shock to the system and resulted in a serious fall in agricultural output and the need to import food products for the first time in many years.

In late 1994, however, the reform programme was in danger of going seriously wrong and it required an even greater degree of urgency – i.e. shock – to address a number of serious financial problems which had been unsuccessfully dealt with earlier. Some commentators were conjecturing that Hungary was facing a financial crisis not unlike Mexico's 1994 financial 'meltdown' as the budget and current account deficits appeared to be getting out of control. A package of 'mini shock' austerity measures were introduced in March 1995, which were well received both domestically and by the international community, and by mid-1996 Hungary appeared to have ridden out the threat to its post-communist recovery plans.

Perhaps the most important question now facing Hungary is whether or not a business culture has emerged which is appropriate to a real market economy. The extent and sophistication of the entrepreneurship exhibited in post-communist Hungary has been impressive, particularly with regard to the development of smaller-scale manufacturing. The government has contributed to this by taking full advantage of the international assistance offered to the transition economies to construct a comprehensive support system for entrepreneurial activity throughout Hungary. It has even taken its first tentative steps towards creating the sort of inter-enterprise linkages which have underpinned so much of the economic success of the East Asian economies, by passing a procurement law which offers enterprises with significant local linkages (i.e. with over 50 per cent local content) better prices from the government purchasing arm.

In this chapter we will outline how the business environment has changed in Hungary and how it has built upon these earlier experiences of reform and post-communist transition to emerge as having one of the region's most modern, sophisticated and entrepreneurial business cultures.

Business and government

In common with nearly all the other then-communist economies, and in spite of meaningful economic reforms and liberalization under communism, the Hungarian economy deteriorated sharply in the 1980s. It finally became clear to many Hungarians that the communist economic and political system was nearing the end of its life. One facet clearly indicating the impending economic collapse was the alarming rise in the foreign debt, which doubled between 1985 and 1987 (Batt, 1991), and which signalled the end of the 'last gasp' strategy of communist economic development using foreign (capitalist) capital.

As a response to the pressure for reform sweeping the country, the Hungarian Constitution was substantially amended in October 1989 to provide for elections to a unicameral parliament with members elected for a four-year term of office. After protracted negotiations between the party in power, the Hungarian Socialist Workers Party (HSWP) and a range of opposition parties and groupings which had arisen in the increasingly liberal political climate since 1987, a democratic government was elected in April 1990. This first government was a centre-right coalition led by the Democratic Forum (HDF) which gained 165 parliamentary seats out of the total 386, in partnership with the Independent Smallholders Party which gained 44 seats and the Christian Democrats with 21 seats. The more progressive elements in the old HSWP, which had reconstituted themselves into the Hungarian Socialist Party (HSP), won 33 seats. The old hardline communists retained the old party name, but failed to obtain any seats in parliament since their party was unable to clear the minimum threshold of votes set at 4 per cent. It looked set for oblivion in common with the other former communist parties (name changes notwithstanding) in Eastern Europe. But the May 1994 elections saw a reversal of fortune, resulting in the Hungarian Socialist Party (the old HSWP) returning to win 208 seats in parliament out of the 386, followed by the Alliance of Free Democrats with 70 seats. A coalition government was formed with Gyula Horn as prime minister. The general feeling was that the Hungarian population was suffering from 'reform fatigue' and wished for a measure of stability and a slowing down of the reform programme.

In spite of the ideological differences between the first two democratic governments, government policy has consistently been driven by the need to effect the transition from 'guided market' to free market economy. Differences between governments have therefore consisted more in *how* to achieve this rather than in what needed to be done. Key planks of government policy have been (a) the privatization of state-owned enterprises (b) minimizing unemployment and (c) reducing foreign indebtedness. A related issue has been Hungary's economic relationship with its neighbours and, in particular, with the European Union (EU).

The desire to create a free-market economy has, however, come face to face with the realities of the economic situation in Hungary, especially the massive investment required to achieve successful privatization. This has slowed down as the companies remaining to be privatized become less and less attractive to domestic and foreign investors. Moreover, there is a relative scarcity of domestic and foreign investment as well as increasing competition from other countries in the region, such as the Czech Republic and Poland. As with the other transition economies, Hungary is finally running up against the problem of a shortage of capital with which to build a market economy.

The political decision to contain unemployment has also slowed down the privatization process and many enterprises continue to be financially supported, rather than let go to the wall, in spite of one of the most rigorous bankruptcy laws in the transition economies. With unemployment running at around 11–12 per cent in 1995, the government was unwilling to undertake any actions which would further aggravate the situation. This has meant that many enterprises continue to be owned, even if indirectly, by the state, with shareholdings in the hands of banks and local government bodies.

A key role taken on by the government has been that of creating an environment attractive for new investors and new business activity. There is a danger that one focuses too much on the dire problems of former state-owned enterprises rather than on the success and expansion of the new private sector. Government policy has been consistent in reducing and limiting inflation. The need to service the foreign debt has also brought home the need to produce goods and services of a quality that can earn foreign currency. Domestically, this has been accompanied by policies that keep wages depressed and Hungarian wage levels have been a significant source of competitive advantage, even though they are virtually the highest in the region.

The government has also been very keen to regularize Hungary's place in the international community. Hungary had already adhered to the GATT in 1973, and joined the IMF and the World Bank in 1982. In spite of the size of the foreign debt, Hungary has always paid promptly and is regarded as an exemplary client by the IMF and other creditors. With the collapse of COMECON Hungary has sought to re-orientate itself to western markets, while maintaining trading links with some of its regional partners. Hungary is a signatory of the Central European Free Trade Agreement which was also signed by the Czech Republic, Poland and Slovakia (the Visegrad group) in 1991. Furthermore, Hungary signed an association agreement with the EU in 1991 and EU countries are now a major market for Hungarian exports.

Business and economic reform

Earlier attempts at reform

In common with the economies emerging from the former Yugoslavia, Croatia and Slovenia, Hungary really commenced the transition to a market economy well before the collapse of communism in 1990. The key feature was the introduction in 1968 of the so-called New Economic Mechanism (NEM), which was meant to introduce a clear break with the Soviet-style planned economy framework. The NEM has been described as a 'guided market' model in contrast to the Soviet 'directive' model. Key features of the NEM concept included the replacement of central planning by indicative enterprise plans and enhanced enterprise autonomy, an onus on enterprises to become profitable, the freeing of many formerly centrally fixed prices and the liberalization of foreign trade.

The NEM met with considerable criticism, however, from orthodox party members who saw it as a fundamental break with Soviet practice, and incorporating aspects of the Yugoslav model of worker self-management which, at that time, remained ideologically suspect. The Hungarian communists accepted the NEM only because they were more concerned to maintain at least the passive support of the population by providing sufficient material well-being, which they were increasingly unable to do through a strict central planning regime.

The NEM did engender a few years of improved economic performance, but it proved to be a short-lived phenomenon, for a number of reasons. First, in the mainly monopolistic structure of industry and relative absence of competition, firms retained market power even though they were more responsive to consumer demands than before. Second, although the pricing system was relaxed, many prices were still fixed centrally and subsidies were widespread, resulting in the kinds of inefficient behaviour associated with 'soft budget constraints'. Third, many industries were considered of strategic significance and remained subordinated to ministry control. Fourth, Hungary remained a part of COMECON and enterprises were in no position to renege on their agreed obligations. The major problem, however, remained Hungary's detachment from the world economy. Increasing consumer aspirations could be satisfied only by increasing imports. Because of their relative uncompetitiveness, more and more Hungarian goods were needed to pay for these imports. When these proved insufficient, Hungary began to borrow on the western markets and built up a substantial foreign debt. In an attempt to improve the performance of Hungarian enterprises, joint ventures with western companies were sanctioned and encouraged.

State-owned enterprises themselves, moreover, were unable to provide the range of products and services to which Hungarians aspired. In order to accommodate these aspirations, at least in part, the regime allowed private enterprise to expand. The supply of agricultural produce from private sources played an important role in ensuring a plentiful and, compared to other COMECON countries, attractive range of foodstuffs. In industry, enterprises sub-contracted parts of their production to private organizations formed by their own workers. Additionally, private enterprise began to provide a number of commercial services not offered by the state. This legal second economy was paralleled by an illegal second economy which operated outside the framework laid down by the state. Illegal operations were particularly prevalent in housing construction and motor vehicle maintenance. The development and expansion of the second economy permitted a continuing rise in living standards. However, in order to pay for this, as per capita wages declined in the 1980s, many Hungarians needed to have more than one job. This meant that Hungarians were paying for their standard of living by working long (and longer) hours.

To a greater degree than in other COMECON countries, however, the introduction of the NEM fostered the development of managers who were not largely political appointees or administrators, which had been the case while the Soviet-style planning system had been in operation. With the NEM, enterprise managements enjoyed greater discretion to direct and manage their enterprises. In fact there was considerable material motivation for managers to improve the performance of their organizations, although their efforts often ran counter to the national interest and aroused popular resentment. Perhaps more than elsewhere in Soviet-controlled Central and Eastern Europe, Hungarian managers became more skilled in identifying and implementing enterprise goals and in pursuing personal advantage. Fischer (1992, page 35) goes so far as to say that the most important result of the NEM was that it created 'Eastern Europe's most advanced "management culture".'

Nevertheless, the NEM failed to deliver what it had promised and the Hungarian economy at the end of the 1980s was still not competitive by international standards. Furthermore it could no longer sustain the standard of living of the population and had accumulated an enormous degree of indebtedness.

Transition to the market

Taking a longer view, the transition from a communist regime to a market economy and democratic system of government has been less abrupt in Hungary than in other Central European countries. The Hungarian government recognized at an early stage the deficiencies of the Soviet model and the need to introduce market mechanisms in the running of the economy. It was the communist regime which had instituted liberalizing measures in the 1980s with the aim of raising economic performance. Sizable legislation relating to private enterprise, company reform and foreign investment was also put in place well before the collapse of communism. The regime also took a relatively relaxed stance towards unofficial economic activity. One important result of all this was significant growth in the private sector and in entrepreneurship, both officially-sanctioned and unofficial, prior to the collapse of communism.

Post-communist Hungary was also seen as the first to embark on what became known as the 'gradualist' path to the market economy. There were good political reasons to continue the gradual reform initiated by the reforms of the 1980s: it was important to promise the Hungarian electorate that change would be brought in gradually to preserve the comparatively high living standards of the Hungarian population. Hungarians, so many thought, would not accept the psychological and social pressures which could be inflicted by the kind of 'shock therapy' reform programme being advocated by international funding agencies, such as the IMF, and by western advisors working elsewhere in Eastern Europe. Moreover, the economic situation in Hungary looked better than elsewhere, since liberalization and marketizing reforms under communism had created the foundation upon which a full-blooded market economy could be established.

Ultimately, however, the more positive elements of the communist inheritance did not allow the Hungarian government to avoid painful shock therapy measures along the lines of those being implemented elsewhere. For a start, there was an urgent problem to tackle in the shape of the growing budget deficit, which was largely being financed by money creation and thus helped to drive the accelerating inflation rate in late 1989 and 1990. The IMF was the main architect of an early austerity/anti-inflationary programme and it demanded large and immediate reductions in subsidies as a precondition for giving Hungary financial support. The government thus tightened monetary policy on several fronts and simultaneously cut back on expenditure. The result was that inflation was brought largely under control, or at least prevented from going 'hyper'. Inflation appeared to have peaked in 1991 at 35 per cent, thereafter gradually declining (EBRD, 1995).

The success of this aspect of the reform must, however, be seen alongside the sizeable fall in industrial output registered in the period 1990–92 and the dramatic rise in unemployment from 2.5 per cent in 1990 to 8 per cent in 1991 and a year later to 12.3 per cent (EBRD, 1995). This was a shock to Hungarians used to full employment and job security, and it created a political backlash against the early reforming administration. Such a dramatic rise had unpleasant social effects and represented a significant burden for the welfare services, as well as emphasizing just how much 'shock' there was to the immediate post-communist reform package. However, the level of unemployment appears to be having positive effects, leading to reorganization and better performance of enterprises. Unlike in neighbouring countries, where serious job-shedding has not been matched by productivity improvements, the level of unemployment in Hungary is associated with substantial real productivity improvements made in Hungarian enterprises.

It is appropriate that it was a Hungarian economist, Janos Kornai, who pointed out the role of the 'soft budget constraint' as one of the main causes of inefficiency in the communist economic systems of Eastern Europe. Hungary was particularly active in establishing an extensive regime of enterprise subsidies, and these subsidy schemes have proved very difficult to dismantle. One critical aspect of the early reforms was the government's inability to cut back its expenditure sufficiently on enterprise support and public administration. After so many years of maladministration and inefficiency, the survival of numerous enterprises depended on financial support from the government. The result of this inaction was a mushrooming budget deficit, which was to become one of the most persistent problems facing the government going into the latter half of the 1990s. Even after several years of reform and attempts to trim public spending in the early years of the reform, Hungary still has a very high share of GDP accounted for by public administration (a quarter of total employment is with the government) and social spending (OECD, 1995).

Measures to deal with this problem, as well as with the equally acute current account deficit (see below), were finally brought forward in late 1994 and implemented in 1995. The 'mini-shock' programme involved cuts to many welfare entitlements and a rapid 10 per cent reduction in government employment. These measures, along with revenue generating measures such as an import surcharge, and other one-off factors, such as changes to the social welfare and sickness payments, resulted in some relief for the government. But the continuing process of disentangling the state from the heart of the economy, and cutting back the social welfare system, is creating pockets of poverty and resentment in Hungarian society. Moreover, there is still strong political resistance to the new policy.

Privatization

The key element in the Hungarian reform programme was the introduction of private property, which was to be achieved primarily through a major sell-off of state assets. The Transformation Act of 1989 established the guidelines for the privatization process which led to the setting up of the State Property Agency (SPA) in 1990 and, through a subsequent act, the State Asset Holding Company (SAHC) in 1992. The SPA was set up with the purpose of disposing of state-owned enterprises in the medium-term, while the SAHC had the job of administering those companies which were to remain predominantly in state ownership.

The Hungarian privatization programme began in 1990 with large-scale privatization and the target of disposing of twenty of the largest enterprises. This first phase was widely considered a failure. The SPA was unable to get rid of the enterprises quick enough, partly because it was expecting too high a price to be paid. From then on a variety of privatization methods were used, so that by late 1994 around two-thirds of the state property held by the SPA in 1990 had gone. Further rounds of privatization continued. By mid-1995 the SPA had disposed of much of its initial portfolio of 1862 companies, with state ownership reduced to below 50 per cent in 902 of these companies and 542 others in liquidation (EBRD, 1995, page 44). The SAHC was also making progress in reducing the share of state ownership in its portfolio of companies.

Hungary's privatization programme was somewhat different to those of its Visegrad neighbours, the former Czechoslovakia and Poland, since it was based on the outright sale of assets instead of the use of vouchers and share give-aways to the population. Moreover it was unique in many other aspects, as Canning and Hare (1994, page 177) note, 'in its pragmatism, in the astonishing variety of models and approaches, in the high degree of apparent responsiveness and flexibility on the part of government and its agencies'. Hungary's approach was influenced by the financial circumstances of the early years of the transition: a growing budget deficit (and pressure from the IMF to reduce it) and a shortage of domestic investment capital with which to upgrade industry and also by the readiness of foreign capital to invest in Hungary. The first point dictated that state enterprises be sold off in order to raise cash, while the constraint represented by the latter two points effectively meant that the only investors with any money would be foreigners.

Not surprisingly, the main feature of the early years of the programme, apart from the fact that it proceeded much slower than originally intended, was that foreign participation in the purchase of state assets was very high. Bakos (1993, page 18) estimates that foreign investors purchased 71 per cent, 81 per cent and 61 per cent of total state assets put up for sale in the three years 1991–93 alone. The revenue generated was substantial (for example, 63 billion forints in 1992) and was intended to be directed towards the budget and the restructuring of state enterprises in difficulty. There was a problem of corrupt behaviour on the part of managers in state-owned enterprises who were taking state assets into their own hands at below their market value – what was called 'spontaneous privatization'. This activity was made possible by the freedom given to enterprise managers to initiate the privatization of their own enterprise. It was followed by some renationalizations of already privatized enterprises and the introduction of a stricter privatization regime. A final and increasingly important aspect of Hungarian privatization has been the extent of worker ownership it has generated.

As the programme proceeded more changes were made. In May 1995 a new Privatization Law merged the SPA and SAHC to constitute a new State Privatization and Asset Management Company (APVRt). The law is noteworthy in that it lays down a number of areas where state ownership (full and part) is to be maintained, not just in the conventional sectors such as transport and communications (railways) and energy (electricity, nuclear power) but also in the banking sector and in a wide range of companies. It provides for the government to dispose of its remaining assets, around 900 firms, and to sell its remaining shareholdings in around a 100 other firms. Larger state-owned firms deemed to be important from the point of view of the national interest can be privatized only with government approval and with part of the equity held back. Foreign strategic shareholdings have been encouraged and, indeed, fought over by many western multinationals. The pharmaceutical sector, for example, once the main production centre for the entire CMEA, has seen numerous western buy-ins (*Central European*, March 1996). The remaining medium and small sized companies in state ownership are being privatized by the APVRt in cooperation with the managers of the companies concerned. One aspect of the new programme is the establishment of special equity funds to provide an investment opportunity for the owners of compensation vouchers given to those having lost property under the former communist regime. The value of these had reached 114 billion forints by the end of 1994 (OECD, 1995).

A large contribution has been made to the development of a burgeoning private sector by the growth and expansion of new start-up enterprises and small-scale entrepreneurship in Hungary. One of the chief gains from the earlier start to liberalization made in Hungary was that entrepreneurship was encouraged and allowed to gain a foothold in the economic system. Earlier reforms allowed workers to establish 'workers economic associations' which could operate after the normal working day on sub-contracting and other work obtained from outside, or from their own enterprise, using the equipment of the parent enterprise. Such associations allowed for greater productivity and creativity because the workers profited directly, as well as utilizing assets which would otherwise be idle. It also inculcated an appreciation of efficiency and entrepreneurship among those workers who took advantage of the scheme which they were to make good use of later on when the remaining obstacles to private enterprise were abolished. Gacs *et al.* (1993, page 76) report that of those entrepreneurs purchasing business units in the small-scale privatization programme underway in the early 1990s, about half had previous experience of private business in the 1980s, and over 40 per cent continued to operate one or more of those businesses. This prior experience may account for the apparent greater participation of Hungarian entrepreneurs in manufacturing activities, as opposed to simple trading and exchange, compared to their counterparts in other transition economies such as the Czech Republic and Poland (Johnson, 1994).

Changing legal structure

Legislation intended to improve the performance of Hungarian companies predates the collapse of the communist regime and numerous measures were put into place before a democratically elected government was in power. The 1988 Companies Act established the legal forms by which business entities were to be organized. Six legal forms were stipulated. German practice has been a strong influence on four of the legal forms:

- Public limited company (Részvénytársaság – Rt)
- Limited company (Korlátolt felelössegü társaság – Kft)
- General partnership (Közkerseti társaság – Kkt)
- Limited partnership (Betéti társaság – Bt)

The other permissible forms are trade association (Egyesülés) and joint venture (Közös vállalat – Kv). The joint venture need not include a foreign partner.

All firms have to register with the registry court of the county in which they are located and are subject to its supervision. The great majority of companies have opted for the Kft form which has a two-tier board system based on the German GmbH. Basic requirements include a minimum share capital of 1 million Hungarian forints (HUF). If the share capital is greater than 20 million HUF, or the company has more than twenty-five shareholders or more than 200 full-time employees, the company must appoint a supervisory board of at least three members. Two thirds of members are elected by shareholders and one-third by the employees. The supervisory board reports to the shareholders' meeting.

Legislation on bankruptcy was initially promulgated in 1986 and was replaced by a new Act on Bankruptcy and Liquidation in 1992. While the initial act, although a novelty under a communist regime, was implemented only sporadically, the 1992 Act has had an enormous impact on the way business is conducted. Unlike in many of the other transition economies, the law has facilitated a real change and restructuring: nearly 6000 enterprises have filed for bankruptcy since 1992, with a third of these undergoing liquidation procedures, and a wave of mergers and consolidations has followed actual and threatened liquidations, especially in the textiles, building materials and agro-processing sectors (*Business Central Europe*, Jan. 1996, page 44).

As might be expected in the change-over from one economic system to another, there has been a substantial volume of legislation covering taxation, foreign investment, competition, property rights, intellectual property, consumer protection, banking, labour and accounting. All this legislation has played an important role in shaping the business environment, regulating behaviour and creating the institutions necessary for the effective operation of a market economy. Nevertheless some aspects of legislation are considered weak and poorly enforced.

An important consideration in legislation has been to prepare the ground for Hungary's desired accession to the EU. Since 1992, for example, accounting procedures have in all substantial elements followed the relevant European directives. In fact, Hungary implemented these new accounting procedures even before they became accepted practice in all member states of the EU.

As the relationship between business and the law has evolved over the last decade, and as the legal framework has been constructed to support the activities of companies in a market economy, EU legislation and practice have consistently been taken as a model, with German influence especially evident.[1]

Business and the economy

Hungary has a relatively smaller industrial sector than other transition economies, including its Visegrad neighbours, which reflects the greater diversity of the Hungarian economy. The major components of the manufacturing sector are chemicals, food and engineering products. All these areas, in line with the overall economy, have suffered absolute declines since the collapse of the communist regime. Together these three areas account for around two-thirds of industrial output. Hungary has limited natural resources. Bauxite, for the production of aluminium, is mined and there are limited reserves of hard coal. There is also gas and oil. The production of all these natural resources has been declining.

Agriculture was a key sector under communism and was favoured in many ways in order to support the material well-being of the population. Table 2.1 indicates that agriculture accounted for nearly 6 per cent of GDP. It also accounts for over 10 per cent of the workforce, with many industrial workers undertaking agricultural jobs as a secondary activity, and for more than 20 per cent of exports. It is relatively less heavily subsidized than many neighbouring states, and especially compared to the European Union. Under the previous regime Hungarians were considered to enjoy the best standard of living in COMECON, and the agricultural sector made a large contribution to this. This sector has, however, been seriously affected by recent economic changes and by a series of severe droughts. Restructuring of the agricultural sector, as well as the difficulties of finding new markets for agricultural products, have resulted in great problems. The situation has been worsened by a lack of finance and investment and by the EU's refusal to open up its markets

[1] See Randlesome, C. (1994) *The Business Culture in Germany*. Butterworth-Heinemann, Oxford.

Table 2.1 *Structure of GDP in Hungary in 1993 (per cent)*

Agriculture, forestry	5.6
Industry	23.1
Construction	5.3
Transport and communications	7.0
Services	20.5
Trade	11.0
Other	27.5
Total	100.0

Source: Central Statistical Office.

more extensively to Hungarian products. Output and employment have consequently declined considerably.

In the service sector, tourism plays an important foreign currency earning role. Hungary was a popular tourist venue under communism and is now faced with the challenge of competing with other lower-cost holiday destinations. Tourists from Eastern Europe have declined considerably in number as a result of increased freedom of movement, and sizeable investment is being undertaken in order to increase Hungary's attractiveness as a holiday and business destination. Another area of services, which has experienced substantial growth and upgrading, is retailing. Foreign investment in a variety of forms (acquisitions, majority shareholdings and franchising) has helped to modernize Hungary's retailing structure and offer consumers a range of products similar in standard to those of Western Europe.

The Hungarian economy has attracted much more foreign investment than the other East European post-communist states. It has been estimated that cumulative foreign investment by the end of 1993 amounted to more than US$ 7 billion (*Doing Business in Hungary*, Citibank/Price Waterhouse, 1994). Hungary received US$ 5.6 billion of investment in the period 1989–93 compared to US$ 3 billion received by Poland and US$ 2.2 billion by the Czech Republic. However, the rate of foreign investment has since decreased and there are indications that investors are looking more widely in the region for investment opportunities.

By 1995 private companies accounted for the bulk of economic activity, although almost half of the economy remained in state hands. The growth of small companies, many with less than twenty employees, has made a substantial contribution to the expansion of private sector output. Official statistics, moreover, fail to take account of the so-called 'grey' economy, which is reputed to amount to about one-third of reported GDP.

Post-communist Hungary inherited an industry structure which was inappropriate to its domestic and international requirements. Although the communist regime had been keen to foster its own brand of 'goulash communism' – more freedom for enterprises and more emphasis on light industry and agriculture – the main focus of the economy remained rigidly planned Soviet-style heavy industry producing capital goods. Trading relations had been largely with the Soviet Union and other COMECON partners. The collapse of communism highlighted these features, and subsequent developments have been concerned to address structural inadequacies and raise company performance. This has been a particular problem with the large monopolistic enterprises. In many cases these have been broken up and privatized in smaller units. Often the most attractive parts were acquired by foreign investors. This left the remaining companies in limbo and uncertain of their role. The difficulty of privatizing some companies in old sectors such as iron and steel, aluminium, mining and chemicals induced the centre-right government to take twelve companies back into state ownership rather than adding 80,000 people to the ranks of the unemployed.

The private sector is, however, expanding and an increasing range of services (both for business and private consumption) has become available. Small firms with under fifty employees numbered less than 8000 in 1989 but had already increased to over 55,000 by 1992, with the majority in trade and services. Local entrepreneurs have played a major role in the expansion of the private sector, although foreign companies have had a highly visible role. GEC's acquisition of Tungsram and the investments made in Hungary by Ford, General Motors and Suzuki are examples.

Although a small country, Hungary has its own internal divide. The areas bordering Austria to the west and north are economically more advanced than the east and south of the country, where agriculture and older industries predominate. For example, the Miskolc region, known as Hungary's 'Ruhr', is characterized by traditional heavy industries such as steel, chemicals and mining and by unemployment rates 50 per cent above the national average. Furthermore, while overall unemployment has levelled off or even started to fall, in this area it continued to increase in the first half of 1994. In order to alleviate such disparities central and local government instituted regional development measures, for example, setting up duty-free zones and industrial parks and by encouraging investment and the creation of small businesses.

Substantial changes are taking place in the structure of the Hungarian economy, in particular in the shape of a shift away from heavy industry and from predominant trading relations with former COMECON partners. A result of this shift has been substantial internal turbulence in the economy as old structures have eroded and new companies – both domestic and foreign – have been established. It is likely that the adjustment process will continue for some time, especially in view of the growing importance of the EU in Hungary's economic activity.

Foreign trade

The collapse of communism has brought about a dramatic shift in the orientation of Hungarian business. For forty-five years the primary focus was on the Soviet Union and the other members of COMECON. Since 1989, however, Hungarian business has turned increasingly westward and by 1993 over 40 per cent of trade was with the EU, with Germany alone accounting for over half of this. Table 2.2 illustrates the amount of foreign trade and Hungary's main trading partners.

Hungarian exports to the EU are concentrated in four main areas: agricultural products, textiles and clothing, machinery and transport equipment on their own account for nearly half the total. The Association Agreement signed with the European Community in March 1992, however, places a number of restrictions and limitations on Hungary's major exports. This has caused some resentment. The EU is seen as a model for the future development of Hungary and there is a powerful aspiration to become a full member. Hungarians feel that the EU has helped to provide markets for Hungarian products, but that more could have and could still be done. The official position of the EU, that Hungary must put its own house in order before being granted full membership, is comprehensible but not particularly appealing to Hungarians.

Table 2.2 *Foreign trade in 1994 (US$ millions)*

	Imports	Exports
Former communist bloc of which:	3490	2473
Russia and CIS	2193	1241
Czech Republic	347	198
Slovak Republic	356	144
Poland	193	222
Romania	119	197
EU countries of which:	6600	5457
Germany	3403	3082
Italy	1017	906
Others	2180	1469
EFTA countries of which:	2702	1548
Austria	1748	1164
Others	954	384
Others:	1762	1223
Total	14 554	10 701

Source: Ministry of Industry and Trade, Budapest.

Some Hungarian companies have responded to the difficulty of penetrating Western European markets by reviving contacts with former trading partners in Russia and elsewhere in the former Soviet bloc in order to find alternative customers and to avoid the trap of being excessively reliant on one or a few markets. Although Hungary was principally preoccupied with its relationship with the EU in 1993, it also entered into free trade agreements with EFTA and with the Visegrad group of countries. In spite of the inroads made into Western European markets and the conclusion of agreements with its former CMEA partners, however, Hungary has been unable to avoid problems with the current account deficit, which by 1993 had reached US$ 3.5 bn (EBRD, 1995).

Looking at both sides of the trade equation in turn, we can see that on the export side the collapse of CMEA markets forced a quite successful reorientation towards the western economies. This export redirection worked itself out by 1992, to leave Hungary's exports to the west mainly composed of basic industrial products such as food and drink, textiles, agricultural produce, chemicals and raw materials. Some manufacturing sectors, such as electrical engineering and other metal products, have recovered and have done reasonably well, though some exporting companies have gone under as a result of the harsher financial climate and the enforcement of tough bankruptcy laws. A key factor in the successful export performance of many Hungarian firms has been the large amount of foreign investment: foreign-owned firms in Hungary have consistently out-performed local firms in export markets.

It is problems with imports which are considered to be the main cause of the worsening current account deficit. These problems have their origins in the extensive liberalization of imports during the first two years of the reforms, when some 90 per cent of imports became free and local market share was lost by most Hungarian companies. Imports of consumer goods doubled between 1989 and 1991. Local manufacturing companies simply did not have sufficient time to restructure in order to meet the foreign competition, and the Hungarian government paid little attention to implementing an industrial policy. After 1992 the import of investment goods and industrial inputs became relatively much more substantial, and this was interpreted as a sign of industrial regeneration based on the use of foreign technology (OECD, 1995). But some commentators were a little less sanguine about the effects of this development, pointing out that import-led industrialization should be the hallmark policy of a non-industrialized country, which has no domestic capacity to produce capital goods, rather than an industrial country undergoing systemic change such as Hungary, and which had a significant capability to produce many of the required capital goods (Amsden *et al.*, 1994).

In 1995 the Hungarian government was finally forced to confront the current account deficit problem with a drastic package of reforms. In March that year it brought in a series of 'mini-shock' reforms, principally intended to narrow the gap between imports and exports. The two main components were an 8 per cent surcharge on imports, and an immediate 9 per cent devaluation of the forint, to be followed by monthly reductions. The reform was well received by the financial community and the indications by early 1996 were that, even though the package could be stimulating inflation through higher prices on imported goods, it nevertheless looks set to reduce the current account deficit over the next few years. A number of other factors could assist the process: Hungarian wage levels have fallen; successful company restructuring has led to increases in productivity; and the Dayton Peace Agreement signed in late 1995 by the main warring parties in the Yugoslav successor states seems set to establish a new peaceful order in the Balkans, and a period of economic reconstruction and development.

Business and finance

As in other areas, the first real reforms to the financial sector were undertaken by the former regime, which initiated a reform of the banks in 1987 to create a two-tier banking system. The National Bank of Hungary retained its role as the central bank but passed on its commercial banking activities to a set of new commercial banks including the Hungarian Credit Bank, the Commercial and Credit Bank and the Budapest Bank. A further reform was introduced in 1991 with the passing of the Financial Institutions Act which, with subsequent amendments, laid down the regulatory and supervisory framework.

The Financial Institutions Act specified the types of banking institutions permitted to operate in Hungary and the legal requirements for these operations. The Act specifies four types of bank: (1) commercial banks offering a more or less full range of services, (2) investment banks, (3) specialist providers such as factoring houses and (4) savings banks.

The banks face a range of problems as they adapt their services and operations to the requirements of an advanced market economy. The most serious one initially was the large amount of bad loans. Banks tended to retain a close relationship with their enterprise customers and were reluctant to 'get tough' with them, hoping instead to forge a mutually beneficial link with them in the new market economy as in the German model. The bad loans problem was tackled through a bank consolidation programme implemented first in early 1993, which swapped bad debts in the banking system for government bonds repayable over a twenty-year time period. Further tranches of government bonds were introduced in late 1993 and mid-1994, pulling the banking system at least partly out of the mess it inherited from the old regime. Other changes to the banking system have been made. For example, the Credit Guarantee Corporation was established to support the financial requirements of the small business sector, and the Hungarian Export–Import Bank was established in early 1994 to facilitate Hungarian exports and capital goods imports.

Although there is increasing foreign participation in the banking system, many banks are still awaiting privatization. A December 1997 deadline has been set for the privatization of the large banks but the process has gone very slowly. Part of the reason is that the predominance of foreign capital in the privatization process so far has led to unease over possible foreign control of the banking system. A recent opinion poll showed over 85 per cent of Hungarians are opposed to the sale of MOL, one of the country's largest gas utililities (*Central European*, September 1995, page 7). In addition, the banks are closely involved with state-owned enterprises, either as shareholders or as creditors. In many cases this means that the banks have loaned money to or are owners of shares in companies which are only marginally viable, if at all. This reduces the scope for the banks to provide investment funds for other companies in Hungary. Many banks are also considered to be undercapitalized.

Nevertheless, although the driving force still remains foreign direct investment, domestic investment in the economy is rising. A further barrier to domestic investment is the high rate of interest charged by the banks. The National Bank has set high rates of interest in order to contain inflation. The interbank interest rate was 22 per cent in 1993 and the end of year average for 1994 was estimated to be 31 per cent (*Economics of Transition*, 1995 (1): 140). Borrowing money from Hungarian banks can thus be very costly, and foreign companies tend not to do so.

An alternative source of finance is through quotation on the Budapest Stock Exchange, which was opened in June 1990. The Exchange has remained small, and most of its activity involves trading in the treasury bills which have been used by the government to finance the budget deficit. However, recent successful privatizations have invigorated it. The government floated the country's national savings bank in August 1995, increasing the market by 20 per cent, but it is the programme to privatize the main utilities which is expected to have the biggest effect on the stock exchange. Major state-owned enterprises in the gas, electricity and telecommunications sectors are set for flotation in 1996 and 1997, and this should increase the overall size of the market substantially.

Taxation

Reform in the Hungarian taxation system pre-dated the collapse of communism. Hungary introduced a value added tax and personal income tax in January 1988, and corporate taxation exactly a year later.

Personal income tax is progressive, and currently rises to 44 per cent of income, while corporate tax was recently reduced from 36 per cent to 18 per cent, with shareholders having to pay for much of the reduction through a new tax of 23 per cent on dividends (EBRD, 1995, page 45).

Part of the reason for the heavy inflow of foreign investment in the early years of the transition was the very propitious taxation regime granted to foreign investors. This initially provided for sizable reductions in the corporate tax rate, and even complete tax holidays for investments deemed critical to the economy. Other features were a faster depreciation rate and a generous interpretation of which machinery and equipment was eligible for such favourable treatment. At the end of 1993 the system was almost completely phased out, having achieved most of its original purpose, though some advantages are still available to foreign investors in key sectors.

Business, the labour market and trade unions

Employment

One of the major 'shocks' of the transition has been in the labour market. The communist system guaranteed employment for all, even if this signified the creation of unnecessary positions or under-employment. Many jobs were also created for specific political reasons, rather than for economic ones. Under communism labour was cheap and enterprises often hoarded labour just in case it might be needed. Labour shortages were endemic, and in Hungary there was a high degree of labour turnover as workers moved from company to company in order to obtain higher wages.

The transition has had a wide-ranging impact on employment. Unemployment rates have risen dramatically, from 2.5 per cent in 1990 to around 12 per cent in 1992 and 1993, before declining somewhat to 10.4 per cent in 1994 (EBRD, 1995, page 197). Unemployment now appears to have levelled off and is forecast to fall as new jobs are created.

The labour market can be divided into four main areas:

1. The public sector (i.e. government bodies, education, etc.)
2. State-owned enterprises
3. Domestically owned private companies
4. Foreign companies.

The public sector, with over 900,000 employees, is a major employer, although wages are relatively low. It is not unusual for public sector employees to have more than one job (officially or unofficially). Employment in the remaining state-owned enterprises is possibly the most insecure in Hungary, in view of the uncertain future of many companies.

These are often firms which are unattractive to private investors or which have been kept alive in order not to aggravate unemployment. Restructuring has already had a dramatic impact on certain industries. For example, employment in the defence industry has shrunk from 30,000 in 1988 to only 5000 in 1994. However, if the private sector continues to expand there will be increasing opportunities for those currently employed in state-owned companies provided they have the requisite knowledge and skills and can adapt to the new environment.

The private sector has in general attracted the better qualified and more energetic and entrepreneurial sections of the labour force. Wages are usually higher than in the public sector and in state-owned companies, with the highest wages being paid by foreign companies. The corollary of higher wages are higher expectations and demands on the part of employers, many of whom are accustomed to working according to Western European or American practice.

In general, wages have stayed more or less in line with inflation, although productivity gains have meant that the unit cost of labour to companies has fallen. This has enabled companies to retain their international competitiveness and the cost and quality of labour remains a distinctive source of national competitive advantage for Hungary (the average monthly wage was just over US$300 in mid-1995). There is also a ready pool of labour because of unemployment and continuing restructuring. Hungarians are regarded as well qualified and skilled workers with a strong work discipline. Many foreign companies are attracted to Hungary because of the low cost of labour. However, the cost of labour can be misleading if other costs are not taken into account. For example, low labour costs can be eroded by low productivity, need for supervision by expatriate managers, and transport costs. Hungarian workers, because of their education and training, are considered to be quick at acquiring new skills and to require limited supervision. Hungarians are also regarded as being competent to carry out many managerial functions, although a managerial deficit still exists.

Trade unions

Under the former regime the unitary trades union association co-operated actively at national level with the ruling communist party, while within the workplace the trades union organization worked closely with enterprise management. The communist National Council of Trades Unions (SzOT), membership of which was virtually universal, was not immune to the dissatisfactions in Hungarian society. Towards the end of the 1980s SzOT's position was increasingly challenged by new trade unions not linked to the ruling party. In 1990 SzOT was reconstituted and renamed the National Confederation of Hungarian Trades Unions (MSzOSz). MSzOSz also declared its independence from any political party, although it is still closely linked to the Hungarian Socialist Party (the former communists).

Even though MSzOSz faces a challenge from a number of other trade union bodies, some formerly in SzOT, it remains the major trade union organization. Although trade union membership is no longer mandatory, membership levels remain relatively high with approximately 60 per cent of the workforce unionized. The sixty-five or so unions affiliated to MSzOSz have a total membership approaching 1.3 million, which represents almost one third of the workforce. Other major trade union federations are SzEF (Trade Union Coordination Forum) with 500,000 members and ASzOK (Autonomous Trade Unions) with 400,000 members.

The decline in union membership is attributable in part to the collapse of the communist system. Individuals are no longer compulsorily enrolled. Furthermore, the post-communist environment and the growth of the private sector are less conducive to trade union activities. In the state-owned sector, too, the depressed situation of many companies limits the scope for action by the trades unions.

There are also a number of organizations representing the views of employers, of which the National Federation of Entrepreneurs (VOSz) is possibly the leading example. Other organizations include the Association of Hungarian Manufacturers (GYOSz) and bodies representing various types of co-operative and the self-employed. The lack of coherent organization is understandable in view of the clear differences of interest between state-owned and private companies and between domestic and foreign employers.

The National Council for the Reconciliation of Interests was set up in 1988 to act as a wage-negotiation body and has since developed as a body in which employer and employee representatives and government can discuss labour and social issues. However, the fragmentation of interest groups, with seven officially recognized trades unions and nine employer organizations, has tended to frustrate any attempt to achieve a consensus.

The legal framework for employee participation in companies is laid down in the 1992 Labour Code. According to this company sites with more than fifty employees must establish a Work Council based on the German model. Employers are obliged to consult the Work Council on a range of issues affecting employees, including reorganization, training and early retirement.

Declining membership, trade union diversity, high unemployment and the general climate of change and uncertainty have tended to act against the trade unions adopting an aggressive role. When industrial action has been taken by the unions, as in the coal industry in 1992–93, the aim has been essentially to influence government policy rather than to challenge company management.

Business, education and training

The Hungarian education system is generally regarded as providing a good level of education. The education sector is largely state-run, although there an increasing number of foreign and private providers have appeared since 1989. Under communism the education system played an overtly ideological as well as an educational role. Nowadays the system appears largely neutral politically.

Education is compulsory between the ages of 6 and 16 and nursery education caters for about one-third of 3- to 6-year-olds. Approximately 75 per cent of the age group are enrolled in secondary schools, with 15 per cent of the age group proceeding to higher education. Secondary schools include grammar (gymnasium) and technical schools. Education is highly regarded and there is a strong demand for places in higher education. The education system has been adapting to the new post-communist environment, but developments have been hampered by limited finances. Salaries of university teachers, for example, are low and many academics have multiple jobs. A government proposal in 1995 to introduce tuition fees met with a loud negative response from the public.

The major university centre is Budapest, with its range of specialist universities (e.g. University of Economic Sciences, Technical University). Other notable centres are Debrecen, Pécs and Szeged. There are also technical universities in Miskolc and Veszprém. However, a major deficiency of the current provision of education and training relates to providing the competencies necessary to work in a market economy, e.g. in management, accounting and finance and marketing. For example, many engineers need to acquire managerial skills in order to enhance their employability. Some steps were already being undertaken in the 1980s and with the transition there has been an expansion in provision of business and management courses. Courses are often provided by foreign university institutions, sometimes in conjunction with local public and private organizations. There is particular interest in obtaining credible foreign qualifications, such as the MBA, which are seen as improving employment prospects.

Business and the environment

Hungary suffered in a similar way to the other countries of Central and Eastern Europe from environmental degradation. Communist regimes, focusing on meeting production targets, took little account of the impact on the environment of air, land and water pollution. Untreated sewage is still being released into local rivers in some major urban centres.

The negative impact on the environment was aggravated by the inefficiency of industry, which caused higher rates of energy consumption and pollution in comparison to more advanced and more efficient operators. It is not only the physical environment which has been affected by the absence of pollution control. The health of the population has also been severely affected and the high incidence of many diseases (for example, heart ailments and cancer) has been linked with the intensity of pollution.

Companies now have to cope with more stringent pollution regulations and associated public expectations. For both domestic and foreign companies, making good the damage caused in the past (for example, to polluted land), and investment in equipment meeting today's standards can be a costly exercise. Treatment of waste is often regarded by many of them as an expensive extra, and there is a need to develop a stronger sense of corporate responsibility towards the environment.

Nevertheless, there has been a growing public awareness of environmental issues. An example is the continuing opposition to the Danube Dam project planned by Hungary and Slovakia. Hungary and Czechoslovakia agreed under the former regimes to co-operate in the construction of a dam at Gabcikovo-Nagymaros. Hungary, however, subsequently decided to pull out of the project after recognition of the damage that would be caused to the environment. The dispute soured the relationship between Budapest and Bratislava to such an extent that the dispute was referred to the International Court of Justice in 1993.

A key factor in attempts to reduce pollution in Hungary has been the aspiration to emulate practice in Western Europe and prepare the way for accession to the EU. Hungary is keen to meet the increasingly demanding requirements of EU environmental legislation by 1999. In order to achieve this a decision has been taken to invest substantial sums of money in projects such as the modernization of the country's oil refineries.

Conclusion

Hungary is conventionally seen as one of the few transition economies to have seriously experimented with a 'gradualist' reform strategy. In a broader sense, the introduction of meaningful reforms in the 1960s and 1980s, followed by more far-reaching reforms in the post-communist period, means that there has effectively been a current of gradual reform throughout the last thirty years. At the same time, focusing on the post-communist period, Hungary can be considered a member of the 'shock therapy' group of transition economies, because *inter alia* it very quickly implemented radical import liberalization, reduced subsidies and created a competitive market environment which quickly induced bankruptcy and painful restructuring.

How has this reform strategy, however we wish to categorize it, affected the emerging business culture in Hungary? First, the point must be made that the early reforms and private sector experience under communism greatly helped to underpin the subsequent rapid growth of entrepreneurship in Hungary after 1989. It is widely known that the bulk of those entering and succeeding in the private sector after 1989 were also those who had previously had substantial experience in the legalized private sector in the 1980s. Moreover, an unofficial economy of some considerable size and sophistication was tolerated within the interstices of the official economy, and this too underpinned much of the entrepreneurial activity after 1989. The early reforms also served to develop an advanced management culture within the larger enterprise sector, because the old bureaucratic system of management was increasingly being sidelined in favour of a more independent and creative managerial stratum capable of reacting to the new freedoms and responsibilities engendered by the reforms. There was also a significant amount of dissaggregation and spin-off activity both before and after the collapse of communism, which further entrenched the new managerial styles within Hungarian society.

But the emerging world of business in Hungary has been much more influenced by the post-communist reforms and the introduction of the market economy with fully legitimate private entrepreneurship. The new freedoms catalysed the shift of many more people into business and the prevailing economic stability offered a propitious business environment. The privatization programme and support for new start enterprises has created a dynamic market-oriented sector which continues to expand and to provide much needed competitive pressure on the remaining state sector. In addition, there was the inflow of ideas, capital, technology and innovations in the first wave of foreign investment into Hungary in 1990–93. Over 2200 joint ventures were formed in the first nine months of 1990 alone, and the numbers grew rapidly thereafter. As many surveys have pointed out, joint ventures have had a major impact on Hungary's economic performance, especially with regard to export performance and inducing competitiveness through forced emulation and technology and managerial skills transfer.

A business culture is therefore emerging in Hungary which is sophisticated, entrepreneurial and open to new ideas and influences. The country has benefited greatly from earlier marketization than in other states in the region, and it has retained remarkably little from the bureaucratic management system operating under communism. If it can finally settle the legacies of financial mismanagement under communism identified by Janos Kornai, then Hungary stands well placed to emerge as one of the most open, forward looking and business-friendly economies to have emerged from the collapse of communism in Eastern Europe.

References and suggestions for further reading

Amsden, A., Kochanowicz, J. and Taylor, L. (1994) *The Market Meets its Match: Restructuring the Economies of Eastern Europe.* Harvard University Press, Cambridge, Mass, USA.

Bakos, G. (1993) *Hungarian transition after three years.* Paper presented at the Inaugural Symposium of the Centre for European Studies, Nansan University, Nagoya, Japan, 15 December.

Batt, J. (1991) *East Central Europe from Reform to Transformation.* Royal Institute of International Affairs, London.

Business Central Europe, (various issues).

Canning, A. and Hare, P. (1994) The privatisation process – economic and political aspects of the Hungarian approach, in Estrin, S. (ed.) (1994) *Privatisation in Central and Eastern Europe.* Longman, London.

Central European (various issues) Euromoney Publications, London.

Citibank/Price Waterhouse (1993) *Doing Business in Hungary.*

Citibank/Price Waterhouse (1994) *Doing Business in Hungary: supplement.*

Drost, H. (1995) *What's What and Who's Who in Europe.* Cassell.

EBRD (1995) *Transition Report.* EBRD, London.

Economist Intelligence Unit (various) *Quarterly Country Survey: Hungary.*

Estrin, S. (ed.) (1994) *Privatisation in Central and Eastern Europe.* Longman, London.

Fischer, B. (1992) *Large privatisation in Poland, Hungary and Czechoslovakia.* RFE/RL reseach report, Vol. 1, No. 44, 6 November.

Gacs, J., Karimov, I. O. and Schneider, C. M. (1993) Small scale privatization in Eastern Europe and Russia: a historical and comparative perspective. *Communist Economies and Economic Transformation,* Vol. 5, No. 1.

Johnson, S. (1994) Private business in Eastern Europe, in Blanchard, O., Froot, K. and Sachs, J. (eds) (1994) *The Transition in Eastern Europe,* Vol. 2, University of Chicago Press, Chicago.

Kilényi, G. and Lamm, V. (eds) (1990) *New Tendencies in the Hungarian Economy.* Akadémiai Kiadó.

OECD (various) *OECD Economic Surveys: Hungary.* OECD, Paris.

Okolicsanyi, K. (1993) *Private sector gains little from high Hungarian savings.* RFE/RL research report, Vol. 2, No. 15, 9 April.

Swain, N. (1992) *Hungary, The Rise and Fall of Feasible Socialism.* Verso.

Tovias, A. (1994) Modernizing Hungary's industrial structure: the contribution of the EC, in Buckley, P.J. and Ghauri, P.N. (eds) (1994) *The Economics of Change in East and Central Europe.* Academic Press.

3 The business culture in Poland

George Blazyca

Introduction

As elsewhere in the former Soviet bloc, the business culture in Poland has undergone immense change since the revolutions of 1989. Although the pace of change across the old centrally planned economies is uneven, Poland appears to be one the region's success stories. Indeed one long established UK-based investment trust, Foreign & Colonial, described Poland in the summer of 1995 as a 'tiger' economy. Even allowing for the usual marketing hype there was little doubt that, by 1995, Poland commanded increasing investor enthusiasm. This is not to say that the emergence of a new business culture in Poland has followed a smooth trajectory – far from it, a considerable number of 'downs' have accompanied the 'ups' – but the centre of economic and business gravity has tipped decisively towards enterprise, initiative and the market. Indeed it might be argued that in the short period since 1989 a genuine business culture has emerged for the first time in forty years. This is no small achievement. It is also one that confounds those critics who argued that central-planning habits would be an enduring impediment to business development.

One of the clearest features of the Polish business scene in the 1990s was the dynamism of a new sector of small private enterprise, but by mid decade there was evidence too of innovative response to changed circumstances on the part of many managers of state-owned firms. People, especially of course the young, learn quickly how to adapt to new possibilities and opportunities. Moreover, Poland had a history of small-scale legal private business activity and trade under communism which was possibly the most extensive of the Soviet-style centrally planned economies. This experience itself usefully underpinned the massive expansion of the private business sector and entrepreneurialism after 1990.

Of course a new business culture has not been transplanted with clinical precision in place of the old. It is very likely that Poland, for the foreseeable future, will be a country with multiple business cultures: one will be dynamic, private, market-based and legal; another inhabiting the interstices of the economy – its darker 'grey' corners – will be dynamic, private, market based but unofficial and semi-legal; yet another will be state run and will be more or less dynamic depending on government policy and the strength of sectoral competitive pressures. As elsewhere in Eastern Europe, the business culture will adapt to the prevailing business environment, emerging with elements of the 'old' fused on to the 'new'.

Business and government

Government and political parties

Poland is noted for its exciting political life. Six governments appeared in the interval between 1989 and 1995 and a seventh was being formed at the time of writing in early 1996. But the general election of September 1993 appeared to be something of a watershed. It brought into power a coalition of parties (the Social Democratic Alliance – SLD, and Peasants' Party – PSL) with roots in the communist tradition. A combination of better organization, better discipline, much less fractiousness and a new voting mechanism meant that the SLD-PSL's 36 per cent of the popular vote was rewarded with 66 per cent of parliamentary seats. The surprise for some in this election was that voters rejected the two major Solidarity

Table 3.1 *General election results – September 1993*

Party	Votes (per cent share)	Seats (per cent share)	Seats (number)
SLD	20.4	37.2	171
PSL	15.4	28.7	132
UD	10.6	16.1	74
UP	7.3	8.9	41
KPN	5.8	4.8	22
BBWR	5.4	3.5	16
Others	0.9	0.8	4
Total	65.8	100.0	460

Notes: SLD, Sojusz Lewicy Demokratycznej; PSL, Polskie Stronnictwo Ludowe; UD, Unia Demokratyczny; UP, Unia Pracy; KPN, Konfederacji Polski Niepodleglej; BBWR, Bezpartyjny Blok Wspierania Reform.
'Others' refers to organizations representing minorities, especially Germans, for which the 5 per cent threshold (share of vote needed to enter parliament) did not apply.

Source: Rzeczpospolita, 27 September 1993

parties, the Democratic Union (*Unia Demokratyczna* – *UD*) and Congress of Liberal Democrats (*Kongres Liberalno-Demokratyczny* – *KLD*), parties which later merged into the Freedom Union (*Unia Wolnosci* – *UW*) led, until April 1995, by former prime minister Tadeusz Mazowiecki, and from then by Leszek Balcerowicz who jumped from economics to a new career in politics. These parties had shaped economic policy from 1989 and the September 1993 vote was widely interpreted as a rejection of aggressive liberalism. Meanwhile the post-Solidarity right, although with 28 per cent of voters, found it paid a high price for its fragmentation: its only parliamentary representation was the KPN's (the ultra right Confederation for an Independent Poland) 4.8 per cent of seats.

Managing the economy – institutions

Economic and social policy is shaped by the government through the council of ministers – the Cabinet. Parliament, the Sejm, with 460 deputies is the supreme political authority although it is to some extent constrained by the 100 strong Senate and by ill-defined limits on presidential powers. The president is the head of state and guardian of the constitution but should exercise little direct influence over business and economic affairs. In the so-called 'small constitution' established in the post-communist vacuum, the then Solidarity-held presidency was given direct authority over three areas of government: the ministries of defence, foreign and internal affairs. An understanding existed that the president would nominate ministers only to these posts and would let the government get on with running the country, and especially the economy. But in the period from September 1993 through to 1995, with a non-Solidarity government in power, President Lech Walesa was given to spontaneous and frequently mischievous interventions over economic matters. This persistent interference may in part have contributed to Walesa's defeat in the November 1995 presidential elections by the reformed Communist Alexander Kwasniewski.

Returning, however, to institutions which bear heavily on the business culture, the finance ministry (*Ministerstwo Finansow*) and the National Bank of Poland (*Narodowy Bank Polski*), have become pre-eminent in economic policy making since 1989. The old apparatus of central economic administration, especially the Planning Commission and branch ministries, have withered away or been transformed unrecogniz-ably. The central planning office (*Centralny Urzad Planowania* – *CUP*) is a forecasting and survey bureau which publishes regular commentaries on the economy and the industrial mood. The labour and social policy ministry (*Ministerstwo Pracy i Polityki Socjalnej*), given high unemploy-ment, restructuring effects and its responsibility for the country's nine million pensioners, has a high profile political role and one that is likely to remain important in the foreseeable future. Poland's commitment to

At Butterworth-Heinemann we are determined to provide you with a quality service. To help supply you with information on relevant titles as soon as it is available, please fill in the form below and return to us using the FREEPOST facility. Thank you for your help and we look forward to hearing from you.

What title have you purchased? _____

Where was the purchase made? _____

When was the purchase made? _____

Name (Please Print): _____

Job Title: _____

Street: _____

Town: _____

County: _____ Postcode: _____

Country: _____ Telephone: _____

Company Activity: _____

Signature: _____ Date: _____

(FOR OFFICE USE ONLY)

BUTTERWORTH
HEINEMANN

Butterworth-Heinemann Limited – Registered Office: Michelin House. 81 Fulham Road, London, SW3 6RB. Registered in England 194771. VAT number GB: 340 242992

Direct Mail Department
Butterworth-Heinemann
FREEPOST
OXFORD
OX2 8BR

UK

trade 'openness', its network of international agreements and, since May 1995, the partial floating of the zloty, all conspire to reduce the direct influence on business of the ministry for foreign economic relations (*Ministerstwo Wspolpracy Gospodarczej z Zagranica*).

The privatization ministry (*Ministerstwo Przeksztalcen Wlasnosciowych – MPW*) is a new and major player on the business scene. It is also worth noting the potentially important role played by the Anti-Monopoly Office (*Urzad Antimonopolowy*) which was energetically run from its inception in 1990 until early 1995 by a Lodz-based academic economist, Anna Fornalczyk. Following her departure the office appears to have played a more subdued and certainly less high profile role in business regulation.

Some sectoral ministries continue to exist although a major reform of the central administration was begun in 1994 and intended to be fully implemented in 1996. However, in early 1996 these sectoral institutions with some influence on business include: industry and trade (*Ministerstwo Przemyslu i Handlu*), agriculture (*Ministerstwo Rolnictwa i Gospodarki Zywniosciowej*), construction (*Ministerstwo Gospodarki Przestrzennej i Budownictwa*), transport (*Ministerstwo Transportu i Gospodarki Morskiej*), and communications (*Ministerstwo Lacznosci*). Whatever happens to central administration, the environment ministry (*Ministry Ochrony Srodowiska Zasobow Naturalnych i Lesnictwa*) may be expected to play an increasingly important role in the future especially in applying EU norms to business activity. Despite the existence of government departments with sector responsibilities throughout the early 1990s, in all cases it was hard to locate new or decisive sectoral policy initiatives. The important lesson for business is that the policy-making centre of gravity has shifted away from sectoral branches towards the finance ministry, central bank and also to privatization, although the latter should eventually do itself out of a job.

Another functional body whose role should not be overlooked is the central statistical office (*Glowny Urzad Statystyczny – GUS*). GUS publishes some of the fullest and perhaps most reliable economic data in Eastern Europe. It also produces a useful detailed monthly communique on economic performance. One other important aspect in the development of a new business culture in Poland since 1989 is the emergence of independent economic forecasters and business consultants. Research organizations like the Gdansk Institute for Market Economics, as well as some academic institutions, have entered the forecasting business. Where the business culture, such as it was under central planning, was characterized by a central monopoly of information, one of the most significant changes in the post-1989 climate is the multiplicity and variety in information for business decision-making. As the scope of managerial discretion (even in state firms) has widened so too has the supply of business information.

At the regional and local level some authorities have, since 1989, shown striking enterprise in economic matters, particularly in trying to attract inward investment. Others however have been slower to respond to the new environment while some have made life awkward for new private enterprise. Some regions however face, or will face, major economic difficulty in restructuring production. This is true of major conurbations such as Silesia with its heavy industry, Lodz with its concentration of textiles as well as of smaller 'one-plant' towns such as Starachowice, south of Warsaw, with its 'Star' truck plant, or Mielec, dependent on the production of light aircraft the Defence Ministry no longer wishes to purchase.

Polish local government is structured on forty-nine major regions or vovoidships which group 2483 self-governing 'communes' (*gminy*). The vovoidship has tended to play a less important role in local economic policy making than might be expected, and city and town councils at the commune level have, where they have chosen to act, made a greater impact.

Business and economic reform

The fall of communism in 1989 was not entirely a neat affair and this had its impact on economic management and the business climate. Often reform legislation moved through parliament at an agonisingly slow pace and some critical economic policy instruments, in particular the annual state budget, were almost always bitterly contested. These political struggles did considerable damage to Poland's standing with potential inward investors. At first, and until the general election of October 1991, it was the dominant influence of communist MPs in parliament that guaranteed reform legislation a tortuous passage. But later a parliament inhabited by an immense variety of post-Solidarity groupings, yet dominated by none of them, created another volatile mix and further problems for economic legislation.

In the more recent period, from 1993 to the end of 1995, the post-communist dominated parliament was no longer an obstacle to legislation; instead, the president, Lech Walesa, could be counted on to challenge many of the Sejm's economic and business initiatives. Sometimes the challenge was well founded but often it was no more than part of Walesa's continuing crusade against (post) communism. Of course, as the November 1995 presidential election drew closer it became increasingly difficult to disentangle the two motives. After Alexander Kwasniewski's victory, with both presidency and parliament in SLD hands, most commentators expected the legislative process to become smoother. Needless to say the post-Solidarity political opposition viewed this development in less sanguine terms. Returning to Poland's business culture, no understanding of the forces shaping it during the 1990s is possible without an appreciation of the shock to the business climate that came in early 1990 with the launch of the Balcerowicz plan.

The Balcerowicz plan

In August 1989, as the first Solidarity government, led by Tadeusz Mazowiecki, came to power, some forty years of communist rule and Soviet style economic management officially ended in Poland. Central economic planning, which had in any case by that time ceased to function effectively, was abandoned and the move to the market started. This transformation was planned by the newly appointed finance minister, Leszek Balcerowicz, whose famous 'Balcerowicz plan', a shock therapy to extinguish Poland's hyper-inflation, came into effect on 1 January 1990.

The new government's policy intentions were both clear and ambitious. The aim was to create as speedily as possible a western style market economy. Following what later became standard IMF advice on the economics of transformation, the Polish programme had three strands: stabilization, restructuring and privatization. But with late 1989 monthly inflation running at over 30 per cent, it was clear that stabilization was the priority task. Thus, although Mazowiecki and Balcerowicz were both committed to privatization, the new government's economic policy initially was best known for its firm deflationary stance, for its 'shock therapy'.

The Balcerowicz plan had three key features:

- It cut subsidies and public spending and aimed for a Maastricht-like control over the budget deficit.
- It opened with a dramatic 32 per cent zloty devaluation and a promise, in a move to boost confidence in the currency, to defend the new rate for the foreseeable future. In order to give this confidence a sound foundation, a zloty stabilization fund worth US$1 bn was created by Poland's official creditors in the west. The zloty became 'internally convertible': this meant that although firms were obliged to sell foreign exchange earnings to the National Bank at the official rate, the authorities guaranteed to supply business with hard currency to cover all current needs. The complex administrative rationing of foreign exchange ended. The zloty devaluation served two other purposes. It encouraged a shift of resources into exports while the promise of exchange rate stability provided anti-inflation policy with a vitally important 'anchor'.

- A tough tax-based incomes policy, was another crucial feature of the Balcerowicz plan. This was its second 'anchor'. The intention was to break price-wage inflationary push, a spiral very much a feature of Polish economic life and one that threatened to explode as subsidies were reduced and prices liberalized.

Another crucial aspect of 'Balcerowicz' was its insistence on opening Poland to the world economy. As trade barriers were all but dismantled Poland was for a time (1990 and into 1991) one of the world's most open economies. Strong producer pressures for protection were resisted more successfully than is usual in the west.

During 1990 and 1991 the output side of the economy took the brunt of the deflationary force of the Balcerowicz plan. In the two years 1990–91 GDP fell by 17.8 per cent and industrial sales by 33 per cent. Inflation however was reduced to manageable proportions, from 251 per cent on average in 1989 and 586 per cent in 1990, to 70.3 per cent in 1991, and 43 per cent in 1992. The success of the plan's anti-inflationary focus is better seen through average monthly inflation figures, which fell from 11 per cent in 1990 to only 3.1 per cent during 1992.

One of the central achievements of the Balcerowicz plan was the elimination of 'shortage'. More or less chronic shortage, queuing and black market activity were continual features of central planning wherever it existed. Poland's price liberalization immediately ended shortage. If this simply displaced one rationing device by another there would perhaps be little to trumpet. However price liberalization in Poland was accompanied by a flurry of mainly private sector activity which aimed to meet, albeit depressed, market demand. Even if *privatization* was slower than hoped from the start of the Balcerowicz plan in 1990, *the private sector*, as we report in more detail below, was on the move.

Table 3.2   *Polish growth rates and inflation, 1989–95*

Percentage change on previous year	1989	1990	1991	1992	1993	1994	1995
Real GDP	0.2	–11.6	–7.6	2.6	3.8	5.2	6.5
Industrial production							
(old series)	–0.5	–24.2	–11.9	3.9	7.3		
(new series)			–8.0	2.9	6.4	12.1	10.2
Consumer prices	251	586	70.3	43.0	35.3	32.2	27.8

Sources: Rocznik Statystyczny 1994, 1995, (GUS, Warsaw, 1994). Press reports for initial 1995 estimates.

However, policy makers were initially disappointed by the tardy response of state firms to new economic conditions. The first reaction of largely monopolistic producers facing declining demand was typically to raise prices and restrict output. And although state producers must have contributed to the export success story in 1990 (see again below) this was nevertheless in the context of a steep fall in overall production. There is no doubt that Poland's remarkable recovery took place thanks to the private sector. In 1991 and 1992 private industry pushed sales up by 25.4 per cent and then by 23.4 per cent. This continued into 1993 and 1994 with sales growth of 34.7 per cent and 22.7 per cent respectively. By contrast, state sector performance was sluggish; during 1991–93 its sales fell respectively each year by 19.5 per cent, 3.3 per cent and 6.5 per cent and it was not until 1994 when for the first time since 1989 public sector sales increased (by 5.8 per cent).

The changing legal structure

In the central-planning period, state firms had little need or incentive to appeal to any legal code in regulating business affairs. The *de facto* situation was that state owned business was obliged to meet tasks and targets handed down by central planners. With the collapse of planning and economic liberalization and as independent economic entities came into being the authorities turned to the pre-war commercial code (*Kodeks Handlowy*) for a body of law to fill the gap. The commercial code sets out the legal requirements for various forms of business organization and operation. In Poland these include the following: the fully state-owned enterprise, the (private or state) joint-stock company, limited liability companies, private partnerships and individually privately owned concerns. The number of registered economic units (excluding family farms) rocketed from 0.9 million in 1989 to 1.9 million in 1993, almost entirely the result of liberalization and the growth in small private concerns. The number of state-owned businesses fell but those that remain are of course very much larger concerns with an important weight in the economy, particularly in industry.

Foreign investors can establish operations in Poland by setting up wholly owned limited liability or joint stock companies or by entering into joint ventures with Polish partners, perhaps by buying shares in a going Polish concern. Foreign-owned companies have no difficulty in repatriating after-tax profits. They can also purchase land in Poland after obtaining interior ministry approval. As Poland geared up for entry to the OECD in 1996, further liberalization was promised removing virtually all restrictions on foreign concerns setting up in Poland.

Table 3.3   *The growth of private sector employment in Poland 1989–93*

Percentage share of private employment in total	1989	1993
Non-agricultural economy	30.8	46.2
Industry	29.1	46.0
Construction	37.4	78.2
Transport	14.3	25.4
Trade	72.7	89.1

Note: Employment is defined as simple headcount by place of employment end year.

Sources: *Rocznik Statystyczny 1991*, (GUS, Warszawa, 1991), p. xv and Rocznik Statystyczny 1995 (GUS, Warszawa, 1995), p. xxxvi.

Privatization

Over the period 1990–94 privatization of state assets made substantial headway in Poland. The number of state enterprises fell from 8441 at the end of 1990 to 3827 at the end of 1994. And, as noted earlier, Poland was transformed from a predominantly state-run economy to an economy with most activity located in the private sector. Notwithstanding the successes of the Polish privatization programme, it quickly became apparent that the development of a new dynamic, albeit small-scale, private sector was the main factor responsible for tipping the economic balance from state to market.

Poland's first step towards developing a privatization policy after the fall of communism occurred in July 1990 with legislation which opened the way to so-called 'capital privatization', whereby successful larger state enterprises, after detailed valuation studies (usually by western consultants and accountants), were publicly floated. This conventionally individual approach, tried and tested in the UK, proved to be expensive, time consuming and something of a side issue: other privatization routes were subsequently opened up which produced more impressive results. Between 1990 and the end of 1994 only 135 firms were privatized through the 'capital' route. Some of these were publicly floated on the newly-opened Warsaw stock exchange while others were disposed of to major investors. In all cases 20 per cent of shares were reserved for employees.

Alongside 'capital privatization' a process of privatization through liquidation also operated which had far greater significance. This involved two distinct legal procedures, one based on the 1981 law on state enterprises, the other on the 1990 law on privatization. The latter, the so-called 'Article 37' route, permitted the sale or leasing of firms in good financial condition. The former, the 'Article 19' route, was used to dispose of firms in poor health. Not surprisingly, Article 37 privatizations were the most numerous, involving 897 firms between 1990 and 1994. Article 19 privatizations totalled only 293. Article 37 privatizations also proceeded at a fast pace with an 86 per cent 'completion rate' compared to 23 per cent for Article 19 starts and 19 per cent for capital privatization. Privatization through liquidation also became a vehicle for worker-manager buy-out, the predominant new form of ownership to emerge in Poland in the early 1990s.

Privatization styles shifted and changed with the passage of time and privatization ministers. One privatization approach which became more popular was the deliberate seeking out of 'western' strategic investors invited to tender for controlling stakes in individual Polish concerns. These included General Motors (with Warsaw's FSO cars, later superseded by the South Korea Daewoo Corporation), International Paper (with the giant Kwidzyn cellulose-paper plant), Fiat (with FSM cars), Lever (the Pollena soap powders enterprise), Pilkington (the Sandomierz glassworks), Michelin (the Stomil, Olsztyn tyre company), BAT (the Augustosz tobacco concern), Pepsico (the Weder chocolate firm) and many more.

During the presidential election campaign of summer–autumn 1990, Lech Walesa raised the stakes over privatization, pointing to the need for its 'acceleration', a theme he was to return to when, in one of his final presidential acts, he demanded an early 1996 privatization referendum. A discussion on mass privatization followed. Initial plans for mass privatization were developed by Janusz Lewandowski in his first stint as privatization minister in the Bielecki administration in 1991. But the inconclusive general election of that October and the paralysis of government that followed under the premiership of Jan Olszewski froze further developments. It was only when the government lead by Hanna Suchocka was formed in mid-1992, with Lewandowski back at privatization, that a renewed mass privatization momentum was generated.

In early August 1992 the government published draft proposals for mass privatization. These centred on the creation of a layer of fifteen investment funds (*Narodowe Funduszy Inwestycyjne – NFI*) which were to hold shares in, and manage the affairs of, anything up to 600 leading state firms. The NFI were to be jointly run by a consortium of western and Polish managers under a majority Polish board with a Polish chair. Shares in each of the state firms to be privatized were initially to be distributed as follows:

- 33 per cent to a 'lead' NFI to take special responsibility for that enterprise;
- 27 per cent allocated among remaining NFIs;
- 10 per cent for employees;
- 30 per cent for the state treasury, to be used later for a variety of purposes such as reprivatization bonds, a fund to pay for public sector wage increases or to support state pensions.

When the scheme eventually saw the light of day, the employee share was increased to 15 per cent and the state share reduced to 25 per cent. Each adult Pole would be able to purchase for a nominal sum a share in an NFI. The key feature of the scheme, unique among privatization approaches in the region, was to create speedily, through the intermediary of the NFI, effective corporate governance agents able to push through enterprise restructuring. The scheme was however a casualty of bitter parliamentary political in-fighting. Eventually, in early 1993, the appropriate legislation was passed. Considerable organizational headway was made in the summer of 1994 but the scheme almost foundered later that year when prime minister Waldemar Pawlak delayed approving the final plan.

It was only after a major government reshuffle in February 1995 which ousted Mr Pawlak that mass privatization was brought back on track. Fund management agreements were approved by the Minister of Privatization in July 1995 involving fifteen NFIs, and a little later each fund was randomly allocated a selection of lead shareholdings out of the over 400 enterprises to be privatized. Already some of the NFIs are increasing their strategic shareholdings via purchases from each other and from employees.

Finally, from 22 November 1995 each Polish citizen was able to purchase a share certificate (*swiadectwo udzialowe*) for zl 20 ($8) and so take part in this phase of the privatization programme. Each *swiadectwo* gave the holder the right notionally to one share in each NFI. A brisk market in certificates began immediately, the *swiadectwo* changing hands initially at up to three times face value. The result on the programme will not be known for some time but already it looks as though it has avoided many of the pitfalls of mass privatization experienced elsewhere in the transition economies. The problem, for example with Russian mass privatization, was that it was by no means clear that new owners able to take effective control over enterprises generally emerged. Even if they did appear they were often associated with less desirable elements in society (see Chapter 5). Enterprise 'insiders', especially managers, may have been able to use privatization simply to increase the room for managerial discretion. In the Czech case, where citizens could use points to bid for enterprise shares, it appears that most shares ended up with state banks thus raising the question, how successful was Czech voucher privatization in creating new owners able effectively to manage enterprise assets (see Chapter 1).

Competition policy

The first Solidarity government formed in 1989 recognized that the move to building a market economy also required a regulatory apparatus. An anti-monopoly office (*Urzad Antimonopolowy*) was established in a new legal act of early 1990 and, under the leadership of its first president,

Anna Fornalczyk, it was not slow to speak out against what it considered to be restrictive business practices. The main problem facing the regulators was the political strength of those it accused of 'bad behaviour'. These included not only state businesses but also some leading western concerns such as Fiat, blamed for excessive price increases, and General Motors of the USA which lobbied for substantial import protection in return for its investment in FSO cars.

Business and the economy

Performance and economic structure

Poland first emerged from recession in 1992 when GDP increased by 2.6 per cent. In 1993 it expanded by a further 3.8 per cent and in 1994 by 5.3 per cent. This boom continued into 1995 when GDP increased by around 6.5 per cent. Alongside this robust output recovery the average annual rate of price inflation was brought down to 43 per cent in 1992, then to 35.3 per cent in 1993 but slowed only marginally in 1994 to 32.2 per cent and 27.8 per cent in 1995. Recovery was based initially on consumption which increased faster than GDP in both 1992 and 1993. Then, in 1994, a significant change in the balance of demand took place as investment and exports replaced consumption as the motor driving the economy. After a steep decline over 1989–91, total investment spending increased in 1992–93 and its growth accelerated to 6 per cent in 1994 (up by 12 per cent in the 'enterprise' or business sector excluding co-operative housing construction) and to 15 per cent in 1995. Expenditure on machinery and equipment, a barometer of modernization, began also to accelerate, with growth of 14 per cent in 1994. As for foreign trade, the National Bank of Poland reported an increase (measured on a payments basis) in the dollar value of exports of 24.8 per cent in 1994 with imports up by 12 per cent. GUS, recording trade on a customs basis (tracking goods rather than payments), reported an increase in the dollar value of exports of 20.5 per cent and in imports of 13.5 per cent. In 1995 the trade boom continued, the total value of turnover exceeding US$ 50 bn for the first time in Poland's history.

In terms of industrial structure, Poland is well known for its raw materials (especially coal, copper, sulphur) and agricultural produce but industry is the most important economic sector. Of course, all centrally planned economies had a bloated industrial sector. In Poland in the late 1980s industry accounted for around 44 per cent of GDP, a figure considerably greater than typical for developed capitalist economies, where shares in the range 25 to 35 per cent are more common. It was thus to be expected that one consequence of the fall of communism would be a re-balancing of economic structure. By 1994 industry's share in GDP had fallen to 32 per cent. In the late 1980s Poland's highly protected agriculture accounted for around 13 per cent of GDP but a very sharp dose of price liberalization, removal of foodstuffs subsidies and international openness meant that the sector faced much greater competition as domestic demand fell. Polish farmers weathered this storm badly and agriculture's share in GDP was whittled down to little more than 6 per cent by 1994. Construction was also squeezed from a late 1980s' 10 per cent of GDP to only 5.7 per cent in 1994. As might be expected, one other consequence of the shifts taking place in the Polish economy is the expansion of services, a sector much neglected under central planning. In the late 1980s services (other than trade) accounted for only around 12 per cent of GDP and by 1994 this share more than doubled to almost 30 per cent.

Components of GDP measured in current prices, as above, certainly point to important shifts taking place in economic structure but in a period when price movements have been dramatic it is useful also to track the economy through other variables. The changing pattern of employment also reveals the beginning of a deep economic restructuring. In the late 1980s agriculture had 26 per cent of total employment, a share similar to that of industry with 29 per cent. By 1993 agriculture and

Table 3.4   *The structure of the Polish economy in 1994*

	Percentage shares of GDP	Employment
Industry	32.2	24.9
Agriculture and forestry	6.2	27.1
Construction	5.7	6.2
Transport	6.0	3.9
Trade	13.5	13.9
Total including others	100.0	100.0
State	42.5	41.7
Private	57.5	58.3
Total	100.0	100.0
Totals		
(Zl bn)	210 407.3	
($ mn)	92 284	
$ per capita[a]	2 416	

[a]At the average exchange rate of zl2.28 per $. On a purchasing power parity basis the zloty is undervalued. One Polish author estimates GDP/capita in 1994 to be $2430 at official rates and at least $4500 on a PPP basis.

Sources: Rocnik Statystyczny 1995 (GUS, Warszawa, 1995), page 528: press reports, see also R. Rapacki, Development Trends and Economic Policy, (Warsaw School of Economics, mimeo, 1995).

industry each accounted for around 25 per cent of employment and in 1994 agriculture's share rose to 27.1 per cent while industry's fell to 24.9 per cent. Agriculture's employment share is also remarkably high in international terms. Just over 38 per cent of the Polish population live in the countryside. The important consequence of these observations is that agriculture and rural politics are likely to have a profound bearing on government and therefore also on business for some time.

Heavy industry

Heavy industry, that is, fuel, energy and metallurgy, had a privileged role in Poland during most of the post-war period but its importance is diminishing. Fuel and energy had 21.8 per cent of industrial sales in 1993 and 16.2 per cent of employment. This high share in sales reflects early 1990s price liberalization. With sales measured in constant 1990 prices fuel-energy had 15 per cent of all industry sales in 1993. In this sector where prices remain regulated by the state, where heavy losses are still made and privatization least advanced, the business culture has perhaps changed least since 1989.

Coal

Coal-mining is still important in employment and accounted in 1993 for 354,300 jobs (10.7%) in an industry total of 3.3 million. In 1989, by comparison, coal employed 489,900 workers (12.2%) in a fuel-energy industry total of just over 4 million. Coal production slumped from a peak of 193 million tonnes in 1980 to 133 million tonnes in 1994 and it has long since lost its pre-eminence in Polish exports, its share down from 13 per cent in 1985 to 7 per cent in 1990 and around 5 per cent in 1993. Almost all coal mines are located in the upper Silesian industrial region where the process of industry restructuring is making patchy progress. Some labour shedding has certainly taken place and since Silesia does not (yet) suffer disproportionate unemployment (it was between 8 and 10 per cent in March 1995 when the national average was 15.4 per cent – 2.7 million people – of the economically active labour force) some new employment opportunities have emerged. But coal still faces much restructuring and is again a sector where the business culture is closest to the old planning model.

Petrol and oil

While Poland sits on enormous coal reserves the country has virtually no oil of its own and although there is a limited amount of exploration both in the Baltic and on land the country must rely on oil imports to meet its needs. In the past these came almost exclusively from the former Soviet

Union, but in the short time since 1989 sources of supply have been considerably diversified. In 1990 the former USSR still accounted for the bulk of Polish oil and supplied 83 per cent of the country's needs, but a year later in 1991 this share had fallen to 55 per cent. Almost all oil imports and exports were handled during this period by the foreign trading organization CIECH.

Throughout the period from the very early post-war years to early 1996, the organizational structure of the industry changed little. This is another sector where the business culture is heavily swayed by central steer. The retail side was dominated by the state-owned CPN network which in 1994 had 1371 filling stations. On the production side seven refineries operated in 1994. The two major refineries are *Rafinaria Gdansk SA*, with its newly developed port facilities permitting much larger imports from Middle East suppliers, and *Petrochemia Plock SA* on the Vistula north-west of Warsaw. The third refinery, *Rafineria Poludnie*, is actually a grouping of five smaller plants in the south of the country. Two major pipelines cross the country: one runs from north to south from Gdansk to Plock while the other, the well known, 'Friendship' pipeline runs across the country from Russia to Germany, again through Plock. Major redevelopment is underway as refining struggles to modernize to meet EU competition by the end of the decade.

The first serious plans for restructuring the sector were drawn up in July 1993 by Andrzej Olechowski, later a Polish foreign minister. These recommended the hiving off and sale of a substantial chunk of CPN's filling stations to inward investors as an inducement to take a share in refineries and contribute to refinery modernization. This, it was thought, would be an effective way of luring major investment into the refining end of the Polish industry. But with the fall of the Suchocka Government in 1993 these plans were shelved: the incoming PSL-SLD coalition government determined to produce its own vision of the industry's future. The Pawlak administration duly established an inter-ministerial group to produce a new plan. This was ready towards the end of 1994 but the government delayed making a final decision partly because of what appears to have been intense lobbying on the part of the CIECH concern for a more prominent role in the restructured sector. The role of industrial and other pressure groups in lobbying to promote their own narrow interests is becoming an interesting feature of Polish business life. These 'lobbies' are certainly different from those in the planning period and may, as we noted earlier, even involve leading western businesses.

The new plan built on the Olechowski scheme but in keeping with the coalition's predilection for strong national firms it argued for the creation of a vertically integrated Polish business under the umbrella of a new company, *Nafta Polska*, which was to own pipelines and storage facilities, have a 70 to 80 per cent share in the refineries and 33 per cent of the CPN's retail network. The refineries were to hold the remaining 67 per cent of CPN assets. Foreign investors would be able to buy up to a 30 per cent stake in the refineries and so get a toe-hold in the lucrative retail end of the market. Later, that share could increase to 50 per cent. In early 1996 a detailed timetable for the construction of *Nafta Polska* was revealed.

Demand for petrol and fuel oil is expected to grow rapidly, from something in the region of 4.6 million tonnes of petrol in 1995 to 9 million tonnes by the year 2010 and for diesel from around 5.1 million tonnes to 7.3 million tonnes over the same period. The prospect of this rapidly growing market was likely to attract investors. During the early 1990s a number of western firms including DuPont Conoco, Total, the Finnish Neste and Norwegian Statoil, expressed interest in the Polish industry, and some have moved into the retail business. It is clear however that the Polish authorities, fearful of the impact of western European competition on Poland's refining capacity, were determined to link access to a booming demand for oil products to commitment to invest in the industry's future.

Steel

Metallurgy employed 164,600 people in 1993, 5 per cent of all industrial employment, and down from 204,000 in 1989. As with coal, steel industry restructuring proceeds patchily. Employment in steel fell from 144,000 in 1989 to 111,000 in 1993. But this 23 per cent decline in employment was overshadowed by a drop in steel output of 38.3 per cent over the same period. Since then demand for steel has increased. Industrial relations in the steel industry remain volatile. During 1994 bitter and lengthy strikes erupted first in the giant Huta Katowice steelworks and then over the summer at Huta Lucchini in Warsaw. In 1992 the Lucchini company bought a controlling stake in the Warsaw steelworks This was one of the largest western investments of the early 1990s and very much tied up with the production of steel for the motor industry, especially for Fiat at Bielsko-Biala in Poland's south west.

Steel industry restructuring plans were originally formulated by Canadian consultants who produced a scheme to reduce steel employment to 40,000 by the year 2002. This involved the part closure of seven out of twenty-six steelworks. Capacity was to be trimmed from 20 million tonnes to 10 million tonnes over ten years. The plan also proposed the merger of the Katowice and Sendzimir steelworks (formerly Nowa Huta) near Krakow. These two account for around 60 per cent of Polish steel output. Since steel demand has increased over 1994–95 the long term restructuring plan has been allowed to gather dust. A particularly acute problem in the steel sector is how to meet commitments in EU agreements. While Poland could sell more crude steel to western Europe it certainly could not meet western European competition in higher-quality steels.

Copper

Poland stands on a substantial non-ferrous (especially copper) metals industry. Copper ore extraction withstood the recession remarkably well. Production fell from 26.6 million tonnes in 1980 to 24.4 million tonnes in 1990 before rising in 1991 to 25.7 million tonnes and then to 27.1 million tonnes in 1993. The World Bank identified Polish copper as a profitable industry, in some part due to the silver which is extracted as a copper by-product. A number of western concerns are eager to get in on the privatization of the giant Polish Copper Combine (the Lublin based KGHM), one of Poland's largest enterprises and the monopolistic producer in the sector, a privatization which was due to begin in 1996.

Electrical and mechanical engineering

In 1993 the vast electrical and mechanical engineering sector, the manufacturing heart of Poland, accounted for 20.8 per cent of all industry sales and 27.5 per cent of employment, some 926,000 industrial jobs. The major sub-sectors are machine making with 347,800 jobs, transport equipment with 265,500 and metal manufacture with 217,600. As in other centrally planned economies, the engineering sector was developed to service the needs of heavy industry and the defence sectors. It played a prominent part in exports, especially in exports to the thirsty Comecon and Soviet markets but it was far less successful in exporting to more demanding and competitive markets in the west. Indeed one of the striking features of Polish engineering was that, alongside the engineering sectors of the other CMEA economies, it singularly failed to penetrate markets in the industrialized west. Moreover, from the 1970s it became plain that centrally planned economies, for all their industrial strength, were being rapidly overtaken by the newly industrializing economies (NICs) of south-east Asia. By the 1980s it was evident to all that central planning's capacity for innovation, quality and productivity in this crucial industrial sector was fatally low.

Very few manufacturing sectors were penetrated by western capital during the planning period. One of these however was the motor industry where Fiat was the leading player in East European markets. The Italian concern built on its long standing involvement in the Polish motor industry to establish, in 1992, Fiat Auto Poland. This was the rejuvenated FSM car plant where Fiat had been involved in small car production for many years. Fiat Auto Poland at FSM was to become the firm's major European small car (Cinquecento) production base.

Polish attempts to attract investment into medium-sized car production proceeded less smoothly but after protracted negotiations General Motors took a majority stake in a joint venture based on the FSO factory in Warsaw. The FSO plant had operated, like FSM, on the basis of a Fiat licence during

Table 3.5 *Polish industrial structure 1993*

	Sales	Per cent shares in employment
Fuel and energy	21.8	16.2
Metallurgy	6.9	4.9
Electrical and mechanical engineering	20.8	27.6
Chemicals	9.0	7.2
Construction materials	4.1	5.6
Wood and paper	5.7	6.9
Light industry	6.9	14.3
Food industry	22.8	14.4
Industry total (including others)	100.0	100.0

Note: Percentage of sales in current prices.

Source: Maly Rocznik Statystyczny 1994, (GUS, Warszawa), pp. 210–211, p. 188.

the 1970s but Fiat's attempts to retain its influence were rebuffed on anti-monopoly grounds. During 1995 the South Korean Daewoo concern expressed its interest in moving into FSO where management had become disillusioned with GM's small assembly operation. A substantial deal was subsequently agreed which caused GM to up its Polish commitment by searching for a location for a large greenfield investment.

Chemicals

The chemicals sector, like the rest of Polish industry, is in the grip of adjustment to new conditions. Much of chemical production in Poland is based on raw materials and bulk products, especially sulphur, sulphuric acid, caustic soda and fertilizers. In line with industry generally chemicals production fell sharply in 1990–91 but since then recovery has been reasonably rapid although not in the bulk sectors. Production growth since 1991 was based on pesticides, plastics, soap powders and household chemicals. Pharmaceutical production was badly hit by the loss of Comecon markets. Leading western pharmaceutical concerns made a strong pitch for the Polish market following the collapse in local production but based mainly on aggressive sales and exports. Western investors were fast to move in on some chemicals sectors especially at the consumer end of the market. This was the case, for example, in soap powders where Lever bought out the Pollena plant at Bydgoszcz using it to produce a range of products marketed in the country by Lever-Polska. Proctor and Gamble as well as Colgate-Palmolive have also established Polish operations.

Food and drink

The Polish food industry was relatively neglected in the old planning system despite the country's extensive agricultural base and a clear food sector potential. But by the early 1990s food industry sales comprised a significant proportion (22.8 per cent in 1993) of the industry total and the sector accounted for substantial and increasing industrial employment, 485,600 jobs, or 14.4 per cent of total industrial employment in 1993. Food and drink also attracted immediate western investor interest and a steady flow of capital. Coca-Cola Poland, for example, was quick to open a number of new bottling plants. Pepsico Foods bought into the Wedel confectionary concern. Heineken moved into beer production with a stake in the well-known Zywiec brewery. Fast food retailers like McDonald's, Pizza Hut and Burger King were also quick to create a Polish presence.

Construction

The striking development in the Polish construction sector during the early 1990s was the collapse of public enterprise and the surge in private activity. By 1993 the great bulk of construction (77 per cent) was in private hands. This was almost exactly the reverse of the situation in industry where 70 per cent of sales in 1993 were still due to the state sector. Construction sales fell sharply in 1990 and then made a modest recovery in the years that followed. Housing, according to official data, was the construction sector to suffer most during the early 1990s: in 1994 completions were reported to be at their lowest level since the mid-1950s. However the official figures sit uncomfortably alongside everyday evidence (at least in major towns and cities) of building work. It may be that many housing starts now take place technically illegally without planning permission. But there is no doubt that the construction of giant edge-of-town housing schemes has come to an end in favour of building, at least in more prosperous parts of the country, on a more human scale. Construction faces great business opportunities in Poland in the mid-1990s, especially as major infrastructure projects (particularly motorway building) get underway.

Agriculture

Economic liberalization in 1989 plunged Polish agriculture into intense difficulties and it remains in a weak state. Since 1989 the sector had to contend with falling demand, withdrawal of subsidies, increased competition, not to mention volatile environmental conditions which generated a drought in 1992 and a summer heatwave in 1994, both of which devastated crop production. Depressed agricultural incomes meant lack of funds for investment and even simple industrial inputs which, in turn, magnified the damaging impact of adverse weather conditions.

Poland's mainly peasant farm sector has had a hard time in meeting the sweeping changes in economic conditions introduced in the early 1990s. In economic terms the last years of communist rule were reasonably good for Poland's farmers. The price liberalization for foodstuffs and farm products introduced in 1989 by communist premier Mieczyslaw Rakowski released a produce price push which far outstripped the growth in prices of industrial products. As a result, the 'prices scissors' opened widely in farmers' favour as agriculture's terms of trade with industry improved by 12 percentage points in 1989. This leap in agricultural trading conditions was however short-lived: in 1990, the first year of the more general price liberalization introduced by Balcerowicz, agriculture's terms of trade with industry deteriorated by 45 percentage points. The macroeconomic squeeze depressed demand; agricultural incomes slumped. By the summer of 1990 nation-wide farmers' protests, including road-blocks, hit the headlines. Since then the squeeze on farm incomes has been a more or less constant feature of economic transformation and rural families have been among the hardest hit of social groups. A 1994 government report on agriculture to the year 2000 estimates that the average income per person in agriculture in 1993 was only 77 per cent of that in the rest of the economy and only 57 per cent of its 1985 level.

Polish agriculture is predominantly private and small scale. In 1993 the average farm had an area of only 6.3 hectares. The sector employed around 3.7 million people of which the great majority (3.4 million or 92 per cent) were in the private sector. The small state and co-operative sector has virtually disappeared, its employment falling from 700,000 in 1989 to 300,000 in 1993. In the northern and western parts of the country where state farms predominated, rural unemployment is a serious problem.

In employment terms agriculture is immensely important. Its 3.7 million 'employees' – virtually the same number as in industry in 1993 – account for one quarter of all employment. While its employment share has changed little since 1989, sharply falling production has cut its share in GDP from 11.8 per cent (1989) to 6.8 per cent in 1993. A deep decline in output alongside a less pronounced fall in employment implies of course a large drop in productivity. Profitability is poor and few farmers are able to accumulate resources for investment. Indeed the farm sector has found it hard enough to set aside resources for purchases of inputs such as fertilizer, where the application rate fell sharply in the early 1990s. Farmers with little money for equipment created added difficulties for the troubled agricultural machinery producing sector.

Poland has moved from net exporter to importer of food and agricultural produce. The share of agriculture and food in total exports fell from 13.5 per cent in 1990 to 10.9 per cent in 1993 when the food and agriculture trade balance slipped into a substantial US$477 million deficit. Nevertheless with exports of US$1.5 billion in 1993 the sector is clearly an important one and its 1993 exports may have been unusually small, hit by the previous year's drought when the crop harvest fell by just over 23 per cent. There are high expectations too that as the Russian economy recovers, Polish farmers and food producers will find a strong demand for their output in the east.

Until recently the Polish authorities appeared to have had no policy for agriculture other than to leave the sector to a market based adjustment stimulated by strong import competition bereft of virtually any prices or incomes support. To the extent that they exist at all, state policies towards agricultural have evolved in a fragmented way. Solidarity governments, ever fearful of 'capture' by the farming lobby, were determined to stay at arm's length from agriculture and interventions where they occurred were piecemeal and modest. Fear that the PSL-SLD coalition, after its 1993 election, would quickly succumb to agricultural pressure turned out to be largely unfounded although in 1994 a system of minimum prices for some imports was initiated in a micro version of the European Union's CAP. At the same time, as noted earlier, agriculture has a powerful political presence which cannot be ignored.

Clearly, with so much employment tied to the land, creating a modern, larger scale and more efficient agriculture is a delicate yet pressing matter in Poland. All the more so since Poland's eventual EU membership is likely be delayed until either a radical reform of the CAP itself or until a much smaller farm sector emerges in Poland. One recent western estimate suggests that the entry into the EU of the 'Visegrad 4' countries (Poland, Hungary, the Czech and Slovak Republics) will add a further ECU 63.6 bn to the EU's annual budget, of which CAP support alone would account for ECU 47 bn. (The CAP is reported to consume ECU 36 bn per annum, a sum, in the early 1990s, equivalent to 50 per cent of the EU budget.)

Foreign trade

Polish business at first suffered greatly from the CMEA collapse in 1991. The sudden loss of markets created a gap in order books that it was simply impossible for many firms to fill. This was especially true for heavy industry, steel-making, shipbuilding, machinery and transport equipment. But the data reveal that somehow a remarkable transformation took place over the short period 1989–92. As Comecon collapsed the EC became Poland's major trading partner. The EC share in Polish exports increased from 32.1 per cent in 1989 to 57.9 per cent in 1992 while the EC share in Polish imports rose from 33.8 per cent to 53.2 per cent. Germany replaced the former Soviet Union as Poland's number one trading partner in a trade reorientation that took Poland in the early 1990s back to a trade pattern more characteristic of 1939.

Table 3.6 *The EU share in Polish trade 1989–92*

	Percentage shares of	
	Exports	Imports
1989	32.1	33.8
1990	46.8	42.5
1991	55.6	49.9
1992	57.9	53.2

Source: Rynki Zagraniczne, 12 July 1993.

Given the uncompetitive structure of the economy, Polish exports' performance was surprisingly good after 1989. The year 1990 saw exports' growth (in dollar value terms using National Bank data) of 43.4 per cent to $10,863 million and a trade surplus of $2214 million. A further 17.5 per cent growth in 1991 pushed exports to $12,760 million. In 1992 exports increased by 9.7 per cent to $13,997 million. In 1993 however exports were extremely poor, falling in dollar value by 3 per cent and prompting a devaluation of the zloty. But by 1994 European recovery came to Poland's aid and exports performance was, once more, surprisingly strong. This continued in 1995 although real zloty appreciation may, towards the year end, have had some impact in slowing exports.

As for imports, recession and devaluation in 1990 ensured their growth would at first, compared to exports, be limited: they increased by 17.9 per cent to $8646 million. But by late 1990 and into the first half of 1991 real zloty appreciation generated a substantial increase (47 per cent) in

Table 3.7 *Polish foreign trade 1989–94*

	1989	1990	1991	1992	1993	1994
Convertible currency trade, $ mn						
Exports	7,575	10,863	12,760	13,997	13,585	16,950
Imports	7,335	8,649	12,709	13,485	15,878	17,786
Balance	240	2,214	51	512	−2,293	−836

Note: Trade flows are also estimated by the Central Statistical Office, GUS, through customs declarations and those estimates differ from the payments data reported here by the National Bank.

Source: Balance of payments data from the National Bank of Poland reported in Statistical Yearbooks and in *Rzeczpospolita*, 10 February 1995.

imports taking the total import bill to $12,709 million. This led, in May 1991, to the first devaluation of the zloty since the Balcerowicz plan was launched. A further devaluation in February 1992 gave exports another boost. But as economic growth picked up in 1993 imports began to be sucked in at a fast rate and export weaknesses became more apparent. According to NBP data Polish trade fell into a substantial deficit of $2.3 billion in 1993, the first deficit recorded by the bank since before 1989. In 1994, thanks mainly to German economic recovery export performance was, as noted earlier, extraordinarily strong.

Another striking feature of business development in foreign trade post-1989 was the sudden emergence of private trade. Initially this was especially noticeable on the imports side as predominantly small traders rushed to fill gaps on the market. Later, private trade began to make a stronger impact on exports, and in 1994 and 1995 so-called tourist or 'cross-border' trade was playing a major part in closing the official trade gap. Indeed, some estimates suggest that this trade in 1995 may have been worth $6 bn and most of that net exports.

Business and finance

The banks

The banking system has changed substantially since 1989 when nine independent but state-owned banks were carved out from the National Bank of Poland (NBP). These banks were 'commercialized', that is, transformed into state-owned joint stock companies, with privatization in mind. Since then the NBP has taken on the role of traditional central bank, concerned with anti-inflation policy, monetary policy and the exchange rate. It has operated with remarkable independence but has also been embroiled in political disputes with the finance ministry during 1994–95. Poland appears to have dealt reasonably successfully with the 'bad debt' problem which plagues the East European banking system. Banks were recapitalized in a one-off measure during 1993–94 *provided* that they took steps to clean up their balance sheets. Most initial surveys of the impact of this programme are reasonably optimistic that a fundamental change has taken place in their operations.

The Poznan-based *Wielkopolski Bank Kredytowy SA* was the first of the nine regional banks to be privatized, in 1993. It was followed by the controversial privatization in February 1994 of the Katowice-based *Bank Slaski*. Since then the enthusiasm for further privatizations has abated somewhat and the authorities began to moot the possibility of merging some of the remaining, generally smaller and weaker banks, with a view to creating a banking group that might better withstand competition. By 1995 foreign banks played only a modest role on the edges of the Polish market.

The Warsaw Stock Exchange

The Warsaw Stock Exchange was established in April 1991 when it quoted prices in the shares of the first five Polish privatized companies. By 1996 shares in more than forty companies were traded regularly on the exchange. But given the still small number of firms involved, the exchange still had a largely symbolic significance. Share price movements tended to be exceptionally volatile as those with savings use it for little more than a gamble. The authorities wavered during 1994–95 over the introduction of a stock exchange trading and capital gains tax.

Business and the labour market

The Polish labour market in the early 1990s had a number of characteristic features. First, the level of unemployment was high although economic growth in 1994–95 had at least halted its increase. Second, unemployment was greatly differentiated by region. Third, the grey economy provided a safety net of employment 'opportunities' without which a social and political crisis would surely have emerged. Fourth, wages remained low by international standards although national insurance costs (at around 40 per cent of wages) to employers were among the highest in the region. Fifth, the labour force was generally well educated. Sixth, the trade union scene was dominated by three players, Solidarity, the OPZZ and Solidarity 80, each of which operated with boundless ill-feeling for its rivals.

Some regional and social dimensions of unemployment have established a new map of uneven economic development. These are worth noting. The bleakest areas are in the north and east of Poland. In October 1994 the Slupsk province to the west of Gdansk had the highest unemployment rate – 30.5 per cent. Meanwhile Olsztyn, further to the east, experienced unemployment of 28.9 per cent and neighbouring Suwalski, which borders Russia and Lithuania, had unemployment of 28.3 per cent. This was a far cry from the relative success of Warsaw with its 7.8 per cent end-of-October unemployment rate, or of Krakow with 8.4 per cent, Poznan with 9 per cent and Katowice with 10.2 per cent.

Unemployment has hit the young and the less well qualified particularly badly. In 1994 unemployment in the 15–24 year age group was twice the national average. Another noticeable feature of unemployment was the growth in long-term unemployment alongside the repeated return to the register of some groups of workers. In September 1994, 45.8 per cent of the unemployed had been job-seeking for over a year and of the 1.6 million unemployed to register during the first nine months of the year over one-third (580,000) had been on the register on some previous occasion. Women too face severe difficulties in finding work.

The grey economy is estimated to provide anything from 700,000 to 1.1 million jobs, additional to the 14.7 million officially recorded in September 1994. The availability of such employment opportunities, although probably concentrated in some parts of the country – booming metropolitan areas, as well, perhaps, as those close to the Russian and other eastern frontiers (the cross-border trade factor) – may make high official unemployment rates just tolerable.

Trade unions

The trade union scene, as noted above, is highly fragmented but the two leading unions are the OPZZ and Solidarity. The former has the largest membership and its own MPs (part of the SLD parliamentary grouping). Following the 1993 election Solidarity lost its parliamentary representation. During 1994–95 the OPZZ was reluctant to make more trouble for the coalition than that already being caused by Lech Walesa in the run-up to the presidential election. Although activists occasionally work together at shop floor level, the political gulf between OPZZ and Solidarity at the national level appears unbridgeable. A number of other smaller but sometimes very noisy unions also exist. The 'Solidarity 80' union for example with a mere handful of members succeeded in bringing the giant Huta Katowice steelworks out on strike for several weeks in the early summer of 1994.

Since 1992 the Polish authorities have tried to use a tripartite commission of unions, employers and government to settle wage and other issues in the public sector. The commission meets and makes declarations but has some severe structural deficiencies, the major one being that unions are split and therefore weak while employers are hardly distinguishable from government. Nevertheless this 'social pact' mechanism, originally devised by Jacek Kuron when he was labour minister, may be a useful forum for discussion. In contemporary Poland the trade unions make little secret of the fact that their actions are usually tied up with fairly clear political objectives.

Business, education and training

One of the features of the communist system was its highly developed education system. It was however a system geared to the needs of the centrally planned economy. In terms of its focus, engineering subjects, in the service of heavy industry and machine building, were particularly favoured. This was the educational background sought in enterprise managers, who were valued for their skills in keeping production to target rather than in making profits or minimizing losses. It is no surprise therefore that in parallel with wider economic transformation the educational system is in the throes of adapting to new circumstances. The problem, as with the rest of industry, is that it is doing this at a time when a huge resource squeeze is affecting the public sector.

Education was in crisis in Poland in the mid-1990s. As the country's universities struggled with profound changes in curricula and over-hauled syllabuses they faced a growing staffing problem as the real value of academic salaries plummeted. Academic moonlighting was common.

Business and management education is new to Poland. The development of MBA programmes is perhaps illustrative of the wider problem. In mid-1995 this country with over 38 million inhabitants had only 13 MBA courses on offer. Nevertheless the management training and education deficit is slowly being filled by a reorientation in state establishments often backed by western resources (such as the EU's PHARE programme), by the emergence of new private schools, and by enterprises themselves (especially those with foreign involvement) as they mount their own training efforts.

Business and the environment

Environmental degradation on an enormous scale was a well known legacy and universal feature of central planning. Poland had, even in the old system, a panoply of environmental legislation but it was rarely enforced. The ascendancy of the plan's output targets meant that environmentalism counted for little. Air, land and water were free resources to be used at will in plan fulfilment. But in the 1990s as Poland moved slowly towards EU membership it also started to embrace EU rules and norms. Increasingly business should expect to find in Poland similar approaches to environmental issues as those in the EU.

The appalling intensity of environmental damage causes investors to exercise the utmost caution in taking on many existing Polish industrial businesses and especially industrial land. Clean-up costs can be hefty and under EU rules become the responsibility of new owners. This leads many inward investors to prefer green-field solutions.

Conclusion

As in many other transforming economies the business scene in Poland has undergone huge change in the short period since 1989. By the mid-1990s Poland was already a country where business activity could take place in much the same style that is typical of the western mixed economy that Polish policy-makers are uniformly committed to building. That this is so is very much an achievement of Poland's first Solidarity finance minister, Leszek Balcerowicz, whose stabilization plan introduced the economic liberalization which permitted a surge in private business development. It was this, much more than government inspired plans for privatization of existing state assets or for sectoral restructuring (both of which proceeded patchily), that was the decisive factor in tipping the economy in a new direction.

In addition to liberalization of prices and the conditions for business start-up, the dismantling of Poland's state foreign trading system also opened the country to fierce international competition. Polish producers began to operate for the first time in the post-war period in a gale of competitive pressure and, slowly, even the managers of state-owned businesses began to adjust to meet market pressures that they had previously been shielded from.

So, two striking features of the new economic situation in the country were, first, the boom in private business (even if these were mainly activities on a very small scale) and second, the emergence of competition as a real pressure on the managers of many state enterprises. Western capitalism then began to make a more direct influence felt, contributing through its investment to shaping a new business culture.

After finding that Poland was a good export market, a growing number of western firms, in time honoured fashion, began to explore investment possibilities in the country. In global terms the sums involved were paltry, especially over 1990–94, but in 1995 the FDI flow accelerated. It was highly differentiated by sector and region. Some parts of the country (Warsaw, Poznan, Krakow, Gdansk) reaped benefits quickly as did mainly consumer goods sectors in production. With the inward investment came, again as was to be expected, new ways of doing business, new management interest in matters (the customer, promotion, accounting and, of course, the bottom-line profits) traditionally neglected in the old planning system. Some of this rubbed off on state businesses most of which, ever since 1990 or 1991, knew that they faced 'hard budget constraints'. Indeed it was a remarkable feature of the Balcerowicz plan that it succeeded in only eighteen months in virtually wiping out 'soft budgets' (coal is the remaining problem area) – something that twenty years of economic reform experiments had singularly failed to achieve.

If the new economic dispensation is very much more typical in the mid-1990s of a market economy pockets of old-style management obviously remain, particularly in heavy industry. In such sectors – coal and steel – the business culture is more akin to that prevailing under planning although no-one today is setting targets and the state, unwilling to face the prospect of huge and regionally concentrated increases in unemployment, simply has to pick up the tab. Elsewhere, the influx of western business has brought with it some new pressures, such as demands for protection and privilege in return for investment, and the Polish authorities may not yet be well equipped to meet such challenges. While the neo-liberal economic policy pursued by the Balcerowicz team was immensely successful in creating a new business climate Solidarity governments had an almost palpable fear of the resurgence of the 'lobby', the organized pressure group demanding privilege – 'rent-seekers' as economists would put it. The response was a strictly 'hands-off' attitude towards business and the economy. This meant that the authorities found it difficult to engage with and develop almost any sectoral policies whether for agriculture or industry. This surely will change in the years ahead but the dangers of 'regulatory capture' are real and the hostage takers are as likely to be western as local interests in Poland's still rapidly evolving business culture. But perhaps when all is said and done this simply testifies to the fact that Poland in the mid-1990s is practically a 'normal' place in which to do business.

References and suggestions for further reading

Blanchard, O. *et al.* (1993) *Post-Communist reform: pain and progress.* MIT Press.

Blazyca, G. and Dabrowski, J.M. (1995) *Monitoring Economic Transition: The Polish Case.* Avebury.

Blazyca, G. and Rapacki, R. (eds) (1991) *Poland into the 1990s: economy and society in transition.* Pinter, London.

Economist Intelligence Unit (quarterly), *Poland Country Report.* The Economist Intelligence Unit, London.

Gomulka, S. (1994) Economic and political constraints during transition. *Europe-Asia Studies,* Vol. 46, 1.

Millard, F. (1994) *The anatomy of the new Poland.* Edward Elgar.

Poznanski, K. (ed.) (1993) *Stabilisation and privatization in Poland: An economic evaluation of the shock therapy programme.* Kluwer Press.

Sachs, J. (1993) *Poland's Jump to the Market Economy.* MIT Press.

Schaffer, M. (1993) Polish economic transition: from recession to recovery and the challenges ahead. *Business Strategy Review,* Vol. 4, 3.

Winters, L. Alan (ed.) (1995) *Foundations of an open economy: trade laws and institutions for Eastern Europe.* CEPR, London.

4 The business culture in Croatia and Slovenia

Will Bartlett and Milford Bateman

Introduction

In this chapter we consider together the case of Croatia and Slovenia, the two southern European republics which emerged to become independent in 1991 out of the bloody dissolution of the Socialist Federative Republic of Yugoslavia. Croatia and Slovenia were the two most technologically advanced and westernized of the republics of former Yugoslavia – and, probably, in Eastern Europe as a whole. Both republics faced the prospect of independence with significant goodwill on the part of their respective populations, the majority of whom were very keen to move towards a market economy and in favour of reducing their historic links with their Slav neighbours. Moreover, Croatia and Slovenia also share the legacy of a specific type of communism established within former Yugoslavia – the system of worker self-management. This was a path-breaking attempt to create a 'Third way' between Soviet-style communism and free-market capitalism. Though it was watered down substantially by the authorities and gravely compromised by excessive political interference, it nevertheless demonstrated that more democratic forms of management and industrial organization were workable. Indeed, for a period in the 1950s and 1960s, Yugoslavia experienced an 'economic miracle' and became one of the fastest growing economies in the world – not too dissimilar, it has been said, to the so-called 'Asian tigers' of the 1970s and 1980s. The system of worker self-management clearly had some part to play in this success story.

In one crucial respect, however, the common experience of Croatia and Slovenia differs. As the two countries extricated themselves from the remains of former Yugoslavia, Croatia alone was plunged into major conflict. The ensuing war cost this small, newly-independent country around $22 billion in physical damage as well as severely undermining its remaining economic and industrial capacity. There was also the enormous cost of maintaining the ability to fight and having to provide for several years for up to 400,000 refugees displaced from elsewhere in Croatia and parts of former Yugoslavia. Slovenia, on the other hand, after a minor incursion into its territory by the remnants of the Yugoslav National Army, escaped serious conflict. It did have to endure the economic dislocation and loss of markets associated with the break-up of former Yugoslavia as well as the disruption caused by the move to a more market-based economy, but this was not compounded by the need to fight for independence.

Because they had to endure the consequences of the dissolution of a state, of the abandonment of an entire economic system, and then to face the ensuing conflict and economic dislocation which this precipitated, both Croatia and Slovenia have to be seen separately from the other transition economies under consideration in this volume. Today, Croatia and Slovenia are some way along the road to a market economy. In a relatively short space of time, and under the most difficult of conditions, they have established the foundations necessary for economic recovery and progress. In many senses, they are far ahead of the other transition economies considered here. In terms of living standards, and in the appreciation of business and technical skills, they are probably closer to the western economies than to their neighbouring transition economies. And in the development of an advanced business culture, they are also well ahead and set to profit from the greater head start made under the old system in former Yugoslavia.

Former Yugoslavia

An introduction to the pre-reform situation in Croatia and Slovenia means an introduction to the economic system of former Yugoslavia. At the end of the Second World War Yugoslavia lay devastated. Branko Horvat (1976), one of the most respected of Yugoslav economists, gave some indication of the enormity of the damage Yugoslavia had suffered when he noted that it 'amounted to 17 per cent of the total war damage suffered by eighteen countries represented at the Paris Reparations Conference in 1945'. Notwithstanding the physical damage, the Yugoslav population retained a very high morale and a real willingness to rebuild their shattered country as soon as possible. One reason for this almost revolutionary fervour was the fact that the Yugoslavs were virtually the only nation in Eastern Europe to free themselves from the occupying Nazis largely through their own efforts. The communist partisans were thus a well respected force in Yugoslavia because of their leadership of the resistance effort, and especially Marshal Tito, the communist partisan leader who became the president of Yugoslavia. The fact that the partisans were genuinely popular throughout the country was important to the future course of events, because the Yugoslavs were soon caught up in a dispute with the Soviet Union which was to have far-reaching consequences.

After the successful conclusion of the Second World War, Stalin set about consolidating his control over the newly-created communist states, including Yugoslavia. However, unlike in the other Eastern European communist states, Stalin and the Soviet Red Army were not largely involved in winning the war on Yugoslav territory. Crucially, this obviated any need for the partisans to pay homage to the Soviet Union or to curry favour with Stalin in order to remain in power. But they were only able to do this because they had the support of the population in general, who were also in no mood to relinquish one would-be conqueror – Hitler – for another in the shape of Stalin.

Nevertheless, along with the other communist states in Eastern Europe after the war, Yugoslavia fell into line with the pattern set by the Soviet Union and introduced a centrally-planned economy. Unlike the other communist states, however, Yugoslavia only persevered with central planning until 1950. A dispute with the Soviet Union over the extent of its influence in Yugoslav internal affairs precipitated a radical upheaval in the Yugoslav economic system, and the system of worker self-management was the result. It was an idea born out of political expediency on the part of the ruling Yugoslav communists who wished to remain in power in spite of their dispute with the Soviet Union. The Yugoslav leadership felt that to retain their legitimacy they had to offer up to the population a more popular version of a communist economic and political system and, hopefully, a more efficient one. It was also the first real attempt to bring about 'the withering away of the state' which Karl Marx had predicted would be the inevitable outcome of communism.

The basic features of the system evolved over time, but the central principle was that an enterprise should be controlled by its workers, rather than by the planners (or by capitalists). A regulated or guided market mechanism would be used to influence the enterprise's activities and the state would only overtly intervene at the macro-economic level. From the system's inception in 1950, enterprises were gradually removed from state control and put under the direction of a workers' council. This body was composed of employees from the enterprise nominated by their fellow employees and given the right to appoint and oversee a board of managers. A general manager was given overall responsibility for the management of the enterprise, which included carrying out the day-to-day decisions agreed with the board of management and strategic decisions decided upon by the workers' council. Initially, the state retained some control over an enterprise's activities and so the general manager also had to respond to various government decrees and directions. The apparatus of central planning was essentially dissolved as early as 1951, though other state bodies took over some co-ordinating responsibilities. Finally, as the state no longer claimed ownership of industry, and yet private ownership remained anathema, a new type of ownership had effectively been introduced. This was termed 'social ownership', a system whereby workers and managers had control over the use of assets, but no right of sale. Radical change also affected the political system. The principles of worker self-management were applied to political bodies so that workers could have, in theory, both economic and political democracy. New institutions for worker participation were introduced at all levels of government and the Yugoslav Communist Party became the League of Communists of Yugoslavia (LCY) in 1952, an indication that it was genuine in wanting to change its role within Yugoslav society away from control and towards becoming a mass education and propagandizing movement.

Significant changes to the economic system took place in 1965 to create a more market-oriented environment and to strengthen enterprise autonomy. These changes were successful and the economy continued to grow and achieved relative prosperity. Enterprise democracy was functioning reasonably well, growth rates were some of the highest in the world and living standards were rising fast. Yugoslavia began to differentiate itself significantly from other communist countries with its apparently successful blend of the market and basic socialist principles of worker empowerment. Another factor was the open-door policy to the Western European labour market, which reduced expenditure on the unemployed, provided remittance income and released social tensions.

However, in the 1970s it was apparent that there were problems with both the design and practice of the self-management system. It increasingly suffered from the poorly developed concept of social ownership, which discouraged reinvestment of internally generated funds and the use of external funds wherever possible, in contrast with other more robust systems of employee participation, such as the Mondragon co-operatives and German co-determination.[1] The authorities permitted this over time, resulting in a 'budget constraint' every bit as 'soft' as in other Eastern European countries. Moreover, the self-management system was undermined by the increasing power of senior management and directors within the enterprises *vis-à-vis* the workers. Worker self-management began significantly to tail off as managers asserted their professionalism and authority over the workforce and began to pay increasingly less attention to the systems providing for worker involvement within the enterprise, including the workers' council. The LCY saw these developments as eventually leading to a managerial elite which would undermine the system and, what they most feared, their ultimate power. Disguising their real intentions behind a package of seemingly democratizing measures, they took steps to reassert control over the economy and society. These democratizing measures were in the form of two major pieces of legislation in 1974 and 1976 which

[1] See Randlesome, C. (1990) *Business Cultures in Europe*. Butterworth-Heinemann, Oxford.

introduced two key changes. First, the reforms broke the enterprise up into smaller units, each having its own democratic body and each negotiating its relationship with the other units through so-called self-management agreements. This reduced the power of the top management to act independently. Second, the increasingly 'free' market economy was cut down and reshaped into a 'managed' market, with the introduction of negotiated market agreements between enterprises, and between enterprises and the political authorities, termed social compacts.

Very soon after the introduction of the 1974 and 1976 reforms, the system of worker self-management began to collapse. Managers and workers balked at the sheer weight and complexity of the new bureaucratic procedures, negotiated agreements and excessive political intervention. And the renewed authority of the political authorities at all levels of Yugoslav society – factory, locality, nationally – also meant undermining the pretence that workers 'self-managed': they did not, and they knew it. The system thus lost its legitimacy, and the workers lost their motivation. The workers increasingly exercised what remaining power they could muster within the enterprise in pushing to award themselves as much as possible of the enterprise's profit in the form of wages. At the same time, with no effective sanctioning from a management class also lacking in motivation, workers increasingly took to spending time away from their enterprise on second jobs, or simply as relaxation – termed *'pauza'*. Economic performance thus took a major turn for the worse in the late 1970s.

The final episode in Yugoslavia's history was marked by the abandonment of self-management and social ownership. The Law on Enterprises passed in December 1988 saw the system of worker self-management substantially revised in favour of management control. Social ownership was dealt with by the Law on Social Capital passed in December 1989, which paved the way for private ownership and the the privatization of social assets. In addition, Yugoslavia saw the introduction of the first 'shock therapy' programme in Eastern Europe, the Markovic programme, put together by the then Prime Minister Ante Markovic. This was an attempt to deal with a rapidly disintegrating economy, characterized by stag-flation and chronic indebtedness. A strict anti-inflation policy was brought in, consisting of the conversion of the old dinar to a new dinar (equal to 10,000 old dinars) which was pegged to the Deutschmark, a freeze on incomes and a temporary price freeze. However, by mid-1990 the reform programme was beginning to be undermined by the tensions within the country as it began to pull itself apart, and very shortly afterwards it was abandoned when the Federal government lost power to the various republics.

In spite of its ultimate demise, the system of worker self-management did prove to be a major inspiration within the communist economies, and in the wider world. It provided a version of reform communism quite palatable to those seeking change within Eastern Europe, such as Hungary's reformers in the late 1960s and Poland's Solidarity movement in the 1980s. It also interested many socialists in Western Europe seeking an attainable, and more humane and democratic, middle way between free-market capitalism and Soviet style communism. Not unlike the famous Mondragon co-operative complex in the Basque country of northern Spain,[2] it was an experiment in industrial democracy which exhibited numerous faults, but which nevertheless still indicated that the idea of worker self-management could form the basis for an industrial system which embodied the principles of fairness and equity. As we shall see below, it has also influenced many aspects of the economic and business systems emerging out of the ruins of the Yugoslav Federation in the newly independent countries of Croatia and Slovenia.

Croatia

Introduction

Croatia should have emerged from the collapse of communism and the break-up of the Yugoslav Federation in 1991, to become one of the new post-communist economies 'most likely to succeed'. It stood to inherit a reasonably competitive industrial structure, a developed agricultural sector, excellent potential in tourism, good trade prospects, a highly-educated workforce and a rich diaspora now interested to return. Croatia was also westernized and technologically advanced and has benefited greatly from its close economic and business contacts with neighbours Italy and Austria, and also Germany. At the same time, the Croats had in the past been far more pragmatic in their acceptance of the worker self-management system than the other republics in former Yugoslavia, with the possible exception of Slovenia. When the system became over-complicated and excessively cumbersome from the mid-1970s onwards, they took to by-passing many of the more inefficient requirements and regulations. As a result, many Croatian enterprises retained a reasonable competitive edge and were quite successful on world markets.

However, the transition to independence did not come about peacefully and Croatia was forced into a conflict which, though it was to reach a military conclusion at the end of 1995, will have serious economic and social repercussions well into the next millennium. There has been much discussion over the root of the conflict: whether it was a case of historic

---

[2] For those wishing to become more familiar with the Mondragon experiment, see *Making Mondragon* (1988), W. Foote-Whyte and K. King-Whyte, ILR Press, Ithaca, New York.

inter-ethnic rivalry between the various nationalities in the region, or whether the bad experiences of the Second World War were being expunged, or whether it was the increasing resentment felt by the northern republics at the lack of efficiency of their southerly sister republics. What we can say with some certainty is that it had become obvious at the beginning of the 1990s that Yugoslavia was unsustainable as a federation and that some new arrangement would be required to satisfy its increasingly restless constituent republics, especially Slovenia. In particular, the northern republics more than anything feared the prospect of an increasingly powerful Serbia within the federation, and the likely role of Serbia's powerful leader, Slobodan Milosevic. Even under the relatively friendly pre-war division of power between the republics, many in Croatia resented the overwhelming preponderance of Serbs occupying positions of high authority in the police, army and government administration.

Early negotiations in 1990 centred around the possibility of a peaceful transition to a confederation, but the momentum was moving very fast in favour of outright dissolution and independence for those Republics wanting it. But all the early hopes for an independent Croatia emerging peacefully were effectively scuppered in April 1991 when the Serbian minority in Croatia, representing about 12 per cent of the total population in Croatia, balked at the forthcoming prospect of an independent Croatia, and thus Croatian rule, and declared themselves to be an independent republic. Their real aim was not full independence – the territory is not contiguous and has little economic potential – but eventual future integration into an enlarged Serbia proper. But on 25 June 1991 Croatia declared its independence from Yugoslavia and the bitter Serb–Croat conflict began. The next four years were marked by the presence of UN peacekeepers throughout Croatia attempting to keep the Croats and the rebelling Serbian minority apart and, in the meantime, trying to bring about a peaceful resolution. Negotiation with the Serbian minority did not succeed and so Croatia finally utilized the military option within its own territory. By mid-1995 Croatia had succeeded in regaining control of nearly all the rebellious areas except Eastern Slavonia on the eastern border with Serbia, which is scheduled to be reintegrated into Croatia proper in December 1997.

The conflict in Croatia, as well as Croatia's participation in the wider Balkan conflict centring on Bosnia-Hercegovina, has severely undermined Croatia's plans for economic development and reform. It will be hard indeed to recover from the collapse in GDP which by 1993, at around $7–8 billion, was almost half its pre-war standing of $15 billion. Nevertheless, the economy appears to have successfully entered into a period of physical and systemic reconstruction and development and there is the real possibility that Croatia will emerge in the not too distant future as one of southern Europe's major economic powers. Relations with the other former Yugoslav republics have become warmer, including with Serbia, holding out the prospect of renewed trade and economic co-operation within the region.

Business and government

Government and political parties

The chief architect of Croatian independence was Dr Franjo Tudjman, a Croatian nationalist in the 1960s and later the President of the Socialist Republic of Croatia, a constituent republic within the Yugoslav Federation. The original intent of the Croatian government led by Tudjman at the end of the 1980s had been to steer former Croatia and Yugoslavia towards some form of loose confederation of republics. This proved an impossible goal on account of the divergent objectives of the other major republic within the Yugoslav Federation, Serbia, led by President Slobodan Milosevic. The Serbian government of Milosevic wished to recentralize power in the federal capital Belgrade (which was also the capital of Serbia), an objective which would have clearly strengthened the already powerful Serbian position within the federation.

The first direct presidential elections in August 1992 gave Tudjman representing the Croatian Democratic Union (*Hrvatska Democratska Zajednica, HDZ*) 57 per cent of the votes, some way ahead of Drazen Budisa (22 per cent) of the Croatian Social Liberal Party and Savka Dapcevic-Kucar (6 per cent) of the Croatian People's Party. In view of having steered Croatia through to independence and with the prevailing conflict creating an atmosphere of threat and uncertainty, it was always expected that Tudjman would win. The HDZ became established as the main political party in Croatia, with Tudjman remaining as president. There were some reservations felt about the style adopted by President Tudjman over the subsequent years, with accusations of media manipulation and croneyism in the privatization programme, but he remained a popular figure by and large and the only person many felt would be able to keep the country together throughout the conflict.

But in elections in October 1995, for the Croatian Parliament's House of Representatives and for the city and country of Zagreb, Tudjman and the HDZ received something of a shock. These elections were held only two months after the Croatian army had liberated nearly a quarter of Croatian territory held by Serb rebels, clearly with an eye to the HDZ garnering votes from what was a very successful military operation (completed in a matter of days, with very few casualties on either side). And though the HDZ remains by far the most important political party in Croatia – and they again achieved an overall majority, they lost votes compared with the last election and failed to get the two-thirds majority which would have given them the power to amend the constitution. Moreover, in Zagreb, the capital city and commercial centre of Croatia, and home to

Table 4.1   *Results of the elections to the House of Representatives*
(29 October 1995)

	Number of seats allocated
Croatian Democratic Union	75
Alliance of opposition parties	18
Croatian Social Liberal Party	12
Social Democratic Party	10
Croatian Party of Rights	4
Croatian Independent Democrats	1
Ethnic minorities	7
Total seats available	127

Source: Embassy of the Republic of Croatia, London, February 1996.

over a quarter of the total population, the HDZ lost majority control to a united opposition, and in the other major cities they were well down on their last election results. This result appeared to confirm the growing indications that the HDZ and Tudjman remain most popular in the provincial and rural areas of Croatia, but that the urban classes and intellegentsia are somewhat sceptical. It also appeared to confirm the suspected fragility of Croatian democracy when President Tudjman refused to accept the result of the Zagreb elections and the transfer of power from the HDZ. Shortly after the election Tudjman appointed a new prime minister in Zlatko Matesa, but the indications are that government policy will remain very much the same.

Government structure

In anticipation of the ensuing collapse of the Yugoslav Federation, a constitution was adopted for the Republic of Croatia on 22 December 1990. The constitution mapped out the road to multiparty democracy in Croatia through the introduction of a bicameral parliament (*Sabor*) composed of two houses: a House of Representatives (*Zastupnicki Dom*) and a House of Counties (*Zupanijski Dom*). Members of both houses were to be elected for a four-year term in office. The president of the republic is directly elected for a term of five years and can appoint the government, though he/she must obtain the approval of parliament.

Croatia has a decentralized political and administrative system. Croatia is divided into twenty-one counties, termed *Zupanije*, each having a *Zupan* or governor. Large cities, such as Zagreb and Rijeka, have their own authority and a mayor and have substantial control over their own affairs. At the local level there is both the *Opcina*, traditionally the main body after the central government, and at the ward level, the *Mjesni odbor*. The *Opcina* has wide functional responsibilities which it finances from a range of local taxation powers. The most important tax has traditionally been the Sales Tax, part of which went to the *Opcina* and part to central government. Other sources of revenue are available to cities with over 40,000 inhabitants in the shape of a tax of up to 7.5 per cent of income tax, with the largest city – Zagreb – able to levy a tax at a rate of 22.5 per cent.

Business and economic reform

The reform programme

In 1991 the Croats were forced into action on the economic front to defend their newly-acquired independence, beginning with the monetary system. Croatia introduced its own currency in order to isolate the economy from the massive inflationary pressures coming from the rump of Yugoslavia, which was flooding the economy with newly-printed money in order to finance its military build-up. It was felt that Croatia was being deliberately undermined by such actions and that its chances of moving successfully towards independence were being compromised by the massive inflow of Yugoslav dinars printed in Belgrade. In December 1991, the monetary authorities introduced the Croatian dinar. Old Yugoslav dinars were converted on a one-to-one basis. This action appeared to control the accelerating inflation, though not by much – monthly inflation rates fell from over 20 per cent in December 1991 to around 15 per cent going into March 1992. One of the problems here was that the now independent Croatia had a wide range of financial commitments to make in order to establish itself economically and militarily. This political imperative encouraged the National Bank of Croatia to be somewhat relaxed with the printing of the new Croatian dinar, since this source of cash – the 'inflation tax' – was the only one on offer.

In October 1993 the government introduced a three-stage reform designed to control inflation, promote financial and enterprise discipline and push the economy towards the market model. The first phase was a direct response to an inflation rate accelerating out of control: retail price inflation at the end of 1992 was over 660 per cent and the final figure for 1993 was over 1500 per cent. Monetary policy was substantially tightened, incomes policies were introduced within the socially-owned sectors of the economy to choke off inflation-compensating wage demands and a strong exchange rate was aimed at. The results were quick to see and inflation receded significantly. The stronger than anticipated exchange rate induced a degree of confidence in the Croatian currency and, since Croatia is highly import dependent in terms of consumer goods, imported inflation was reduced dramatically. However, the strong currency had a negative impact on export performance and a persistent growth in inter-enterprise arrears remained.

The second phase of the reform was meant to build upon the success of the first by introducing greater financial discipline throughout the emerging market economy. Privatization was meant to create responsible owners with no need for government subsidy. The tax system was successfully reorganized and tax revenue subsequently increased substantially. Largely as a result of this, the government was able to balance the budget by 1994. To ensure competition, new anti-monopoly regulations were brought out and loss-making enterprises were singled out for special remedial treatment. Finally, the banking system was in need of rehabilitation. The results of this stage are slowly coming into view: privatization has proceeded apace though monopoly remains a major feature of industry structure. The problem of loss-making industries also remains evident, with the twenty largest loss-makers going into 'intensive care' in mid-1995.

The third phase is only slowly becoming operationalized. The intention is that inflation remain low and that GNP be set firmly on an upward path. The apparently successful conclusion of the conflict has given much greater leeway for the government to operate, in particular to reduce its heavy commitment to defence spending (estimated to be around 20 per cent of GDP at the end of 1995). The results of this latest stage are impressive on the monetary front, with inflation falling to a new low of 4.5 per cent in 1995 and the government achieving a balanced budget. On the negative side, there is growing worry over the high rate of unemployment in Croatia, the continuing decline in industrial production and the high interest rates which are choking-off business investment.

Perhaps the most critical issue now facing the government is the gargantuan task of reintegrating the former rebel Serb-held territories back into Croatia proper – a feat very much on a par with the reintegration of the former East Germany into the Federal Republic of Germany. Much of the industrial capacity and infrastructure in these territories has been severely damaged or destroyed as a result of the fighting or because of neglect, and very few people remain, or seem likely to want to return, to assist in what will be a long-term reconstruction project. The impact will be felt on the budget, with pressure mounting to 'soften' the stabilization policy, as the various reconstruction departments bid for funds to create the necessary conditions for life in the territories to begin again. The major issue remains, however, how these areas can be re-populated after they have suffered so much damage, and after a period which has seen the bulk of the refugee population become resident in the capital city, or else living abroad. Clearly, the international aid agencies will have an important role to play over the next few years if these areas are to prosper.

Privatization

As a result of the impending conflict, the privatization programme began hesitantly in 1991. In this year the government passed the Law on the Transformation of Socially-Owned Assets, which was to replace the provisions of the previous laws implemented within former Yugoslavia. Under the new law, enterprises were to prepare themselves for sale as they saw fit, with larger enterprises being instructed to seek approval from the two main government bodies responsible for the privatization process, the Agency for Restructuring and Development and the Croatian Development Fund. Smaller enterprises with a capital asset base below five million Deutschmarks were allowed to enter into and conclude negotiations with potential purchasers on their own.

The new law signified many other changes to the privatization process. First, the government abandoned the earlier idea to use internal shares and instead reverted to conventional shareholdings which could be sold on the secondary capital market. It was intentionally made relatively easy for employees to purchase shares in 'their' enterprise through various discounts, low interest loans and payment by instalment. For a period it was even possible to use the foreign currency accounts which the banking system had 'frozen' (see below). This emphasis upon providing for the employees of soon-to-be privatized enterprises reflected a reluctance to completely abandon the relatively privileged position employees held under the old worker self-management system. Second, it brought in a deadline for enterprise managers to meet in trying to privatize their own enterprise. Those that failed to meet the deadline of 1 July 1992 had their unsold shares placed in the hands of the Croatian Development Fund, the Retirement Fund for Employees and the Retirement Fund for Agricultural Workers. Some of the most profitable enterprises were privatized on time, but the greater proportion of formerly socially-owned property went directly into the hands of the three state funds. By the end of 1993 the first stage of privatization was complete. The bulk of smaller enterprises had been sold off, medium-sized enterprises sold but left with the Croatian Privatization Fund and the other pension funds as minority shareholders, and larger enterprises sold with the CPF and pension funds as majority shareholders. Thus, paradoxically, privatization in Croatia was largely a process of nationalization, at least in the early stages.

According to the CPF, 2346 enterprises were able to register before the 1 July 1992 deadline, with a total share capital of 22 billion Deutschmarks. The CPF retained a majority shareholding in 16 per cent of these new enterprises and a minority shareholding in 37 per cent. The total revenue accruing to the CPF from the privatization process amounted to 1.35 billion Deutschmarks: 0.422 billion Deutschmarks of this figure was in cash with the rest (0.927 billion Deutschmarks) in the form of redeemed foreign currency accounts. These figures are rather modest compared to the total value since most purchases were by the instalment procedure. Also the bulk of purchases were made by the enterprises' own employees and managers, possibly because such a personal shareholding in an enterprise enables an employee to retain his/her employment in the ensuing restructuring phase.

In the next stage of the privatization process in late 1993, the CPF started to sell its various shareholdings through public auctions and invited tenders. It also became possible to legally trade in both fully paid-up and part-paid shares as the CPF realized that some original purchasers were having difficulty meeting the payment schedules. Simultaneously, further discounts were offered to those able to pay up in full for their partly-paid shares. It was hoped that this would increase the amount of cash forthcoming from the privatization process. The CPF also retained a sizable shareholding in order to be able to provide restitution to the previous (i.e. pre-communist) owners and to offer some compensation to the war-disabled and the displaced. Finally, in early 1994 it became possible once more to purchase shares using the foreign currency deposits frozen by the banking system in 1991.

The difficult conditions in Croatia meant that the privatization programme was always likely to be unorthodox relative to other Central and Eastern European economies: and it has been. For a start the government realized that few Croatians would have sufficient personal savings with which to purchase shares in their enterprise. Most had lost all their hard currency savings when the Yugoslav banking system collapsed. Moreover, international investment was unlikely to be any more forthcoming because of regional instability and conflict. This suggested a Czech Republic style 'voucher' privatization scheme for the larger enterprises. But this would have denied to the authorities the possibility of recouping some of the war expenses at some future stage. The chosen solution was for the government to provide for the conversion of social property into nationalized property. Once the various regional conflicts had been resolved and economic growth was in sight, so the argument went, the property could be gradually disposed off at much more favourable prices and with the confidence that an effective market mechanism would be able to promote rapid restructuring and genuine competition. The government also favoured this gradual, two-stage approach because it implied the imposition of fewer social costs upon the already war-weary population. There were also elections to be won. The major social cost was increased unemployment as newly-privatized enterprises sought profits through rationalization and the reduction of over-manning. The retention of many enterprises under government control permitted a choice between supporting their continued operation and meeting the cost of unemployment; by and large they preferred the first option.

New legislation proposed in early 1995 by the government promised to accelerate the transfer of assets from the state towards the entrepreneurial sector. The CPF is being subsumed into a new Ministry of Privatization and the Management of State Assets. The Croatian government will continue for some time to off-load its sizable shareholdings in order to raise revenue. Several large enterprises were floated on the Zagreb stock exchange by mid-1995 and more are planned including HPT, the telephone and postal body, electricity companies, INA, the oil company which is also Croatia's largest company and Pliva, one of the region's most successful pharmaceutical companies. The scheme proposes 25 per cent of the government's holdings be transferred to the pension fund; workers will be given special incentives to buy another 25 per cent and the remainder will be sold off. Foreign participation in the privatization programme still remains limited on account of the legacy of the conflict. But major investors are now beginning to be more bullish on the chances of a speedy return to economic stability, with some seeing 1997 as the year 'things come right'. Several share sales to all-comers attracted no interest, but some major investors have already bought into raw materials and energy facilities, food processors, breweries and tobacco.

Developing entrepreneurship

The development of entrepreneurship and the small business sector, together with the necessary business support infrastructure, is a major concern for the Croatian government. In many senses Croatia does have an extremely propitious environment with respect to small business development. First, it has the enormous benefit of a major tourism industry which is restructuring towards smaller-scale suppliers. Second, the Croatian diaspora and guest-worker population in Western Europe is a major, and continuing, source of new entrepreneurs and finance. Third, the legacy of serious under-representation of small-scale activities in the economy – sometimes termed the 'socialist black hole' – means relatively virgin territory for most new entrepreneurial initiatives.

Policy support for the development of new enterprises, particularly so-called 'micro-enterprises',[3] is mainly being undertaken by local authorities. However, a number of initiatives have been taken by central government through the Ministry of Economy and other government bodies. They have also established the Croatian Guarantee Agency, a body designed to tackle financial barriers to new small-firm entry by guaranteeing loans from the commercial banking sector and by offering subsidies to reduce the cost of any loans given out. Commerical banks are also becoming involved in support schemes for small and medium

[3] Micro-enterprises are generally defined as those enterprises employing less than ten persons.

Table 4.2 *Number and structure of small-scale privately owned enterprises in 1990 and 1994*

Activity	1990	1994
Industry and mining	1032	8284
Agriculture and fisheries	122	1777
Forestry	5	85
Water management	0	2
Construction	456	5062
Transport and communications	157	2411
Trade	4258	41,035
Tourism and catering	462	3944
Housing and communal services	0	193
Financial and business services	0	11,648

Source: Ministry of the Economy, Republic of Croatia, 1996.

sized enterprises (SMEs). Zagrebacka Banka, the largest Croatian bank, was the first to make use of credits provided by the international financial community for lending to SMEs. Table 4.2 illustrates the growth in, and structure of, small- scale[4] private enterprise development in Croatia.

Business and the economy

Croatia is a modern economy with an economic structure quite similar to Western European norms. Manufacturing makes up around 30 per cent of GDP, services around 60 per cent and agriculture 10 per cent. Trade is vital to Croatia since it is a very open economy (see below). GDP declined by around 30 per cent between 1991 and 1993 as a result of both the conflict and the economic dislocation caused by the exit from Yugoslavia. It appears to be stabilizing with just under 2 per cent growth in 1994 and 3 per cent in 1995. Income per capita has fallen drastically: from around US$3300 prior to these events to around US$2500 in 1995. These figures conceal Croatia's substantial 'grey economy' activities (see below) plus substantial remittances from Croats working abroad, principally in Western Europe. Nevertheless, living standards have declined substantially since 1991 and are only now beginning to bottom out.

The major economic areas in Croatia are the following:

[4] Small-scale is taken to mean here an enterprise employing less than 200 workers.

Industry

Around 350,000 people are employed in the manufacturing industry. The two main sectors include food, drinks and tobacco, which in 1991 accounted for around 26 per cent of total manufacturing industry output and metal products accounting for around 27 per cent. Other important sectors include chemicals, textiles, wood products and furniture, ship-building and electrical appliances. The industry structure is similar to that in developed economies, though it is somewhat more resource-dependent than the average.

Tourism

Tourism is of enormous importance to the future development and consolidation of the Croatian economy. Yearly tourist spending in Croatia before the dissolution of former Yugoslavia was of the order of US$2.5–3.5 billion, (which represented around 80 per cent of the total tourist spending in former Yugoslavia) with up to 75 per cent of this by foreigners. Tourism represents the biggest single foreign exchange earner for Croatia, generating an amount equal to nearly 80 per cent of the value of exports. Unofficial earnings from tourism (e.g. room hire, taxi work) also provided a substantial boost to the regions, with many estimates putting the total revenues from tourism at double the official figures (Institute of Tourism). It was one of the major sectors of employment generation. Overall, tourism contributed between 10 per cent and 12 per cent of total GNP.

Clearly, this sector has suffered massively by the prolonged conflict in the region. The number of tourists dropped to roughly a quarter the pre-war level. Tourists are returning slowly. Now that a resolution to the regional disputes appears to have been found, rapid growth in this sector is very likely. Several factors account for this optimistic assessment: first, the sector remains under-developed from the past: second, Croatia has strategic advantages over its main competitors in the form of proximity to the main markets of Western Europe and the results of a high level of environmental protection: third, the possibility exists to diversify into new tourist niches.

Agriculture

Agriculture has greatly declined in importance in Croatia since the Second World War as the country underwent rapid industrialization.

Private ownership has always played an important part in agriculture. Today over four-fifths of cultivated land is private. The main activities are cereals production and cattle-breeding. A high percentage of the population has access to a portion of land, often with a small cottage

Table 4.3   *The farming population as a percentage of total population*

Year	1961	1971	1981	1991
Farming population	44	27	14.5	8.5

Source: Croatian Chamber of Economy, 1995.

attached, and this plays an important role for most families in terms of food supply.

Building and construction

Croatia has a strong tradition in building and construction. At the end of 1994 around 62,000 people were officially employed in the sector, with many more working unofficially on home construction. In spite of the regional conflict in 1994 Croatian companies were able to complete construction contracts abroad worth some US $300 million, an indication of the durability of the sector. Furthermore, the reconstruction of Croatia, and probably Bosnia too, will provide a constant stream of commercial possibilities over the next few years which Croatian firms can tap into to expand their activities.

Foreign trade

Croatia is an open economy and foreign trade represents a significant share of economic activity. In 1993, for example, foreign trade was around 66 per cent of GDP, making Croatia one of the most open economies in Central and Eastern Europe. This situation is a legacy of the liberal foreign trade climate operated under the former Yugoslavia, which provided for the possibility of trade with both the Western and Eastern blocs during the period of the Cold War. Croatia continues today to develop its markets in both west and east, though especially in the former with the countries and regions of the Alp-Adria agreement (southern Austria, northern Italy and Slovenia) and with Germany. Significantly, business relations with Serbia have resumed as a result of the peace agreement of December 1995. Given that Serbia supplied the vast range of raw and semi-processed materials for Croatia's enterprises, and represented a big market for Croatian goods, this could play a major factor in accelerating economic growth.

This openness, on the other hand, makes the economy especially prone to fluctuations in foreign trading conditions. Indeed, it was the break-up of former Yugoslavia and, to a lesser extent, the collapse of the CMEA,

Table 4.4   *Main trading areas in 1994 (figures as a percentage of total)*

	Exports	Imports
European Union	52	51
Germany	22	21
Italy	21	19
Others	9	11
Other developed countries	12	16
Sweden	4	1.5
Austria	3.5	7
USA	2	3
Others	2.5	4.5
Eastern Europe	8	11
Former USSR	4	5
Others	4	6
Former Yugoslav Republics	23	11
Slovenia	13	10.5
Bosnia and Hercegovina	8	0
Macedonia	2	0.5
Lesser developed countries	5	10.5
Total[a]	100	100

[a] Figures may not add up due to rounding.

Source: Croatian Economic Trends, 1/1995.

which delivered one of the worst economic setbacks to the Croatian economy: from 1990 to 1993 total exports collapsed by nearly 60 per cent.[5] The worst appears to be over, however, and the former CMEA countries are being targeted again by their traditional Croatian suppliers. Moreover, the significant inroads made into Western European markets when the two above markets were closed to Croatian goods has created a foundation upon which Croatian enterprises can consolidate and, possibly, expand further.

A further point to note with regard to international trade is that, with a floating exchange rate and only minimal intervention by the National Bank of Croatia, the problem of an over-valued kuna has been a feature of the early years of independence. Schonfelder (1995) argues that the over-valuation of the Kuna between 1992 and 1994 must have exceeded

[5] The 1990 figure includes an estimate of trade with other republics within former Yugoslavia.

50 per cent. This over-valuation obviously put enormous strain on exporters and enterprises producing for the domestic market (see below). Croatian products are among the most expensive in Eastern Europe and it is only a generally perceived 'quality factor', the main advantage Croatia inherited over most of the other transition economies, which maintains its market share in the face of much lower cost competitors. In spite of the 'quality factor', the effects of the strong currency on the trading position were negative in 1995 with a trade deficit around $3 billion. Table 4.4 illustrates the main trading areas of Croatia in 1994.

Exports

Unlike in other communist economies, where enterprises were generally obliged to use a state trading organization, enterprises in former Yugoslavia were allowed to become involved in foreign trade directly, including with the western economies. As a result, a culture of expertise grew and a business presence was built up in many high value-added markets where competition from the developed economies was strong. The value of this previous business expertise was immense: it is a major contributory factor to the sophisticated and internationally aware business culture which has emerged in Croatia.

Croatia has attempted to realign its goods export trade away from the former Eastern bloc and towards the European Union (EU). In terms of the former, exports often took the form of an illicit technology transfer,

Table 4.5 *Exports by branch of industry (in US$ millions) and as a percentage of total exports for 1994*

Branch	Exports	Share of total exports
Textile industry	603	14.2
Basic industry	339	8.0
Production of petroleum products	339	7.9
Shipbuilding	311	7.3
Chemical industry	279	6.6
Leather footware	274	6.4
Food processing	273	6.4
Electrical appliances	246	5.8
Timber and wood	159	3.7
Metal manufacturing	107	2.5
Total exports of Croatia	4260	100.0

Source: Croatian Chamber of Economy, 1995.

passing on western technology and designs incorporated into Croatian products. This avenue is no longer needed of course, which partly accounts for the collapse in exports to Eastern Europe. On the other hand, exports to the EU have increased. As noted above, there is major potential to develop increased trade in services, principally tourism, which in 1990 accounted for just over 40 per cent of its total export revenues.

Imports

The relatively liberal climate in former Yugoslavia meant few restrictions on imports. This relaxed framework has largely been carried over, though not always immediately. Increased duties in 1992, and then again in 1993, were only put into reverse in 1994. The earlier moves reflected the need to rebuild hard currency reserves, rather than as an aspect of competition policy. Competition policy has taken the form of withholding of import licences if foreign goods stand to impinge too much upon so-called strategic industries, or those considered infant industries. In this case the Croatian Chamber of Commerce gets involved in the negotiations as a way of encouraging domestic producers to come forward. Foreign competition is having a positive influence on the quality and price of domestically produced goods, with some estimating that over three-quarters of the domestic economy has been affected by actual and potential competition (Institute of International Relations, 1995). A noted case of the effect of foreign competition was in 1993 when Tesla, a large manufacturer of telecommunications equipment and the only one of its kind in Croatia, became involved in a dispute with the Croatian postal service over the latter's threat to buy cheaper equipment from abroad

Table 4.6 *Imports by branch of industry (in millions of US$) and as a percentage of total imports for 1994*

Branch	Exports	Share of total imports
Petroleum products industry	686	13.1
Textile industry	367	7.0
Food processing industry	297	5.7
Electrical appliances	226	4.3
Basic industry	198	3.8
Chemical industry	80	3.4
Total imports of Croatia	5229	100.0

Source: Croatian Chamber of Economy, 1995.

rather than from Tesla. The dispute was settled with Tesla reducing its prices by more than 30 per cent.[6]

Croatia's policy towards imports remains entrapped in the classic textbook dilemma: on the one hand, it wants to liberalize imports in order to provide an injection of competition into a monopolized industrial structure: yet, on the other hand, it recognizes that the industrial structure remains fragile and many sectors stand to collapse if faced with serious foreign competition. As a result of a generally over-valued kuna, foreign-made goods tend to be cheaper than their Croatian counterparts, and this has led to substantial informal consumer goods trade (smuggling, shopping sprees, etc.) with Croatia's neighbours. Prices for most consumer goods in neighbouring Trieste in Italy were estimated to be around 50 per cent lower on average in 1994 than in Croatia (Schonfelder, 1995). This is having a serious effect upon many of Croatia's producers who cannot hope to compete in such a distorted financial climate.

Business and finance

Banking and equity markets

Given that Croatia is both one of the group of transition economies **and** has suffered from heavy damage as a result of the conflict, it is doubly imperative that it establish a healthy market-based banking system and capital markets. The first task undertaken was to restructure the National Bank of Croatia (NBH). The NBH now has a great deal of independence from the government. The NBH is responsible to parliament (the *Sabor*) rather than government, with the governor being elected by parliament for a six-year term. Though the minister of finance has a seat on the bank's board, he or she has no vote. Thus, it is similar to the German central bank – the Bundesbank. The main aspect of the NBH's independence relates to its perceived role in facilitating the transition process: in particular, however, it relates to the universal transition economy problem of financing expanding budget deficits. Unlike in other transition economies, the NBH is able to avoid the need to finance government budgetary requirements via extensive money creation. First, it is able to counter such requests in its board. Second, the NBHs constitution only allows it to extend credits to the Ministry of Finance up to 5 per cent of the the total budgetary requirement. Moreover, those credits are deliberately structured as short term and to be repaid at the end of the fiscal year, meaning that they cannot be used to plug the budget deficit gap. The credits are really 'bridging loans', filling the seasonal gap between expenditures, which are high in the first half of the year, and revenues which generally pick up in the second half of the year.

[6] Reported in *Vecernji list*, 15 June 1993.

The NBH is not directly involved in setting interest rates. This is left to the commercial banks. However, it does involve itself to some extent in exchange rate management, intervening on occasions to prevent damaging fluctuations.

Turning now to the commercial banking system, the first thing to note is that it benefited from earlier moves toward a two-tier banking system in the mid-1960s. This meant that a commercial and industrial banking system was already in place prior to the onset of the major reforms of the 1990s. The 1993 Law on Banks and Savings Banks removed all remaining restrictions on private and foreign ownership of banks. However, under the previous financial regime in former Yugoslavia the banks were effectively owned by their founders, which were usually enterprises. This gave rise to the predominance of low interest rates and other 'soft' borrowing conditions for enterprises who were using 'their' banks to provide financial support for themselves rather than have the banks carry on their business according to conventional commercial banking criteria (e.g. ensuring a profitable loan portfolio). The commercial banks were therefore nearly all handicapped by extensive portfolios of bad loans to their large enterprise owners. By mid-1995 there were fifty-two commercial banks in operation. The system is highly concentrated: the two largest banks (*Zagrebacka Banka* and *Privredna Banka Zagreb*) account for around 50 per cent of the total sector assets; the six largest account for 84 per cent. The system is also regionalized with the result that several banks are in serious financial difficulty on account of being located in war zones and/or economically depressed areas.

The NBH is assisting in the restructuring of the commercial banks. Charged with overseeing this process is the Agency for the Rehabilitation of Banks with a managing board consisting of three members from the NBH and three from the Ministry of Finance. In conjunction with the Croatian Privatization Fund, two plans were implemented to assist in the restructuring of the banks. The first tackled the problem related to Croatian citizens' hard currency savings accounts which were 'frozen' as Croatia became independent. As the end of former Yugoslavia approached the hard currency deposits registered in the National Bank of Yugoslavia 'disappeared', mainly into the budget for the Yugoslav National Army, which was used against Croatia as it sought to exit from the collapsing Yugoslav Federation. The Croatian government has now taken on responsibility for these 'frozen' accounts and made it possible for them to be used again. Initially, they could be used against the purchase price of housing being privatized by the the state and for shares being issued. Foreign investors were also made eligible to purchase the 'frozen' accounts at 70 per cent of face value in order to use them to buy into Croatian companies being privatized. Finally, a later scheme converting the 'frozen' accounts into ten-year government debt came into effect in mid-1995, but this is being restructured already on account of the vast sums to be paid out. A new more gradual scheme is being prepared for late 1996.

The second scheme to help restructure the banks became known as the 'big bonds scheme'. It involved the government issuing bonds to enterprises with the greatest financial difficulties on condition that they undergo a rehabilitation programme. This package of support was provided in exchange for equity in those enterprises. The enterprises used the government bonds to pay off their debts to the bank. Enterprises had more chance of becoming profitable as they were able to reduce their debts, while the banks became technically solvent on account of holding government bonds instead of non-performing loans. The bonds are of twenty years maturity with an annual interest rate of 20 per cent. There has been some disappointment with this particular scheme, however, since most enterprises included in the scheme continued to run up debts. The minimal level of supervision involved in the rehabilitation pro- grammes has been noted as one of the chief causes of this poor performance. Additional support from the international financial com- munity has been forthcoming too, in the shape of a $100 million loan from the World Bank which will be used to refloat a group of the most indebted banks.

The NBH is supervisor to the commercial banking sector but commercial banks are free to set interest rates as they wish. This freedom has resulted in a fairly typical financial profile for a transition economy: high real interest rates, around the 18 to 20 per cent mark for most of 1995, and very short payback periods of around three months or so. Two main reasons account for this. First, because of the conflict they were forced into attaching a large risk premium on all loans. Second, most of the commercial banks have a portfolio with at least some non-performing loans, and they need to make good profits on those loans which are performing in order to cover those which are not. It may also be the case that profits on commercial trade, especially importing businesses, are so high that the banks are simply attracted into appropriating some of this bounty before other more traditional customers are serviced.

There is a significant savings bank sector in Croatia. By mid-1994 there were sixty-seven such savings banks, usually operating within localities and regulated by the NBH. Additionally, specifically to address the longer-term requirements of the enterprise sector, a new state-owned bank was also established in June 1992 – the Croatian Credit Bank for Reconstruction and Development (HKBO). It was given the task of supporting new businesses and infrastructure through the existing banking system. Its work encompasses the legacy of the current conflict as well as the more longer-term requirements of a market economy. The role model and advisor is the Kreditanstalt fur Wiederaufbau (KfW), a German specialist bank which has been notably successful in supporting small and medium sized enterprises through the provision of low interest finance (Randlesome, 1994). This willingness to establish a genuine development bank contrasts with many of the transition economies where they have effectively been frozen off the agenda by governments keen to see equity markets grow into the role as the main, or even sole source of development finance. Western aid agencies have also been blamed for this tendency (see Chapter 7).

Finally, a stock exchange was first established in Zagreb in 1918, but abandoned once the communists came to power after the Second World War. In 1991 it was re-opened by a supporting group of twenty-five banks to trade in large blocks of shares. As in most transition economies, however, it remains weak and under-developed. It is also in competition from a rival private stock exchange set up in Varazdin in 1993 by local entrepreneurs, and dealing with small shareholder transactions. The onset of war further undermined the Zagreb exchange and, later on, the combination of comparatively very low inflation from 1994 onwards plus high interest rates eroded any remaining incentive for investors to move into the equities market. Now that the war has been brought to a conclusion there is likely to be much more interest in Croatian equities, from foreign companies especially, with the opportunity for the market as a whole to recover and expand. The reinvigorated privatization pro-gramme will also provide a much bigger range of stocks to trade.

Taxation

A further element of the stabilization programme has been the need for fiscal restraint. Specifically, the budget must be balanced through an improved taxation system, including a range of new and higher taxes. Central government continues to raise the bulk (about 65 per cent) of its tax revenue from sales and excise taxes. Sales tax was reduced from 40 to 20 per cent as a prelude to Croatia coming into line with Western Europe and introducing a VAT system, scheduled for January 1997. Excise taxes were introduced in July 1994 on a number of traditional products, such as alcohol, tobacco and petrol products. Customs duties have been reduced to 10 per cent though exemptions have been severely curtailed. It had also been expected to raise cash from privatization sales, but this did not occur and it is only now in the post-war period likely to come on stream.

At the start of 1994 a new profit tax was introduced, pitched at 25 per cent with relief being available for reinvestment and for war damages. Also in 1994, a new income tax was launched. The rate is 25 per cent on taxable income up to three times the minimum annual salary, with a rate of 35 per cent for taxable income in excess of this. In addition to income tax there are a variety of other taxes which must be paid by employees out of the gross wage. The result is an overall rate of personal taxation of between 50 to 70 per cent, making it a comparatively large burden on the individual. The need to fight a war also imposed substantial additional taxes on the population, though these are planned to be withdrawn when feasible. Local and regional governments, and the capital city of Zagreb, also have a wide range of tax-collecting powers.

Business, the labour market and trade unions

Labour market developments

Unemployment has increased since independence and, although there remain pockets of strong demand for particular types of worker, the present level is arousing considerable concern. By the end of 1994 the unemployment rate had touched 20 per cent and it has remained at this figure into 1995 and 1996. Another problem remains the low level of job mobility, as workers generally tend to want to remain in their locality for strong cultural/family reasons and because most workers were allocated a flat through their place of employment. The problem of housing as a barrier to mobility has been somewhat ameliorated over the last few years, as the private housing market has taken root, but buying and selling housing still remains difficult. Moreover, the ongoing demobilization programme will add to the reservoir of unemployed labour.

Job creation measures are of more importance as labour market policy. The establishment of new jobs is proceeding, overwhelmingly in the fast growing small enterprise sector. The larger state enterprises, however, are generally over-manned and should be shedding labour. Few large enterprises have made substantial cutbacks to their workforces. Thus the most important *de facto* feature of labour market policy is represented by the continuing provision of subsidies for most major enterprises (estimated cost in 1994, 5 per cent of GDP) and the unwillingness to force unprofitable ones into bankruptcy. The central government believes that the regional conflict has bitten deep into the social cohesion of Croatia and that a simultaneous job loss programme would be untenable. Increasingly, however, enterprises are implementing voluntary schemes of their own in an attempt to reduce the labour-force. This mainly takes the form of offering workers substantial sums of money to leave and establish their own private business. Such offers are only sporadically taken up, however, since to leave an enterprise voluntarily automatically disqualifies the worker from the array of social benefits available to the working population.

There are a number of other smaller-scale labour market policies which attempt to subsidize the cost of hiring the unemployed or encourage the unemployed into self-employment and new enterprise establishment. A programme started in 1993 gave employers (state or private sector) a six-month wage subsidy for any new worker taken on in the special category of difficult to employ. In this category are included the handicapped and, unfortunately, the growing number of war invalids. Alternatively, they were eligible to receive up to 20,000 Deutschmarks as start-up capital if they wished instead to establish themselves in business. A year later further subsidy schemes were introduced, to provide for labour mobility – encouraging the professional classes to return to the islands – to recruit for dangerous occupations, such as coal-mining, and to alleviate the rise in graduate unemployment by sponsoring the cost of research projects.

Trade unions

Trade unions under the worker self-management system performed a similar role as in other communist states. The *Sindikati* undertook a variety of social functions including the arrangement of holidays, provision of foods, etc. As a result membership was more akin to a social club membership. Since the collapse of communism the rate of trade union membership has remained high in Croatia, around 60 per cent of the total labour force, but this figure partly reflects the fact that they have retained many of their social functions. There is also an element of inertia, with people simply continuing to allow for the deduction of trade union fees, rather than make a deliberate move to leave their union. The trade unions continue to be dogged by the perception that they are a left-over from communism and retain little public affection.

Unions have significant consultation rights, especially over such matters as redundancy. The government has legislated for enterprises to negotiate with the trade unions in the case of those socially-owned enterprises in serious economic difficulty. These enterprises prepare recovery programmes, one critical feature of which is an 'enforced holiday' for a section of the workforce. The precise amount of compensation for these temporarily displaced workers is a matter for negotiation.

Business, education and training

The level of education in Croatia is on a par with its neighbours to the north (Slovenia, Hungary). Table 4.7 indicates the results of the 1991 census.

Students up to the age of 17–18 attend one of two institutions. First, there is the professional school which is geared to technical and professional training and prepares students immediately for a career. Students can choose to study for three years and leave to start their career, or four years to open up the option of applying for a university place. Second, there is the 'gimnazija' which is geared to general subjects – arts, social sciences and so forth – with the intention that students then move on to a university place after four years of study. The prospect of a job after studying at the 'gimnazija' but without a university diploma is very

Table 4.7   *Level of education*

	Total	Percentage
No schooling or unknown	389,014	10.1
4–8 years of elementary school	1,721,119	44.6
Schools for highly skilled and very highly skilled workers	488,491	12.7
Schools for mid-level personnel and secondary schools	899,244	23.3
Technical and vocational schools	156,152	4.0
Universities, advanced schools and arts academies	204,006	5.3
Total	3,858,026	100.0

Source: Croatian Chamber of Economy, 1995.

small, so most students come with the idea of moving on to university.

There are four universities in Croatia: in Zagreb, Osijek, Split and Rijeka and in the year 1993/94 there were 71,000 students enrolled. The spread of subjects offered compares with the western economies, with business and language subjects enjoying rapid growth over the last few years. Standards are traditionally high, and a high percentage opt to go on to post-graduate study. As in all other transition economies, the introduction of MBA (Master in Business Administration) type courses is a feature of the direction of changes in the education system, with courses developing in both the existing state universities and through a number of western-style business schools opening up. But one of the main deficits continues to be the lack of suitable training programmes for entrepreneurs, managers and other employees now working in a market economy.

Business and the environment

Croatia emerged from fifty years or so of rapid industrial development with comparatively few environmental problems, certainly far fewer than most other countries in post-communist Eastern Europe. The greater decentralization employed within Yugoslav enterprises meant that pollution and other environmental hazards which impacted upon the workers themselves and the local community could be argued against in the workers' council and in other political fora in the locality. The process was not perfect – many Yugoslav enterprises were hazardous by western standards – but the element of control held by the employees was very often sufficient to prohibit the worst kind of abuses found elsewhere.

Today, the environment plays a very important role in the Croatian economy compared to other transition economies. This is because of the vital tourist industry, which is likely to prove the mainstay of the economy over the next few years. By far the most important region – the Adriatic – remains one of the cleanest and most tastefully-developed coastlines in southern Europe, and a particular selling point in the attempt to develop a more 'up-market' tourist image for Croatia. Not surprisingly, for a long time there were serious efforts to contain pollution along the coast and several major polluting enterprises were forcibly closed down.

However, one of the major material casualties of the war has been the environment. The immensity of the physical destruction and resulting damage inflicted upon the natural environment is only recently becoming evident, as a result of a number of surveys by international organizations. With damage to the environmental infrastructure – water treatment plants, waste disposal services and so forth – and the actual environmental and physical hazards created by the fighting itself, Croatia has indeed suffered very much. The Plitvice National Park, which was held for several years by Serb separatists and which was the scene of fierce fighting with Croatian forces, will take some years to restore to its original condition. Other regions under control of the rebelling Serb forces are also in a very poor state. One of the main problems has been the leaking of highly-toxic polychlorinated biphenyls (PCBs) from electrical installations damaged as a result of the fighting. In one town alone, the famous resort of Dubrovnik, more than fifty such installations were destroyed and have been leaking PCBs into the soil and local water table, and as a result have contaminated the water supply for many kilometres around (Richardson, 1993). Perhaps the worst case is that of Eastern Slavonia, where a sustained bombardment by the remnants of the Yugoslav National Army in 1991 and 1992 destroyed several of the towns in this border region. Many of these towns have been unable to attempt to repair the damage, with the result that leaking chemicals and toxins have spewed into the local water supply, and damaged industrial plant and raw material supplies continue to contaminate the soil and air.

While the negative social effects of the war will reverberate for many years to come and will require significant investment to counteract, the environmental catastrophe visited upon Croatia is, rightly, also being allocated some financial support. A number of environmental clean-up programmes are going ahead and several international agencies, such as UNIDO, are already working on a number of the most pressing environmental problems. There is some urgency to this task because it is rightly perceived that the huge potential economic value of the tourist industry will not be realized fully until the environmental problems have largely been solved.

Slovenia

Introduction

The origins of the independence movement in Slovenia go back at least to 1986 when the liberal wing of the Slovenian League of Communists under the leadership of Milan Kucan achieved predominance over the conservative faction. Several new political parties were established in the Slovenian Spring of 1988, and the first democratic elections were held in April 1990 which were won by a nationalist grouping of parties known as 'Demos'. A referendum on independence was held on 23 December 1990 and was passed with 88 per cent of the votes in favour. Negotiations to create a confederation of independent states with the rest of Yugoslavia failed to achieve any agreement and the Slovenians made a unilateral declaration of independence on 25 June 1991, putting the final nail in the coffin of the 'Yugoslav Idea'. A brief war with the Yugoslav army followed immediately on this declaration of independence which was decided successfully in the favour of Slovenia when the Yugoslav army withdrew from the territory. Slovenian independence was recognized internationally in January 1992, and since then the country has been at peace and is a safe destination for business and tourism.

Slovenia is a small country of two million people bordering with Italy, Austria and Hungary. Unlike the other successor states of the former Yugoslavia it is ethnically homogeneous with almost nine-tenths of the population being Slovenes. The Slovenian language, although sharing common Slavic roots, is distinct from the Serbo-Croatian spoken elsewhere in the former Yugoslavia. The Slovenes, like the Croats, follow the Roman Catholic religion. These factors contribute to a strong sense of national cohesiveness, and have made Slovene independence a relatively natural development. One reflection of this desire to promote and preserve the national identity is a clause in the constitution which forbids the sale of Slovenian real estate to foreigners. This clause is controversial as it goes against the grain of the general trend towards opening to the outside world. However, since Slovenia is a small country in the initial stages of a delicate process of economic and social transformation this restriction can be readily understood as a sensible measure to preserve national cohesion and consensus through this difficult period.

Business and government

The Constitution of the Republic of Slovenia was adopted on 23 December 1991, and enshrines the principle of democratic government. The highest legislative authority is the National Assembly, which has ninety deputies elected for a four-year period of office. The second chamber is called the National Council. It has forty deputies representing social, economic, professional and local interests and performs an advisory role. The current president of Slovenia is Milan Kucan, who led the country to independence. The president is elected for a term of five years and may serve no more than two consecutive terms of office. In all, there are eight political parties represented in the National Assembly, including the Liberal Democrats (LDS) with the largest number of seats (thirty), the Christian Democrats and the Social Democrats who together form a coalition government. In addition there are two independent deputies representing the Italian and Hungarian minorities.

Since 1993 there have been fifteen separate ministries, including ministries for finance, economic affairs, economic relations and development, labour, the family and social affairs. A number of quangos have also been established including the Agency for Reconstruction and Privatization, the Development Fund, and the Bank Rehabilitation Agency.

Government finances have been reformed and have begun to approach Western European patterns. The personal income tax accounts for 16 per cent of government revenue, and taxes on goods and services account for 28 per cent. A peculiarity of the Slovene public finances is the large share (42 per cent) of government revenue accounted for by social security contributions. This largely stems from the system of very generous pension entitlements for former employees which was inherited from the self-management system, and the widespread use of early retirement as a means of labour force reductions in loss-making enterprises. A reform to the pension system is urgently required if the government finances are to be put on a viable long-term footing for the future.

Business and the economy

Immediately following the break with the former Yugoslavia, Slovenia introduced its own currency, the tolar, in order to pursue its own independent monetary policy and to isolate the country from the inflation raging elsewhere in the former federation. A macroeconomic stabilization policy was successfully introduced, bringing the rate of inflation down from 200 per cent in 1991 to 20 per cent by 1994, and stabilizing the exchange rate which stood at 180 tolars to the pound sterling in June 1995. The stabilization policy did however require restrictions on aggregate demand and unusually high real interest rates. Together with the disruption caused by the loss of markets in the former Yugoslavia, the policy led to a sharp short-run fall in industrial production and in GDP, and an increase in unemployment from virtually zero to 14 per cent of the workforce by 1993. However, the recession was short lived, and economic growth resumed in 1993. During 1994 the GDP increased by 5 per cent, one of the highest growth rates in Europe at the time. Slovenia had always had a relatively open economy even within the former Yugoslavia, and was able to take advantage of pre-existing trading links on western markets, aided by the high level of linguistic skill of the population. This provided a favourable basis for economic recovery. The growth turnaround was largely export led and was based upon a successful reorientation of export trade towards Western European markets, particularly in Germany, Italy and Austria.

The Slovenian economy has a strong manufacturing base accounting for around 27 per cent of GDP. Particular strengths are found in engineering, machinery production, and various light industries such as textiles and wood products. Many of the older heavy industries such as iron and steel manufacturing whose output fell by 50 per cent between 1989 and 1993 have suffered badly during the post-independence recession. These uncompetitive industries will have to be gradually restructured through a process of managed decline. Other industries such as the wood and wood processing industries which are potentially competitive on world markets have also suffered sharp reductions in output. However, such industries can be expected to recover in time and require imaginative policies of restructuring and short term support to help them realize their competitive potential.

The Slovenian government is heavily involved in the restructuring process, and has established a Development Fund to take over and manage some of the worst-affected loss-making companies. In all over one hundred such loss making companies have been taken over by the Development Fund for the purpose of restructuring and eventual privatization. Elsewhere in the economy a successful turnaround is being achieved through the companies' own efforts. For example, the important electrical machinery and appliances sector has registered some of the highest export growth rates. In all, labour productivity in manufacturing is improving rapidly, and registered a growth of 15.3 per cent in the first nine months of 1994.

Along with the growth achieved in the manufacturing sector there have been accompanying trends in electricity production, construction, trade and transport. The tourism sector which suffered badly due to the proximity of the war in Croatia in 1992 and the lack of international awareness of the new state has begun to recover. Over a million tourists spent their holiday in Slovenia in 1994, a growth of 7 per cent over the previous year.

Privatization

The privatization laws introduced in the former Yugoslavia in 1988 created a framework for privatization throughout the whole country. In Slovenia a republican Privatization Agency was established in 1990 to monitor and control the privatization process, and at the same time the Development Fund was established to manage the implementation of the process. In practice its main task was to take over the ownership of ninety-eight large loss-making enterprises and restructure them prior to privatization. After independence the federal law continued to be in use until a new Slovenian privatization law could be agreed upon. This new law was eventually passed at the end of 1992 following a lengthy and controversial debate over the appropriate methods of privatization to be used. Under the new law the self-management system based on the concept of 'social ownership' was to be replaced by more conventional forms of corporate governance. The main method of privatization was to be through the sale of shares at a discount to insider employees and managers of enterprises combined with the exchange of shares, again with priority to insiders, of shares for privatization vouchers which have been distributed to the population. Enterprises had a further option of commercial sale through public offering of shares if they chose not to follow the route of insider privatization, although it was expected that only a minority of larger enterprises whose assets were too great to be bought by employees would take advantage of this possibility. In addition, a tenth of the shares issued by privatized companies were to be reserved for a Pension Fund, a further tenth for a Compensation Fund and two-tenths were to be transferred to the Development Fund. The Development Fund has a key role to play in the privatization process through the use of its resources for enterprise restructuring and the provision of soft loans to private businesses. At the end of the privatization process it is likely that most privatized enterprises in Slovenia will operate under a system of majority employee ownership. While this system has some advantages in terms of providing strong incentives from employees to deliver a high level of productivity, it may also discourage outside investors from placing investment funds in such firms. Whether the employees will retain their share holdings or sell them on the open market when restrictions on sale elapse is an open question but one which will determine the long-term evolution of the industrial structure in Slovenia.

Small business development

The liberalization and deregulation of the private enterprise began to occur within the former Yugoslavia with the passage of the Enterprise Law in 1988. Slovenian entrepreneurs took advantage of the new opportunities and in the following years a large number of new private enterprises have been established. From a base of 6313 small private firms with under fifty employees in 1990, the number of private enterprises, mainly limited liability companies, grew to over 38,000 by the end of 1993. Already there existed a strong private sector in the form of an equally large number of craft enterprises. Recent legislation will result in a reorganization of the craft sector along the lines of the German system of qualified craft work, whilst other former craft enterprises will convert to the limited liability form. Taken together with the previously socially owned enterprises which have undergone privatization, the private sector now generates around 42 per cent of Slovenia's GDP, a proportion which is continually increasing.

The Slovenian government has given more attention and support to the small firms sector than others in the region. It has established a Small Business Development Centre as a public non-profit making institution under the aegis of the Ministry for Economic Affairs. The centre has organized a network of 560 local branches to support small-scale business. Specific measures of support include a 100 per cent profit tax exemption over the first year of operation of a new private business, falling to 66 per cent in the second year, and to 33 per cent in the third year. In some favoured regions the 100 per cent exemption lasts for the full three years, and there are also a number of benefits for employers who take on trainees or new entrants to the labour market. In addition there are special programmes for the encouragement of innovation in small firms, women entrepreneurs, and promotion of small business incubators. A recent development is the establishment of a Small Business Development Fund to provide loan guarantees and subsidized, co-financed loans through the banking system. The Small Business Development Centre is also seeking ways to promote the development of subcontracting by foreign corporations to Slovenian small firms, and has recently established a small firm subcontracting centre with this purpose in mind.

These efforts in the area of private sector business development have been supported and assisted by substantial financial and technical aid from the European Union PHARE programme, which allocated 12.5 million ECU for this purpose in 1994 alone out of a global assistance budget for 1994 of 44 million ECU. In this respect, Slovenia has benefited greatly in comparison with Croatia, which has suffered from 'invisible sanctions' and has been frozen out from the various international assistance programmes which have been available to Slovenia and other Eastern European countries.

Foreign trade and investment

Slovenia is a relatively open economy, and has succeeded in reorienting its trade pattern following the break-up of the former Yugoslavia. Overall, exports account for just under 50 per cent of GDP and grew in real terms by 2 per cent in 1994. Within this, exports to the former Yugoslavia fell by a further 5 per cent in 1994, while exports to the rest of the world rose by 4 per cent. The largest part of foreign trade is carried out with the

European Union (EU), mainly with Germany, Italy and France which together accounted for just over 50 per cent of both import and export trade. However, trade with Eastern Europe may increase in the future following Slovenia's accession to the Central European Free Trade Association (CEFTA) at the end of 1995.

The reorientation of trade to new European markets has underpinned the Slovenian economy's successful turnaround from the economic difficulties experienced following secession from the former Yugoslavia. As a result, in the first nine months of 1994, Slovenia had a current account surplus of US$371 million. However, foreign exchange reserves are growing rapidly, and the stable tolar is becoming over-valued, threatening the export competitiveness of Slovenian manufacturing industry on western markets. Foreign exchange reserves at US$2.5 billion are sufficient to cover four months of imports and exceed the total foreign debt by one-fifth. The external finances of Slovenia are therefore on a sound footing and there is room for some relaxation of the tight monetary policy.

Most sectors of the Slovene economy are open to foreign investment, although wholly-owned foreign companies are not allowed to operate in the military equipment industry, rail and air transport, communications and telecommunications, insurance, publishing or the mass media. Whilst foreign individuals and companies cannot buy real estate in Slovenia, any company with partly Slovenian and partly foreign ownership can do so. There are no restrictions on repatriation of profits by foreign investors. The tax regime for foreign investors is rather favourable. With a 25 per cent tax on profits, Slovenia has one of the lowest corporate tax rates in Europe. Tax deductions are available and include 20 per cent of the sum invested in tangible assets provided they are not sold within three years. By the end of 1993 there were over one thousand foreign direct investment projects underway with a total invested capital of US$750 million. This put Slovenia in second place behind Hungary among Eastern European recipients of foreign direct investment, with a per capita stock of foreign capital invested amounting to US$395. Two-thirds of this capital inflow has gone into manufacturing industries, especially in the car industry, the paper industry and the production of electrical machinery and appliances. European multi-nationals which have made large investments include Bayer, Renault, Citroen, Henkel, Iveco, IBM, Siemens, Semperit and Bosch. A number of Slovenian companies which were put under the management of the Development Fund have been entirely sold off to foreign investors. These include Farrio Slovenia, a manufacturer of carton board which was sold to the Italian Saffa group, with a capital of US$75.4 million. Other foreign investments have been of longer standing, such as the investment by Renault in the Revoz company, which is one of the largest producers of the Renault 5 and Renault Clio in Europe.

The sustainability of Slovenia's favourable recent economic performance depends very much on its ability to integrate its economic and trade relations with the EU. Following on from the formal recognition of Slovenia by the EU in 1992, a co-operation agreement setting out a preferential (and reciprocal) trade regime was signed in April 1993. Further improvements in economic relations with Europe are promised through the adoption of the EU 'Europe Agreements' for Slovenia, which will establish a bilateral association between Slovenia and the EU. The Europe Agreement establishes the basis for Slovenia's eventual membership of the EU and provides for the preferential treatment of trade in agricultural products, and liberalizes trade in many others sectors. It also covers the approximation of legislation, economic co-operation, financial, political and cultural co-operation. The Europe Agreement was 'initialled' in June 1995, but its final signature is being held up by a long-standing dispute over property rights between Italy and Slovenia concerning Italian claims in the Istrian Peninsula. However, it seems only a matter of time before Slovenia is able to take part in serious pre-accession negotiations with the EU.

Business and finance

In 1992 the banking sector which Slovenia inherited from the former Yugoslavia was in a state of crisis, with a large proportion, perhaps as much as 40 per cent, of non-performing loans in its portfolio. The main exposure was to the large loss making enterprises under social ownership. Bank rehabilitation has therefore been forced to await the restructuring and privatization of these companies. Nevertheless, the necessary legal framework for rehabilitation of the banking system was introduced in 1993, and a Bank Rehabilitation Agency has been established to supervise the process. Eventually it is expected that up to six main commercial banks will emerge as the principal financial institutions covering about four-fifths of the banking assets. By mid-1995 the banking system had become modernized and capable of carrying out most regular commercial transactions required by a developing market economy. Banks' costs began to fall and interest rate spreads correspondingly fell from some 18 per cent in 1993 to a more normal 7 per cent in 1995.

Business, the labour market and trade unions

Until the beginning of the move towards a market economy, employees in social sector enterprises were virtually guaranteed a secure job for their whole career. As a result, there was a queue for jobs, and youth unemployment, though frequently unregistered, was high. With the onset of the recession and labour force lay-offs, formal unemployment has risen dramatically from a near zero base to a peak of 14.5 per cent of the labour force in 1994. Labour turnover has also risen by 50 per cent between 1989 and 1993. Unemployment compensation is rather generous with a maximum entitlement of two years' unemployment pay, although a period of nine months previous employment is required to entitle an unemployed person to benefits. As the number of unemployed due to lay-offs has increased so the proportion of the unemployed covered by unemployment benefits has risen from 20 per cent in 1990 to 41 per cent in 1992. The unemployed lose benefit if they refuse a job offer, but this only refers to full-time regular jobs. Unemployed people can legally continue to receive unemployment benefit if they take an irregular part-time job. This feature of the unemployment benefit system has led to the emergence of the practice of 'double-dipping' in which people draw both unemployment benefit and work in low-paid, insecure jobs, and employers avoid paying social security contributions and wage taxes. Recent changes in legislation have attempted to tighten up on these practices.

The Slovenian labour force is well qualified and highly skilled. Two-fifths of the employees have some form of higher educational qualification, and a third are classified as highly skilled workers. The main problems of the Slovenian labour market relate to persistent upward pressure on wages by employees in socially-owned firms. Between 1993 and 1994 net wages increased by 6.8 per cent. Although the trade union movement has become somewhat fragmented since the demise of the communist regime there are still a few relatively large unions. These include the Association of Free Trade Unions of Slovenia (ZSSS) which has 420,000 members, and the Confederation of New Trade Unions – Independence (KNSS) with 135,000 members. Since the Slovenian labour force is 665,000 strong, these two unions between them represent the majority of workers. In addition there are a large number of smaller unions organized on a regional or trade basis. An Agreement on Wage Policy has helped to steady the rise in gross wages, but the fall in social security contributions has been offset by the net wage increase within the same gross wage framework. However, this should be put in perspective in that the biggest pressure on business costs comes from the extremely high level of real interest rates.

Conclusion

From the perspective of the other transition economies, Croatia and Slovenia are to be envied for their economic progress, which has been achieved in spite of enormous difficulties. They have by some way the highest per capita incomes in all of Central and Eastern Europe and stand poised to enter a period of sustained growth as the region recovers from the conflict.

Because of its size, location and unique geography, Slovenia stands to be the most successful of all the transition economies – indeed, as the more hopeful Slovenes would say, the 'Switzerland of southern Europe'. It has a small, well-educated population and it is ideally located near to Italy and Austria, with their large markets being relatively open for Slovenian goods. It also looks likely to take advantage of the recovery in its near neighbour, Croatia, with which it has always had historically good relations and trading ties. Slovenia's unique combination of mountains, valleys and a small part of the Adriatic coastline, make it an ideal tourist destination. Moreover, its transition to the market economy has proceeded effectively, with few of the serious economic dislocations evident elsewhere in Eastern Europe, or in its former Yugoslav sister Republics. It was also insulated from the inter-ethnic conflict raging just to the south, largely because it had a more or less ethnically homogeneous population prior to the dissolution of former Yugoslavia.

But Croatia too has successfully managed the 'double transition' from communism and from former Yugoslavia. It has laid the foundations for a market-based economic system which has already proved durable in facing up to the extreme privations and dislocation forced upon it as a result of the conflict and the disentanglement from the former Yugoslav economic system. The signs are that it too is set for growth and stability and that it will continue to build a market economy capable of becoming one of the strongest in the region. In a number of areas, most notably in the tourism field, it has world-class competitive advantage.

It is clear that the inheritance from former Yugoslavia has been an important influence on the development of both the Slovenian and Croatian business cultures. In the first instance, it is very often understated quite how different Yugoslavia was from the other Eastern European communist economies. In truth, the Yugoslav economic system was a radically different creature from the Soviet-style planned economies, including the reformed planned economies such as Hungary. The political system allowed sufficient scope for international business and employment abroad, while the worker self-management system provided for a high degree of enterprise autonomy and worker involvement. This package proved capable of building up an economic base with a much greater capacity for economic efficiency than in any of its communist neighbours. The conflict may have destroyed some of this inheritance, especially in Croatia, but the quality of infrastructure, capital equipment and technical training, and understanding of the market economy and entrepreneurialism remains significantly above that of any of the other transition economies.

Second, the emerging business culture has been influenced by the extensive social, family and community networks – *veza* – which were widely used by the population to circumvent the more cumbersome bureaucratic procedures and official obstacles prevailing within Yugoslav society. In fact, such networks became almost a defining feature of the former system. As in the Emilia-Romagna region of Italy – the famous 'Third Italy'[7] – in Croatia and Slovenia there is a strong tradition of trust between members of extended families and communities. This has the potential to facilitate economic development by generating a climate of trust and confidence within which information sharing and business transactions can take place. Moreover, another parallel with Emilia-Romagna is that this process is underpinned by strong regional and local governments and other business support organizations in both Croatia and Slovenia, one more legacy of the extensive decentralization which characterized former Yugoslavia. Strong regional and local governments can take a proactive part in economic development within the community, supporting local and regional initiatives through the provision of common services, finance, training, education and premises, as well as a sympathetic business environment. Other business organizations, such as the Chambers of Economy, also have a role to play in business development, particularly with regard to connecting the new entrepreneurial sectors to the large enterprise sector. In Croatia, for example, the Chamber of Economy is a very well resourced organization and active in economic development initiatives at both national and regional levels. A whole host of entrepreneurial societies have also arisen in Croatia and Slovenia which lobby hard for their members and provide a range of business services.

Third, there is the continuing influence upon current management practice of the participatory philosophy of worker self-management. This can be seen in the sizeable growth and deliberate promotion of worker share-ownership and worker-owned companies in both countries. Indeed, Slovenia is well on the way to becoming an economy dominated by worker-owned enterprises. Moreover, there is also the paternal and less aggressive managerial style of most Slovenian and Croatian managers, in comparison with their European counterparts, which was fairly typical of management under the old system. The benefits to be gained from a participative and co-operative workplace are daily becoming more and more self-evident. The stunning success of the

[7] The Emilia-Romagna region is one of the most economically successful regions in Western Europe on account of the numerous clusters of dynamic small businesses. The main elements in the success of the region remain under debate, and may also be culture specific. However, it is universally acknowledged that **two** of the key elements in the regions success story are the high level of trust within the community and the dense network of social and family connections (see, for example, Goodman *et al.*, 1989).

Japanese industrial system is perhaps the most obvious example of a system widely utilizing such principles, but there are many other regional and individual enterprise examples which illustrate that such principles can pay big dividends.

At the same time, the business cultures in Croatia and Slovenia have also been infused with a renewed entrepreneurial vigour as a result of the rapid growth in small businesses and entrepreneurial activities in both countries since 1991. The relatively liberal business climate in former Yugoslavia allowed many official entrepreneurial activities room to become established and, as the remaining legal restraints are gradually being dismantled, many of these early starters have now blossomed. A further major fillip to the rapid growth in entrepreneurial activities has come from the existing and massive unofficial sector of small artisans, landlords, repair services and so forth, especially on the Adriatic coast. These activities served to generate capital and provide experience. Finally, there has been a well-publicized boost to the Croatian business sector, in terms of new capital and ideas, thanks to the vast Croatian diaspora returning home. The end result of the above processes has been to create a business culture in both countries which is a somewhat unique blend of co-operation and participation, yet westernized and forward-looking.

In short, a business culture is emerging in the region which appears to reflect elements of the past but which contains many of the necessary pre-requisites for sustained growth in the future. The expectation is, therefore, that economic success for both Croatia and Slovenia is very much guaranteed.

Acknowledgements

Our thanks to Sanja Malekovic and Mario Polic for their comments on this chapter.

References and suggestions for further reading

Bartlett, W. (1996) From reform to crisis: the economic impact of war, secession and sanctions in former Yugoslavia, in I. Jeffries (ed.) *Economic and political transformation in the Balkans*, Pinter, London.

Bartlett, W. and Prasnikar, J. (1995) Small firms and economic transformation in Slovenia. *Communist Economics and Economic Transformation*, Vol. 7, No. 1.

Bicanic, I. and Skreb, M. (1994) The Yugoslav economy from Amalgamation to Disintegration: failed efforts at moulding a new economic space, in D. Good (ed.), *Economic Transformation in Central and Eastern Europe: lessons and legacies from the past*. Routledge, London.

EIU Country Reports (various issues) Economist Intelligence Unit, London.

Goodman, E., Bamford, J. and Saynor, P. (eds) (1989) *Small Firms and Industrial Districts in Italy.* Routledge, London.

Glisman, H., Capron, H. and Stanovik, P. (1995) Regional challenges of a small open economy: the case of Slovenia, in M. Tykkylainen (ed.) (1995) *Local and regional development during the 1990s transition in Eastern Europe.* Avebury Press.

Gros, D. and Steinherr, A. (1995) *Winds of Change: Economic transition in Central and Eastern Europe.* Longman, London.

Horvat, B. (1976) *The Yugoslav economic system: the first labour-managed economy in the making.* M. E. Sharpe, New York.

Institute for International Relations (1995) *Croatian International Relations Review,* Issue 1.

Karaman-Aksentijevic, N. and Kopal, M. (1995) Regional aspects of Croatian industry restructuring. XI Workshop on Industrial Restructuring and its impact on Regional Development, Rovinj, Croatia, 15–16 September 1995.

Lydall, H. (1984) *Yugoslav Socialism: Theory and practice.* Clarendon Press, Oxford.

Randlesome, C. (1994) *The Business Culture in Germany.* Butterworth-Heinemann, Oxford.

Richardson, M.L. (1993) The assesment of hazards and risks to the environment caused by war damage to industrial installations in Croatia. Proceedings of an International Conference on 'Effects of War on the Environment', Zagreb, 15–17 April, 1993.

Schonfelder, B. (1993) Croatia Between Reform and Post-Communist Populism. *Communist Economies and Economic Transformation,* Vol. 5, No. 3.

Schonfelder, B. (1995) The doubtful blessings of capital imports. Reflections on the fragility of Croatian stabilisation. Freiberg Working Paper 95/23, Technical University Bergakademie Freiberg, Germany.

Woodward, S. (1995) *Socialist Unemployment: the political economy of Yugoslavia from 1950–1990.* Princeton University Press, Princeton, New Jersey.

5 The business culture in Russia

Marta Bruno

Introduction

In a speech delivered in 1939 Sir Winston Churchill declared:

> 'I cannot forecast to you the action of Russia. It is a riddle wrapped
> in a mystery inside an enigma, but perhaps there is a key. That key
> is Russian national interest.'
>
> (Churchill, 1939)

To a certain extent these famous words describe the complexities of the
business culture in present-day Russia. Before the demise of the Soviet
Union and the collapse of the regimes of Eastern Europe, western
knowledge of communist economies was limited to a theoretical analysis
of the command systems. Direct access to operations in Russia was
restricted to a handful of western companies and even then their
operations were severely restricted and regimented by the Russian
government. Furthermore most data and information on Soviet economic
trends and performance was completely unreliable since it was constructed in such a way as to be either the showcase for Soviet
achievements or else to fulfil the expectations (whether they had been
met or not) of the leadership and planners.

Since the Gorbachev reforms in the mid-1980s, western observers as
well as the great majority of Russians have been trying to unravel the
changes brought about by the different waves of political and economic
reforms. The social and cultural configuration of Russia has changed
dramatically in the last few years as Russians responded in various ways
to new concepts and practices such as the free market and democracy.
Given the geographical extension, ethnic, linguistic and religious diversity and social, economic and gender stratification of the Russian
Federation, economic development and new practices are highly uneven.
While an entrepreneurial business culture is becoming established in
places like Moscow and St Petersburg, in other places away from large
urban centres little has changed since the period of stagnation under

Brezhnev. Economic activities are regulated according to an informal but rigid feudal structure controlled by local bureaucratic-administrative elites composed of higher political and economic managers and directors, themselves remnants of the Soviet past. Thus private enterprise and conditions for business vary enormously according to the sector of the economy, the geographical area and the social and political background of the individuals involved. The central state and institutions are often very weak and this has left a vacuum to be filled with corruption, organized crime and what is generally known as 'cowboy capitalism'.

One result is that the new Russian entrepreneurs, for whom quick earnings are a prerequisite for material survival are reluctant to invest in long-term projects in production or agriculture where returns are not immediate. This trend is also the rule within the foreign business community, which is very interested in the vast natural resources of the Russian Federation but wary of the political situation and hindered by the inefficiencies of the infrastructure. The process of privatization and restructuring of state assets and enterprises has created a clear-cut stratification in Russian society characterized by severe labour market problems and declining living standards for the majority of the population. This trend has brought about a process of polarization of society: on the one hand there is a small (in relative numbers) economic elite controlling financial, natural and industrial resources, the so-called 'new Russians'; on the other there is the mass of Russian 'common' people who are often the victims of the harsh socio-economic conditions but are also actively devising survival strategies, thus creating a new and substantial proto-entrepreneurial stratum. The economic disappearance of the traditional Soviet middle class, made up by the technical and professional intelligentsia, has left an army of disgruntled, well-educated people who, if not re-absorbed in the labour market, could prove politically destabilizing.

The issues currently germane to a stable development of the economy and business environment are the process of privatization of state assets, the conversion of the military-industrial complex, the management of natural resources and viable solutions to labour market imbalances. These factors are inevitably linked to the development of a democratic political system sustained by credible and well-respected legal and financial institutions and an articulated and widespread civil society. As shall be analysed in the course of this chapter, many of these features are virtually absent or very fragile in Russian economic and political cultures and environments.

Business and government

The direction of political reform and government policies have been the key factors in the development of business practice in Russia. In the space of a few years the Russian Federation has undergone a transition from a centrally-planned economy where the government exercised dictatorial control over all aspects of political, social and economic life to an apparently democratic system where central institutions are quite weak and political authority uncertain. It is important to analyse briefly some key moments and issues of the process of political reform to see when and how concepts such as 'free market', 'private property' and 'private enterprise' were introduced in Soviet society and how the Soviet public reacted to them.

The Gorbachev years: implementing reform

The main characteristics of the Gorbachev era were determined by attempts at economic and political reform (*radikalnaya reforma*) within the framework of state socialism. The situation of economic crisis required immediate intervention and Gorbachev initially believed that industrial and agricultural production could be boosted by motivating managers and workers to increase productivity by reducing central control and giving enterprises a higher degree of autonomy. *Glasnost* was an attempt to give citizens more information and control over their lives and therefore involve them in the economic destiny of the country. The reform was implemented from above with many sections of the population and interest groups in Soviet society resisting it.

Since the late 1920s and the abandonment of the New Economic Policy (in which some forms of small private enterprises were allowed to operate) the predominant cultural and ideological model to which lip-service had to be paid by everyone, condemned private property, private enterprise and any form of economic activity associated with the free market. The Stalin purges of the 1930s wiped out almost an entire generation of merchants, artisans and entrepreneurs and as a result Russia, unlike other Eastern European countries, has only limited historical memories of an entrepreneurial class which it could use to help reconstruct a business identity and culture. The only experience that Soviet citizens had of anything comparable to market activities was connected with the black market and the second economy. Because of the severe shortages in supplies and services of the Brezhnev years, unofficial economic activities and practices were widespread but the people who engaged in them, even though tolerated, were considered criminals. The gradual introduction of the market and related economic activities has been extremely controversial and to this day 'business' is considered extremely negative by a sizeable section of the Russian population. After some initial enthusiasm and support for the Gorbachev reforms, as the economic crisis set in more heavily, popular attitudes to the 'market' and 'business' underwent severe shifts in different directions.

The Gorbachev period can be roughly divided in four main phases:

- The first period (1985) of the Gorbachev leadership was characterized by the introduction of the reformist notion of *perestroika*. Nevertheless no clear political programme was outlined and few innovative policies implemented.
- In phase two (1986–1987) the debate around the causes of the economic crisis and the nature of restructuring (*perestroika*) was accompanied by the first wave of legislation. The focus was on individuals' responsibility in the management of the economy. Some forms of small-scale private activity were allowed beside full-time jobs; small co-operatives could operate mainly in the service sector and in general, workers were encouraged to participate in enterprise decision-making. Enterprise directors were also supposed to have increased autonomy from the planning bodies and the option to implement organizational and management changes to obtain improved accountability (*khozraschet*). Gorbachev used Lenin's New Economic Policy as a source of inspiration for a mixed economy that would combine a small private sector and an efficient and decentralized state sector to achieve an alternative 'third way'. The 'human factor' was central for overcoming the situation of economic stagnation (*zastoi*) of the Brezhnev era.
- In the following two years (1988–1989) reformist policies were meant to start bearing fruit. This was not the case. As living conditions and the availability of goods and supplies worsened, Gorbachev started to lose popular support. Elite interest groups, afraid of losing their privileges, supported conservative political resistance to Gorbachev, while people who were eager for change supported the nascent democratic movement which pushed for a more radical reform. Gorbachev, in an attempt to accommodate both radicals and conservatives, went two steps forwards and three backwards along the path of reform. It started to become apparent that *perestroika* was more of a declaration of intent implemented by trial and error than a clear-cut reformist policy. In the meantime, the black economy was allowed to run riot, partly to overcome the severe shortages endemic to the Soviet Union as to other Eastern European Communist economies. Economic stratification started to make itself felt and provoked many popular reactions against people operating within the black and grey markets, who were considered speculators and profiteers. While an increased number of people started engaging in private economic activities, especially through the so-called co-operatives, (*kooperativi*), there was a widespread sense that it was something highly immoral.
- In the last two years of *perestroika* (1990–1991) the gap between the pace of cultural and economic reform widened greatly. While money incomes grew, consumption did not follow pace, partly because by 1990 output had started to decline. As the presence of foreigners and of

western consumer goods became a more familiar state of affairs, Soviet citizens were increasingly able to draw comparisons on standards of living. At the same time, they were no longer afraid of political repression as they had been in the past. The polarization of society between conservatives wanting to maintain the *status quo* and radicals promising economic paradise if allowed to have a free-hand at economic reform, increased. When political strife broke out with the August 1991 coup, radicals won the day and Gorbachev was pushed aside.

The Yeltsin years: trials of transition

Under Yeltsin's leadership an entirely new era started for the Russian Federation, that of **transition** as opposed to **reform**. Under Gorbachev, the issue at stake was that of reforming a very complex economic system, clearly undergoing a severe crisis, but still with its own specific historical and functional features. This system was officially rejected under Yeltsin, who led the country through the process of the abandonment of state socialism and towards the establishment of a democratic, capitalist system. The path towards these ideals, a market economy and a developed democracy, nevertheless remains extremely arduous. On the one hand the legacies of the Soviet system on the Russian economy are immense; on the other no established and efficient alternative is yet in place.

The most important political decision that the government took under the Yeltsin leadership was that of adopting a shock therapy approach to transition rather than favouring a slower option that did not entail a radical break with the past. While much computer power has been used by academics and many political careers have thrived on transition theories and debates, the most relevant issue in the context of this chapter is to outline common popular perceptions of transition. In the general understanding, shock therapy entails liberalization of prices, rapid privatization of most state enterprises and assets and the establishment of market mechanisms. The benefits of this approach should be the shorter time needed to carry out the transition process and to achieve a successful and functioning market economy. The negative sides are extreme economic dislocation and higher social costs.

The Russian Federation, the former Soviet Union and the autonomous republics

The major historical event at the start of the phase of transition was the official demise of the Soviet Union. While several republics had already declared independence under Gorbachev, as from 25 December 1991, the end of the USSR became official. Relations between the newly independent states are proving difficult because of the combination of economic inter-dependency and political and national differences. The Russian Federation still holds sway in the area and is very involved in the politics and economics of its former sister republics, generally known, in somewhat colonial tones, as the 'near abroad'.

The Soviet command economy left a legacy of severe uneven regional development, since it had operated by concentrating production in massive plants (sometimes comprising whole cities) supplying specific goods to the rest of the country. Factories were exceedingly specialized, albeit not very technologically advanced in civilian industry, producing parts for machinery or consumer goods that might be assembled in a different republic. Industrial production was concentrated in the north and western parts of the union, while the east and south were generally underdeveloped. This imbalance between different regions and different republics has resulted in a severe economic dependency on the Russian Federation and a protracted colonial link.

The Russian Federation further comprises within its territory eighty-nine republics, regions and federal territories, several of which with a non-Russian titular nationality. Nationalism and disputes over the control of local natural resources weigh heavily on the relationships between the central Moscow government and the periphery, as in the case of the sadly notorious conflict in Chechnya. The new constitution, approved under Yeltsin with a bare majority in December 1993, failed to resolve clearly the issue of autonomy of the regions from the federal government. The Moscow government maintains a great deal of economic clout over the republics as was evident from the case of Tatarstan. To curb the Republic's independentist policies and persuade Tatar leadership to sign a treaty 'On the Delineation of Spheres of Authority and the Mutual Delegation of Powers' the Russian government threatened to close the oil pipeline, thereby hitting one of the Republic's main economic assets. The conflict was resolved very quickly in the federal government's favour, with the Tatar leadership scaling down their original requests. The multi-ethnic nature of the Russian Federation and the differences in languages, religions and cultures are elements that could potentially play a very significant role in the political sphere and, when combined with the issue of economic control over resources, could lead to open conflict between the federal government and the republics.

The Yeltsin leadership and the organization of the federal government

Even though economic issues are considered to be at the forefront of the period of transition, the development of democratic representation and of government are also very important. The model of government implemented by Yeltsin was that of a presidential democracy. A significant moment was represented by the events of October 1993, when the conservative old communist guard in parliament led by the speaker Rutskoi and MP Khasbulatov, tried to depose Yeltsin and bring about a change in the government's political direction by resisting presidential decrees and occupying the White House. Yeltsin abandoned his role of hero of democracy and decided to use military power to repress the uprising.

When Yeltsin had first come to power in 1991, he did so with the public image of a defender of democracy. During the years of *perestroika*, Yeltsin was a popular favourite as the head of the Russian Republic and he led the radical opposition to Gorbachev. He was considered the champion of liberal, democratic reform, freedom and economic development. While Gorbachev was disliked by Russians and loved by the west, Yeltsin was exactly the reverse, suspected by the west as an unreliable demagogue but able to rally political support at home like no other. His initial political moves upon coming to power in 1991 consisted of implementing radical measures in economic reform by supporting the shock therapy approach involving rapid privatization and liberalization of prices. His style of government appeared to be fairly democratic and tolerant of oppositional politics. As parliament started to increase its opposition to Yeltsin's economic measures, the confrontation began to become much harsher. A political impasse was reached around issues regarding the approval of a new constitution. After eighteen months of political struggle ending with the October 1993 White House events, Yeltsin became less tolerant of opposition.

The violence of the struggle brought about a significant shift in Yeltsin's style of government. He prioritized the drafting of a new constitution which would effectively invest him, as president of the federation, with greater powers while subtracting them from parliament. He decided to push the new Constitution through, by means of a referendum at the same time as the parliamentary elections in December 1993, held to replace the rebel parliament. To make absolutely certain that the constitution would be voted in, Yeltsin resorted to strong political pressures on all the parties running for the elections. Candidates were threatened with being banned from the electoral campaign should they criticise the adoption of the constitution. Yeltsin also drastically lowered the level of support needed officially for the adoption of the constitution from the majority of the registered electorate to 50 per cent of those who voted. The draft of the constitution was not made widely available and very little time was left for discussion. The constitution was adopted, although it was effectively supported by only the 30.7 per cent of the total electorate and by 54.8 per cent of those who voted.

While Yeltsin reinforced the authoritarian style of his leadership, the December 1993 election results also made him realize that his popularity was decreasing. While he officially did not give his support to any of the political groupings running in the elections, it was clear that Russia's Choice, the party headed by Deputy Prime Minister Yegor Gaidar was the one he favoured. Despite having Yeltsin's support and therefore more political arenas, television time and finances to conduct the electoral campaign, Russia's Choice failed to secure the majority of seats obtained through proportional representation. By adding the seats won through the single constituency part of the elections it obtained a close majority of 15.6 per cent over the nationalist LDPR party, which obtained 14.2 per cent.

The unexpected victory of the nationalist leader Vladimir Zhirinovski, whose charisma was undoubtedly decisive in his LDPR Party's victory, was an indicator for Yeltsin that his popularity had been severely undermined. The new parliament was much weaker than the previous one and on the whole was also more willing to co-operate with the president. Yeltsin considerably slowed down the pace of reform by supporting Prime Minister Viktor Chernomyrdin's more cautious approach and by getting rid of many of the more radical members of his government. The most significant departure was that of Finance Minister Boris Fedorov, who had been assisted in designing and implementing shock therapy by a team of foreign experts, headed by the American economist Jeffrey Sachs, already an advisor to the Chilean and Polish governments in their initial phases of transition. The dismissal of privatization supremo Anatoli Chubais in early 1996, effectively the last radical in the government, was a further indication of this slowdown.

In an attempt to reconcile government and parliament, Yeltsin proposed a co-operation agreement between the political parties represented in parliament, the government and other representatives of groups and organizations with significant influence in the economic, labour and social spheres. This agreement between civil, economic and political elites was called the Civic Accord and was signed in April 1994. The most significant groups that refused to join were Yavlinski's reformist Yabloko group and Zyuganov's Communist Party. The participants recognized the damage that lack of political stability due to oppositional politics was bringing to the country and decided to try a more conciliatory path to ease stabilization.

Despite these favourable conditions for political stability, Yeltsin seems to be increasing the undemocratic practices of his leadership. He has a large group of staff directly nominated by him who cover positions of considerable responsibility in the central and regional administrations. Through this practice, posts such as mayors and governors are becoming non-elective. Furthermore, Yeltsin has increased the number of government bodies and organizations that have to answer directly to him and are not required to account to parliament. The most significant example is that of the Ministry of Security which was disbanded and replaced by the Federal Counterintelligence Service, accountable only to the president. The way in which military intervention in the break-away Chechen Republic was decided by Yeltsin and a restricted number of his collaborators, without informing parliament, or several members of government, is indicative of the new trend. While most political parties and possibly the majority of the public were opposed to the war, no effective organized political pressure was exercised by parliament on the government.

With Yeltsin busy trying to preserve his political clout, the real authority of state institutions and laws as regulators and guarantors of democracy are substantially decreasing. In a country where the culture and experience of democracy is new, the control of power is mainly in the hands of the old political and economic elites. In many local elections in 1994, old regime power-brokers were voted in again, while in others they had never been voted out. This reality is very meaningful for business practices since it leads to a non-uniform acceptance and enforcement of laws, institutions and regulations: in other words, to an unstable business environment. Furthermore, the weakness of the central state, combined with the increasingly non-democratic practices of the government, raises serious threats to political, and therefore to economic, stability.

The organization of parliament and political parties

As mentioned in the previous section, parliament was reorganized by Yeltsin after the October 1993 events. The new legislature is a bicameral federal assembly constituted by the 178-seat upper house, the Federation Council and the 450-seat lower house, the State Duma. Both assemblies are elective. For the Federation Council, the candidate with more votes than others wins. The State Duma has a double election. Half of the seats are elected on a single-member constituency basis, while the other half are assigned on a proportional basis from federal party lists. Political parties wanting to run in the elections have to collect a total of 100,000 signatures with a minimum number of at least 15,000 in seven different regions or republics. This is to ensure that parties have national, rather than local, support and thus contain the power of the local elites. The minimum turnout required for the elections to be valid was lowered from 50 per cent to 25 per cent of the eligible electorate. Parties have to exceed a 5 per cent barrier in the proportional part of the election, in order to win seats in parliament. This measure was an attempt to homogenize Russian political life and make smaller political groupings unite in larger ones. The political parties which clear the 5 per cent barrier for the proportional election to the State Duma thus become the main players in Russian political life.

The main current political parties are:

- *Russia's Choice (Vybor Rossii)*, headed by then Deputy Prime Minister Yegor Gaidar, was unofficially supported by Yeltsin. Its slogan was 'Freedom, property, law' and its programme was devoted to radical economic reform, democratization and integration in the world community while retaining a strong social conscience. It identified itself with the reforms brought forward by the government and had a strong westernizing style. It received significant financial support from many sources and was given a lot of media attention. It was by far the most prominent party and the fact that it failed to do as well as was generally expected was an unexpected change of direction in public opinion. In the December 1993 elections to the State Duma it came out first winning a total of eighty-seven seats. In 1995 nevertheless it only won nine seats as the government turned away from more radical economic reform to more moderate positions and political actors.

- *Our Home is Russia (Nash Dom Rossiya)*, headed by moderate Prime Minister Viktor Chernomyrdin, who succeeded Yegor Gaidar to the post, did not run in the 1993 elections, but represented the new middle-way approach taken by the government, following the results of the 1993 elections. Nevertheless it failed to do well in the 1995 elections, securing only fifty-four seats, possibly as a result of people's increasing disillusionment with the government's ability to guide the country towards a better economic situation.

- *The Liberal Democratic Party of Russia (LDPR)*, headed by Vladimir Zhirinovski, obtained the second best result at the 1993 elections, with a total of sixty-four seats. In the December 1995 elections, the LDPR lost a few seats, securing a total of fifty-one, possibly losing some protest votes to the Communist Party. Zhirinovski's charisma was certainly fundamental in obtaining so many votes but according to many analysts the vote for this right-wing nationalist party should be considered more as a protest vote than a proper electoral choice. The LDPR's political success had a significant impact on Russian politics. Government politicians were forced to realize that unbridled privatization and cuts in social welfare and employment could provoke a backlash on reform. The other message it brought to the forefront was that patriotism and Russian nationalism were growing in popularity.

- *The Communist Party of the Russian Federation (CPRF)*, headed by Gennadii Zyuganov, came out third in 1993 with forty-two seats, but then did exceptionally well to take first place in the December 1995 elections and absorbed many of the votes of the so-called 'red-brown' areas that previously went to the LDPR. After the collapse of communism the party had converted itself into a supporter of a parliamentary, democratic system and sought to present itself more as a social democratic party. Nevertheless, the CPRF numbered amongst its members people like Anatolii Luk'yanov, accused of taking part in the August 1991 coup and many others who had opposed Gorbachev and *perestroika*. The party's programme advocates the abandonment of shock therapy and the return to certain aspects of the command economy, especially in terms of social protection and work. The CPRF was also extremely hostile to the west and its involvement in Russia and held strong nationalist views.

- *The Agrarian Party of Russia (APR)*, lead by Mikhail Lapshin obtained thirty-seven in 1993. The party, very close to the CPRF, focused mainly on agricultural issues. It was against the sale and resale of collective and state farms and in favour of economic measures such as fixed prices and state subsidies.

The communists, agrarians and close allies obtained a staggering 189 seats in the 1995 elections. While at the time of writing this has not yet resulted in any major shifts in the direction of political and economic reforms, the balance of power has certainly shifted and it is bound to have an impact in the future.

- *The Yavlinsky-Boldyrev-Lukin Bloc (Yabloko)*, led by Grigorii Yavlinsky, obtained twenty-seven seats in 1993 and in December 1995 gained forty-six seats. In 1993 they ran on a democratic-reformist platform but refused, after prolonged discussions, to join forces with Russia's Choice, mainly because of differences on the constitution, excessive pro-western policies and the failure to dismantle state monopolies on the part of the government. Despite Grigorii Yavlinsky's great personal popularity, the party has failed to distinguish itself as clearly as it would have liked amongst the other liberal and reformist groupings.
- *Women of Russia (Zhenshchiny Rossii)*, headed by Alvetina Fedulova, liked to see itself more as a movement than as a proper political party. Many of its activists, all women, were former members of the Women's Union, the Soviet organization which dealt with women's welfare issues. They distanced themselves from feminist positions and were not particularly interested in women's rights. They asked for more gradual reforms, more attention to social welfare issues and education. They lamented the fact that so few women were in Russian politics, since women had a different and possibly better style of management of political problems. They appealed to both men and women with a social conscience to vote for them. They were not taken terribly seriously during the 1993 electoral campaign, becoming the object of many jokes, but their critics were obliged to backtrack when Women of Russia obtained twenty-three seats. It was the same as the very reputable Yabloko party had obtained and it outdid many of the 'serious' parties who failed to make the 5 per cent barrier in the proportional part of the election. In December 1995, however, they failed to make the 5 per cent barrier.
- *The Party of Russian Unity and Accord (PRES)*, headed by Deputy Prime Minister Serghei Shakrai, obtained twenty-one seats in 1993 and had the unofficial support of Prime Minister Viktor Chernomyrdin. Its slogan was 'house, family, Motherland, tradition and continuity' and it

was in favour of market reform with continued subsidies to state industries and a certain degree of protectionism. PRES seemed to have a rather contradictory view of the role of the state since it supported a strong and active centralized state while also being in favour of increased regional autonomy and self-government.

- *The Democratic Party of Russia (DPR)*, headed by Nikolai Travkin, was the main force in the centrist bloc, with 3.3 per cent of the votes cast in 1993. They came in last clearing the 5 per cent barrier in the proportional part of the elections, obtaining 5.52 per cent of the votes. Together with other political groupings, amongst which were Arkadii Vol'sky's Union of Industrialists and Entrepreneurs and rebel vice-president Aleksander Rutskoi's People's Party of Free Russia, they formed an allegiance called the Civic Union for Stability, Justice and Progress. The DPR decided nevertheless to run independently. Their main political requests were the federal organization of the Russian Republic, the abandonment of the model of presidential democracy implemented by Yeltsin in favour of a stronger parliament and economic measures such as protectionism in foreign trade and restrictions on land sales.

The other parties which obtained under 1 per cent of the votes in 1993 but managed to win a few seats in parliament were the Civic Union, the radical Russian Movement for Democratic Reforms (RDDR) led by former St Petersburg mayor, Anatolii Sobchak, the interest group Dignity and Charity made up of the Council of Veterans of War and Labour, The Society of Invalids and the Chernobyl Society. Independents won 141 seats. The one group to retain a lot of political power, albeit having few seats in parliament, is Arkadii Volski's Civic Union. This group constitutes an enormously powerful lobby made up of the industrial complex's directors and managers. Their most prominent role has been to lead the resistance to the radical privatization programme designed by Gaidar. In December 1995, independents obtained seventy-seven seats and liberals, centrists and nationalists a remaining nineteen votes. The new party *Congress of Russian Communities*, headed by charismatic General Lebed, obtained five seats.

Business and economic reform

The evaluation of the performance of the Russian economy and its reaction to the economic reform programmes since 1991 is an issue that causes much disagreement among analysts. Part of the difficulty stems from the fact that there is a paucity of reliable statistical data, and it is therefore extremely difficult to construct a complete picture of what is a very complex and uncharted transitional phase in a country as large as

Russia. Goskomstat, the state central statistical agency, is doing much to improve its data collection methods, with the help of international agencies in some cases, but despite these efforts the data remain very rough and unreliable. The main barrier is represented by the fact that such a consistent amount of Russian economic activity remains unofficial and illegal. A Financial Times Survey (June 27, 1994: II) suggested that Russian GDP could be under-estimated by as much as 15 per cent. It is likely that unemployment is also under-estimated. Thus any statistical information regarding economic, financial and social trends should always be taken with a pinch of salt, as a rough indicator rather than at its face value.

In 1991 Yeltsin's government undertook the enormous task of dismantling the Soviet economy and replacing it with a capitalist, market one. As noted above, the overall policy perspective adopted was that of the shock therapy approach, which considered that rapid transition would best create the necessarily stringent financial environment within which the most efficient enterprises and industrial sectors could flourish at the expense of those enterprises and sectors considered unlikely to have a future in the new market economy. Shock therapy also received political support, being seen as the only way of ensuring that the chances of a return to the old command economy system were precluded.

The three main areas to tackle were considered to be: price liberalization, currency stabilization and the privatization of state enterprises. We start our analysis with price liberalization. Under the Soviet system, prices were centrally controlled by the government. In his time in office, Gorbachev allowed very limited price liberalization of some consumer goods, thus reinforcing the situation of deficit of those goods for which the price was fixed and the expansion of the black market economy. One of the Yeltsin government's main tasks was price liberalization, in order to allow free market mechanisms to establish themselves. Consumer prices had been rising at an annual rate of 8.1 per cent in 1990, of 168.8 per cent in 1991 and of 2510 per cent in 1992. Price liberalization was launched in 1992 and by 1994 the majority of goods and services were sold at free market prices except for some remaining price regulation of the energy and telecommunications sectors at a national level, increasing by about 20 per cent, and of food and utilities (rents, public transport) at a local level, increasing by an estimated 30 per cent. The body which used to regulate prices, the Price Committee, was abolished in January 1994 and its functions were transferred to both the Ministry of the Economy and to the relevant ministries which were granted increased control over their particular spheres of operations. January 1994 also saw the abolition of price controls of goods and services designated as monopolies, other than natural monopolies. Some degree of indirect price control is maintained through profitability limits in the industrial sphere.

The second area of reform was that of currency stabilization and the need for a balanced budget. Once price adjustments had been allowed to run their course, Russia faced enormous problems of currency stabilization. These were manifold. The non-convertibility of the rouble was one of the problems that spurred some of the original attempts to consolidate the value of the currency. While inflation was already a significant phenomenon before the official price liberalization, afterwards it reached worrying levels of hyper-inflation, thus completely eroding rouble working capital and personal savings. The hyper-inflationary spiral increased reliance upon hard-currency supplies on the internal market to such an extent that an estimated US$1.5 billion in cash was thought to be circulating on the Russian market as well as US$20 billion in bank accounts. It is possible that the dollar cash flow exceeds that of roubles. Furthermore, the Russian business environment has developed a significant 'cash preferred' business mentality, in which most transactions rely on immediate liquidity. It is estimated that about 40 per cent of the money circulating in Russia is cash.

While, initially, positive results were reached with the disappearance of two of the major problems of the late *perestroika* period, i.e. the rouble surplus and the shortage economy, soon enterprise managers started raising their prices in order to maintain their cash flows. Hyperinflation was also convenient in the short term since it decreased their outstanding debts. The government and the Central Bank of Russia adopted a lenient attitude, trying to appease the industrial and agricultural lobbies and continued the provision of subsidies by printing currency. Thus, the main obstacle faced by the government in its efforts to effectively curb inflation became the need to finance the budget deficit. In 1992 the budget deficit amounted to 4.7 per cent of the GDP, increasing in 1993 and in 1994 to 9.1 per cent (41 trillion roubles) before appearing to decline to around the 4 per cent mark in 1995. Since as much as 50 per cent of taxes remain uncollected, the government is effectively forced to refinance the deficit by printing money and, to a lesser extent, issuing bonds. This policy has found many critics who argue that the government is running a pyramid scheme with its own financial assets. A crucial moment was reached on 11 October 1994 when the continuing expansion of the money supply brought about a sharp fall of 21 per cent of the rouble against the dollar, the event becoming known as 'Black Tuesday'. 'Black Tuesday' was instrumental in bringing about a major government reshuffle, which affected the Ministers of Finance and of the Economy and the Chairman of the Central Bank. Moreover, the IMF became stricter with its loans, demanding tighter monetary measures and a decrease in the budget deficit. The figure for 1995 indicated above shows some success and matters appear to be coming under control.

Privatization

Since the Gorbachev reforms, the issue of whether and how the bulk of state assets and enterprises should be privatized constituted one of the major battle grounds of Russian politics. The first steps towards privatization were taken in the last three phases of *perestroika*. Gorbachev wanted to maintain state property ownership of productive assets but also needed to revitalize worker and management motivation in the productive process. His other intent was to absorb into the official economy some aspects of the unofficial one, which was in many ways more dynamic and successful. With the **Law on Co-operatives** of 1988, the formation of small enterprises with an average of twenty-five workers was allowed. Co-operatives operated mainly in the service and construction sectors and their assets were in some cases owned by the members and in others leased from the state. Managers (and occasionally workers) of larger enterprises were given the possibility with the **Law on State Enterprises** of 1987 and the **Decree on Leasing and Lease Relations** of 1989 to lease part or the totality of an enterprise and manage it with an increased degree of autonomy from the relevant branch ministry. With the **Law on Ownership** of 1990 it was possible for managers and workers of some enterprises to buy the leased assets; furthermore, smaller enterprises could drop the co-operative format and be privatized. New private firms started increasing in number in the commercial sector. At the same time some municipalities started privatizing residential housing and small plots of land.

Under the Yeltsin leadership, the drive to privatization gathered momentum under the State Committee for the Administration of State Property (*Goskomimuchestvo*) or GKI, at the head of which was appointed the economist Anatolii Chubais. There was a reversal of ownership for some of the enterprises leased under Gorbachev so that all medium and large establishments could be privatized following the same rules. In 1992 the main Government Programme of Privatization for the Russian Federation was approved and was to constitute the core of the privatization process; the first phase of the process was concluded by 1994, with around 11,200 large and medium enterprises having undergone voucher auctions.

Small enterprises – with a maximum of 200 employees and a capital value of under 10 million roubles at January 1992 prices – were privatized separately from medium and large ones and according to different rules. Rather than being privatized through voucher auctions, they were either sold unconditionally to worker collectives and individual investors or, for some enterprises with particular investment or employment requirements that needed to be met by the purchaser, through commercial tenders. In general, both conservative and radical political groupings agreed that small enterprises should be given a fast-track in the privatization process. Enterprises which fell between the categorization of small and medium (under 1000 employees and under 50 million roubles capital value at January 1992 prices) were given the option to choose whether they wanted to be privatized according to the rules for small, or for medium, enterprises. In general, small businesses were owned by the local authorities so privatization was left to them with some supervision by the GKI. Over 200,000 enterprises were earmarked and by the end of 1994 over 70 per cent had been privatized. There was some regional variation, with the regions of Nizhnii Novgorod, Kurgan, Riasan, Irkutsk and Khabarovsk and the Republic of Khakassiya having privatized well over 90 per cent of their small businesses. Only five Russian regions had privatized less than 20 per cent of their small businesses by the deadline (Russian Economic Trends 1994, pages 76–77).

The process of privatization of medium and large enterprises – from 1000 to 10,000 employees and a capital value between 50 and 150 million roubles at January 1992 prices – was much more problematic than the one for small establishments. Political debate ranged over a number of issues. It was clear that a number of enterprises in key sectors needed to remain under state control. Enterprises defined as strategic – especially if with over 10,000 employees and a capital value of over 150 million roubles at January 1992 prices – needed to obtain authorization for privatization from the government. Inevitably there was heated debate over what should be retained under government control and what was better off privatized. The main areas of dispute concerned the energy and the telecommunications sectors and some fringe enterprises of the military-industrial complex.

The other great political dispute was over the format of ownership and control for medium and large enterprises. The reformist camp advocated various models of outsider control whereby the shares of an enterprise would be accessible to both domestic and foreign investors. The conservatives argued for total or partial forms of insider control for both enterprise workers and managers. Ultimately, a compromise was reached whereby individual enterprises were allowed to vote for the preferred option.[1]

The next step of the privatization scheme was to introduce a system of tokens, known as vouchers, in order to transfer a chunk of state assets to the general public. In 1992 Russian citizens were issued each with a voucher of the nominal value of 10,000 roubles, which they could sell, entrust to an investment fund, use to buy shares or to bid in privatization auctions. Vouchers had to be used by 1 July 1994, by which date the voucher part of the privatization programme for medium and large

---

[1] For a detailed discussion of the various options see Bim, Jones and Weisskopf (1994) pp. 264–65.

enterprises was concluded. Several investment funds appeared and started acquiring vouchers, even though restrictions were imposed on the amount of vouchers they could hold and also on the shares of enterprises they could buy which could not exceed 10 per cent. Peter Rutland (1995, page 15) reports that the funds purchased about 25 per cent of the vouchers, with the largest, Prvni Voucher, holding 3.4 million of them at a cash value hovering around 10 US$ each voucher.

By April 1994 over 11,000 enterprises had been sold off in voucher auctions. Large numbers of enterprises took the opportunity to create significant worker-shareholdings, many of which gave worker-manager combinations a controlling interest in the enterprise. In fact, just over 70 per cent of the enterprises had chosen to go for the insider control option, taking advantage of the rule whereby over 51 per cent of enterprises' shares could be sold to their workers at the discounted rate of 1.7 times the book value of the assets. Foreign private and corporate investors were initially severely limited from participating in privatization but several restrictions were lifted in 1994 allowing them to purchase vouchers and also to take part in cash sales. By mid-1995 the commercial banking sector was also becoming increasingly involved in the privatization process, by offering to the cash-strapped Russian government financial support in return for substantial shareholdings in state enterprises being privatized. This development could lead on to German-style bank–industry co-operation in the longer term, though the early indications are that it is simply a short-run profit-making exercise by the banks and they will sell their shareholdings as and when the market picks up.

Business law

The state of business legislation in Russia remains rather chaotic. The problem is twofold. In the first instance Russian laws which are technically operative often clash with each other. There are many Soviet laws which have not been repealed and contradict more recent ones of the Russian Federation. Laws can be federal or local, they can be approved by the parliament or implemented by presidential decrees. This vast body of legislation suffers from inconsistencies, gaps and contradictions. Several laws which in theory should be enforced have never been implemented. In addition to all these problems, and partly because of them, abidance by laws and legality on the part of citizens is often hazy and rather flexible. The numerous loopholes in existing legislation ill define the boundaries of legality, encouraging individuals and enterprises to find ways around problems that would be deemed illegal in several other countries but have been messily spelled out in Russian laws. Even those who want to stay within the margins of legality may find it difficult to do so since by observing one law they may be breaking another one.

Business law suffers from all these structural problems. Given that 'business' is a post-Soviet concept, the laws regulating it have suffered in the last few years from many U-turns and uncertainties. Foreign investors who decided to set up a business venture in Russia under certain conditions may have had those rules completely reversed in the space of a few months. This characteristic makes the environment a high risk one and encourages informal business rules and codes.

Under *perestroika*, foreign firms were allowed to form partnerships with Soviet firms that went under the legal definition of joint ventures. While this term is still very much in use to describe firms with Russian and foreign participation, legally JVs no longer exist. Companies can adopt the following legal organizations:

- Individual/family private enterprise: a family company with limited liability.
- Mixed partnership: a mix of individuals and corporate members – individuals have unlimited liability, corporate members have limited liability.
- General partnership (not a legal entity): a full liability partnership with participators having full liability to the extent of their personal assets.
- Limited partnership/closed joint stock company. Participators have liability to the extent of their stock. The partnership is not available for separate obligations of participators.
- Open joint stock companies. Limited liability company (Morris-Cotterill 1994, page 122).

All enterprises need to be officially registered and recently registration for foreign companies has become very similar to the one for Russian ones. While previously foreign companies had to register centrally, now they can register with authorized ministries in their field of activity. Newly-registered firms have a period of thirty days to register for tax inspection and open a bank account with no less than 50 per cent of the authorized fund.

Business and the economy

The initial phase of privatization brought about the mass transfer of state enterprises into private hands, but it did little to solve the structural problems of productivity and solvency that continue to undermine the Russian economy. Even though a presidential decree on bankruptcy was introduced in late 1993, very few insolvent enterprises have been declared bankrupt to date. It was hoped that the second phase of privatization through cash auctions of shares and investment tenders would attract the necessary capital, both from home and abroad, to recapitalize Russian industry. Unfortunately, industry is finding very few investors. In Russia, there is a dearth of potential buyers with the necessary capital to invest. The majority of Russian citizens are struggling to survive so cannot be expected to provide excess capital through savings that can be re-invested. Domestic banks and the wider financial sector, as will be analysed in the forthcoming section, are still in a very embryonic phase and are finding it difficult to deal with the inherited burden of communism.

Foreign investors, for a number of reasons that range from threats of political instability to difficult and dangerous working conditions, tend to prefer investing in activities with quick returns and which can be easily abandoned, such as services, retail and trade. The excess capital produced in Russia from the new 'mercantile' activities, both legally and illegally, is usually invested abroad or kept in foreign bank accounts. The Russian government has expressed concern for this massive capital flight but has, as yet, found no effective measures to prevent it. One of the hopes is that the excess capital from small enterprises (the so-called 'kiosk economy') might at least be re-invested into the official small business sector. The international financial community has been unable to come up with significant financial assistance, in spite of repeated promises to the contrary if reform were only pursued more vigorously and comprehensively.

The absence of investment capital for newly-privatized medium and large enterprises is but one of the several problems affecting industrial production. Between 1990 and September 1994 industrial production fell by 44 per cent, though in 1995 statistical estimates reported only a 6 per cent decline (EBRD, 1995). The current breakdown in production finds its roots in Soviet industrial organization. In the years of economic stagnation under the Brezhnev leadership, Soviet industrial enterprises were increasingly more concerned with employment than with production. Their primary function was to toe the official party line and help ensure full employment as part of the social contract between the central government and Russian citizens. In exchange for ensuring social and political acquiescence, managers obtained several benefits on the personal level. Production was almost a secondary matter and continued to be inflated on paper to meet the demands of the central planners, while it continued declining in reality. The normal network of supplies and links to the markets which characterize enterprises in western societies was absent from the Soviet enterprise, since most external relations were regimented by central ministries. Furthermore, Soviet industries had been built to mass-produce goods and were heavily mechanized albeit not technologically advanced. The only sector where production was highly sophisticated was the military-industrial complex but this was kept completely separated from civilian industry with very little transfer of technology.

The end of the centrally planned system of supplies, targets of production and sales put the average civilian industry in dire straits. Enterprise directors were often good party people rather than able managers. They had scant knowledge of what came before or after the moment of production in their specific enterprise since it had not been their responsibility. In general they did not have a network of contacts and sufficient know-how to replace the gap left by central planning. When they did, they were only equipped for producing goods of poor quality with obsolete machinery. They had to deal with workers who resisted change and who were used to being taken care of by their workplace. The directors themselves were used to being part of a bureaucratic-administrative elite with numerous privileges which they did not want to forego and were therefore determined to maintain the *status quo*. It thus becomes obvious that the crisis in industrial production in Russia is not wholly a function of the lack of investment or on the breakdown of supply-chains throughout Russia and the CIS, but also of the absence of a pool of managers and workers with the know-how and the entrepreneurial ability to build up the industrial fabric. As an extreme comment, it could be said that Russian industry does not need restructuring but it does need inventing.

The picture of Russian industry at the end of the first phase of the privatization process confirms that it is one of the most unreformed sectors of the new Russia. A phenomenon which has received a lot of attention has been that of the so-called *nomenklatura* privatization. The bureaucratic-administrative elite – i.e. managers and local politicians – have been able to manipulate individual privatization plans so as to ensure control of enterprises for themselves. These practices are very widespread and not necessarily illegal, given the chaotic state of the Russian legal system. An extreme criminal case was that of the director of the Gor'kii's autoworks who used 46 billion roubles in state credits to buy 30 per cent of his firm's shares through fifteen front companies (Rutland, 1995, page 16).

In terms of political pressure the industrial lobby, with the backing of industrial workers who do not want to lose their employment, have managed to elude the implementation of bankruptcy procedures for insolvent enterprises. Furthermore, the government has been pressurized into maintaining the system of state subsidies to unproductive industries. In some cases the withdrawal of cash injections from the state could have meant the collapse of whole sectors of the economy. Feeble attempts have been made to implement more constructive industrial policies. An attempt was made to promote the creation of Financial Industrial Groups (FPG), bringing together banks, suppliers and producers in core sectors of the economy. Around seventy FPGs are planned by the end of 1996.

Energy and fuels

These sectors are considered by far the most prosperous and promising for the Russian economy with electric power constituting 15.2 per cent and fuel 19.5 per cent of the total industrial production. Gas production fell from 643 million cubic metres in 1991 to 352 million cubic metres in 1993 but remained fairly stable in 1994. Russia has considerable gas reserves and Gazprom, the company controlling gas production, controls 94 per cent of the gas industry in Russia, 100 per cent in Eastern Europe, 30 per cent in Western Europe and 30 per cent of the world market.

Oil production fell from 462 million tonnes in 1991 to roughly 251 million tonnes in 1994 but exports rose by 12 per cent in the first ten months of 1994. The oil industry was exempted from privatization in 1992 and is organized in special holding companies. The largest consortia with foreign participants are the MMMSM (USX's Marathon Oil, McDermott International, Mitsui and Co., Royal Dutch/Shell Group and Mitsubishi Corporation) who announced a US$10 billion investment in 1994 to develop oil and gas reserves around Sakhalin Island in the Russian Far East. This and other large projects have nevertheless been severely hindered by changing legislation and extremely high export taxes.

Coal production decreased by 9 per cent in 1993, with an output of 305 million tonnes, and continued to fall in 1994. The problems plaguing the coal industry are the non-profitability of coal compared to the costs of production of other fuels and the rise by almost 80 per cent in transport costs in 1994. The state has severely reduced its subsidies to the coal industry and several mines risk closing with massive prospective unemployment.

The production of electricity is, on the other hand quite stable and between 1990 and 1994 has decreased only by 14 per cent. This datum on energy consumption is seen by some analysts as an indicator that industrial production has fallen less than official statistics seem to indicate. The energy sector obtains substantial financing from the so-called 'investment component' levied on electricity tariffs. Nevertheless, the sector is suffering from non-payment of consumer debt linked with the inter-firm payment crisis. Its outstanding credit was of 3.3 trillion roubles in 1994.

Manufacturing

While the decline in manufacturing has been very severe overall, a distinction can be made between industries producing less highly-processed goods which are performing slightly better than those producing very highly-processed ones. Thus, while non-ferrous metallurgy declined by 16 per cent between 1993 and 1994, the petro-chemical and the machine-building sectors declined respectively by 43 per cent and 44 per cent in the same period. In the non-ferrous metallurgy sector, enterprises increased production of bauxite by 9 per cent, and of copper by 39 per cent thanks to the high exportability of these goods. In the machine-building sector, which constitutes around 19 per cent of total industrial production, the highest decline affected machine tools and agricultural machinery. The decline is mainly due to the fall in demand and the low standards of innovation and technology which dramatically reduce competitiveness both on the home market and abroad. In the car industry, for example, the enterprises Zil and Kamaz which produce trucks have been hit very badly since their two main customers, collective farms and the army, cannot afford their products any longer.[2] Furthermore, the popularity of imported western consumer goods that benefit from competitive prices, aggressive marketing and advertising strategies and generally higher (real or perceived) quality contributes significantly to the decline of the Russian manufacturing sector. The only glimmer of hope comes from investment, mainly domestic but also some foreign, in the small enterprise sector for consumer goods.

Converting the military-industrial complex

The military-industrial complex used to be the *enfant prodige* of the Soviet economy. It was carefully kept apart from the civilian industry and all the best intellectual resources, research programmes and new technologies were siphoned off into the development of the military industry. Unlike in the west, innovation and progress in the military fields did not trickle down and produce technology transfers or covertly subsidize civilian industry. Secrecy and security, as part of the cold war climate, were considered so important as to isolate the military-industrial production into so-called 'closed cities', impressive and gigantic complexes wholly dedicated to the military. Clusters of industries were concentrated to form urban conglomerates and although people working in these complexes had numerous benefits and prestige, they were bound to secrecy and restricted in their social sphere.

All the above characteristics have rendered the conversion and downscaling of the military an extremely arduous task. As the gap between the military and the civilian sectors widened it became obvious by the time of *perestroika* that this division contributed significantly to the worsening of the economic crisis. With the slowing down of the cold war arms race, there was an ever diminishing need for such a large and expensive military industry. In 1992 a law was passed trying to facilitate conversion of some parts of the military to high-technology exports while other parts faced severe cuts. Employees of the sector, used to being a privileged part of society, put up resistance as entire cities were threatened with mass

[2] *The Economist*, 10 June 1995, p. 86.

redundancy. Part of the problem is the lack of capital to facilitate successful conversion. The great danger posed by this sector, which is increasingly turning into reality, is that with the decentralization of power and the lack of effective regulations, the former military is surviving through indiscriminate and often illegal sales of weapons, technology and rare earths and minerals (such as uranium and plutonium) to the rest of the world; in particular, to developing countries with dictatorial regimes.

Agriculture

As much as the military was the jewel of the Russian economy, agriculture was the problematic sector. Land reform and privatization has been one of the least successful areas of restructuring for the Russian government. The legacies of forced collectivization, the internal passport system preventing work and residence mobility, coupled with the inefficiencies and increasing corruption of the predominantly mono-culture and mono-farming system led to a severe breakdown in workers' motivation and production in rural areas. The whole system of supply and distribution was affected by the inefficiencies of agriculture, food processing, storage, transportation and retailing and a large quantity of food produce was redirected to the informal black-market sector. Politically and culturally the rural population was first repressed and then isolated, with both employment and socialization centred around the farm work-collective. In the 1980s Russia's agricultural sector constituted approximately 16 per cent of the total GDP. It employed 13 per cent of the total labour force and women constituted 36 per cent of all workers in state farms and 45 per cent in collective farms.

Government attempts to reform the agricultural sector have been met with indifference, if not hostility, on the part of the rural population. Younger and more dynamic groups tend to migrate to urban areas and those who stay (including old age pensioners, former collective farm workers) lack entrepreneurial spirit and knowledge of new laws and possibilities. This situation is not facilitated by the often half-hearted and contradictory nature of government reform policies. While formally the reorganization of state and collective farms has been completed, this has produced little effective change in their functioning. In 1992, a total of 138,900 private farms were registered, with five farms closing for every hundred created and in 1993, 101,200 were registered with fifty-two closing for every hundred created. It was estimated that only about one-third of rural workers officially figured as land-owners. Restrictions on land use and sales, only partly eased by the October 1993 legislation, failed to create healthy conditions for the development of a free market. By January 1994, the date by which, in theory, reform of the agricultural sector should have been completed, over 90 per cent of the farms had chosen collective forms of ownership or production (closed joint stock, limited responsibility, co-operative or retaining their previous status of state or collective farms). To make the situation more complicated, regional (*oblast*) governments retain a large authority on land both during and after the privatization process, and illegal practices and corruption are widespread.

International agencies have stepped in to address the crucial issue of agricultural production. In November 1993 a pilot project was initiated with the expertise and financial aid of agencies such as the International Financial Corporation (World Bank), the Know-How Fund (UK) and the US Agency for International Development amongst others, to devise a more efficient model for privatization within the existing legislative framework which would be applicable in other regions. Three farms with different characteristics were chosen in the Nizhnii Novgorod region. Farm land, property and goods were divided into units and farm workers and pensioners were awarded tokens according to various categories of entitlement. The units were then auctioned off after allowing time for deals, barters and partnerships to be made among token holders. Equally, after the auction, time was allowed for adjustments and new agreements. The experiment was reputed to be successful, at least in the short term, and the Russian government is planning to implement it in other regions.

Foreign trade

Russia is one of the few transition economies with a very healthy trade surplus, which was estimated for 1995 to be of the order of $12 billion for non-CIS countries (EBRD, 1995). Clearly, this *largesse* should act as one of the principal springboards from which economic development should be facilitated, both through the investment resources this makes available directly to the exporting enterprises and industries, and through the government being able to use the various revenues generated from export business (export taxes and the like) and the hard currency which eventually makes its way to the central bank.

In terms of exports, the overwhelming feature is the predominance of raw material exports in the overall export profile. Oil and gas are the main individual items, but other important items include coal, timber, nickel and other metals. The bulk of manufacturing exports continue to go to the other transition economies, foremost those of the CIS, but they would in any case not find a market in the western countries. These goods become part of barter deals with the other transition economies also unable to access western markets for their range of potential export items. The statistics on such deals are notoriously unreliable, but it is clear that barter is an important feature of the trading structure of Russia.

Overall, the perceived imbalance in exports in favour of oil and gas has given further credence to the 'Kuwaitization' thesis, implying that Russia is fast moving towards an economic structure wholly geared towards raw material extraction and export with a number of obvious demerits and dangers attached.[3] However, with common sense the oil and gas revenues could be used to recapitalize and develop manufacturing industry, as they have been used to this effect elsewhere.

Turning to imports, in keeping with the general liberalization climate in Russia in 1991, the first moves to open up the trading regime were made with the majority of non-tariff barriers being scrapped. There then followed several years of change in the rate of tariffs applied to goods coming in to Russia, starting from a rate of 5 per cent going up to around 15 per cent by 1994. Industrial policy considerations animate much of the desire for higher tariffs in Russia with the need to protect Russian producers undergoing restructuring from overly aggressive foreign competition. This desire became especially acute following the high-profile difficulties of a number of traditional producers, such as in the vodka industry. According to the EBRD (1994, page 115), however, those industries able to obtain the most tariff protection on industrial policy grounds were also those with the most lobbying power, including defence, micro-electronics, aerospace, motor vehicles and agricultural products. Such tariffs also play an important revenue-raising role in the Russian economy.

From 1994 onwards the tariff structure was set for a gradual reduction in line with its international obligations. This has had some effect on imports, though little in terms of consumer goods imports which continue to be brought into Russia to satisfy consumers starved of most sorts of products – never mind quality products – for so long under communism. Much of this trade remains illegal taking the form of shuttle trade with cheap consumer goods from Asia and the Middle East. It is absent from the statistics and, more importantly, not covered by the various tariffs which would act to make them less competitive. There is also enough legal importation to suggest that consumer goods imports are a major feature of the true import profile. This development, common to the other transition economies, is a source of some discontent with Russian producers who see markets where they should have a real comparative advantage being taken away before they have had the time, or have been able to obtain the investment resources, to respond.

---

[3] A healthy oil and gas sector cannot create the required employment for a country of the size and diversity of the Russian Federation; such a strategy remains at the mercy of world market prices; it is also at the mercy of changing demand patterns, particularly with regard to the development of alternative non-fossil fuel based energy sources; finally, in the longer term, the oil runs out. For a comprehensive analysis of the benefits of oil and gas reserves see Gelb (1988).

Business and finance

The development of the banking system and of financial institutions is of key importance in the creation of markets in Russia but is also very problematic. As is the case in other areas, legislation is hazy and full of gaps and leaves responsibility for many decisions to individual institutions. In theory, a stock market (*birzhe*) is in place in Moscow and others are being organized around the country. Inevitably, such institutions are in a very embryonic phase since the buying and selling of shares is linked to the process of privatization analysed above. Until this process has consolidated and trust in industrial production is re-established, it is difficult to have a healthy and developed stock exchange. Dealings in privatization vouchers, bonds, currency and shares of companies who offer them on the market nevertheless takes place. Foreign currency trading goes through the Moscow Interbank Currency Exchange (MICEX). Banking and finance have been heavily affected by organized crime. Many top bankers have been killed and many others – including Konstantin Borovoj, who set up the Moscow Stock Exchange – narrowly escaped death. In this respect, banking and finance is one of the most dangerous areas of activity in the Russian Federation.

The banking system

Under *perestroika* the Soviet banking system was liberalized and a two-tier system created. Russia inherited these reforms after the dissolution of the USSR. The two main laws regulating the banking system are **The Law on the Central Bank of the Russian Federation** and the **Law on Banks and Banking**. Most of the gaps left by these laws are filled by the Central Bank of Russia (CBR), which is regulated by parliament. As the state bank, the CBR is responsible for supervising and regulating the banking sector, for granting licences to commercial banks and for the money supply. It can apply special requirements for banks with foreign participation. Its role in determining government fiscal and monetary policies as well as the budget is very important. In 1994 the CBR decided to decrease centralized allocations of credit to enterprises and support the increase of the commercial banks' refinancing schemes as well as setting up credit auctions. The first credit auction took place in February 1994 with a total offer of 70 billion roubles of which only 64 per cent was taken up at a monthly interest rate of 17.8 per cent.

Apart from the Central Bank of Russia, the banking sector is made up of over 2000 commercial banks, comprising former Soviet banks such as the Russian Federation Bank of Foreign Trade and the Russian Federation Savings Bank. Other credit institutions are also occasionally granted licences to carry out some banking operations. In the Soviet system different sectors of the economy (agriculture, construction, branches of industry and so forth) used to have their own sector bank. Many of the new commercial banks are based on the former Soviet sector banks. Equally, some large industrial conglomerates, regions or local interest groups have decided to set up their own bank to support individual or local initiatives. Another category of banks are the *Sovzagranbanki*, the banks in Western Europe that used to have Soviet shareholders.

Initially it was extremely easy to set up a bank since the required starting capital was of the order of a few thousand US dollars. The minimum capital requirements were increased, albeit only for new banks, by the Central Bank in March 1994 to two billion roubles subject to indexing according to the inflation rate. A review of banks is planned for 1999 when all banks will be required to have a minimum capital of at least five million ECU.

Commercial banks have different types of licences. Initial licences are granted for rouble operations only. After one year, banks are allowed to apply for a foreign-currency licence. There are three types of foreign currency licences: the most flexible and hardest to obtain is a general licence which allows the conduct of foreign currency operations in Russia and abroad. An extended licence allows Russian banks to have a limited number of correspondent accounts with foreign banks and also offer services to non-residents in Russia, while a domestic licence allows currency operations in Russia and abroad through correspondent accounts with other Russian banks authorized to conduct them.

Commercial banks vary greatly in terms of reliability and efficiency and risk assessment is particularly difficult to establish. The 100 largest banks in Russia comprise all the different types of commercial banks. They also occupy an increasingly large section of commercial banking, controlling around 55 per cent of the market. The three top commercial banks, the Foreign Trade Bank, the Savings Bank and the Agro Industry Bank control over 20 per cent of all assets. Many of the smaller banks are being squeezed out of the market and going bankrupt. The standards of customer service and efficiency are also extremely varied. Some of the more enterprising banks have been training their personnel abroad, importing technology and speeding up their average transaction time. Banks are concentrated in Moscow and in the Central Region and few of them are spread over the territory of the Russian Federation with an appropriate system of branches.

Access to the Russian market has been severely restricted for foreign banks. Russian commercial banks have been lobbying the government to ensure that their control over banking activities would not be threatened by powerful and established foreign banks entering the system. In theory, foreign banks can open both subsidiaries with resident status and the possibility to receive a general licence or branches with offshore status. But in practice the Central Bank has allowed foreign banks to operate on the Russian market only as shareholders in Russian banks.

The most substantial challenge facing Russian commercial banks is that of constructing solid and articulated credit and deposit markets. As far as deposits are concerned, banks need to prove their reliability and build up trust in both corporate and individual customers. Events like the collapse of the former Soviet State Bank (*Vneshekonombank*) and financial scandals like the bankruptcy of the MMM Investment Fund (a financial scam based on the payments of very high interest on deposits by finding new investors according to a pyramid scheme) have severely undermined public trust in financial organizations. In terms of the formation of a developed credit market the problems stem from the constraint in lending operations. Given the high inflation rate and the threats of political instability, there is a widespread reluctance to engage in long-term loans and deposits. Neither depositors nor borrowers are willing to take the risks connected to long-term rouble transactions, despite the very high annual interest rates. The Central Bank, backed by the government and by the International Monetary Fund and the World Bank, has been trying to strengthen the credit market by encouraging enterprise re-financing to go through the commercial sector. Building up banking and financial markets in Russia will require a long time and a fundamental shift in the general public's cultural attitudes.

Taxation

Tax legislation in Russia suffers from all the problems mentioned at the beginning of this section. Taxes can be levied both at federal and local levels and the latter vary a great deal. The amount due through the accumulation of all the different taxes is considered very high for enterprises and the level of tax evasion is enormous. Some firms and some regions refuse point blank to pay, and it is estimated that as much as 50 per cent of taxes are not being collected (Rutland, 1995, page 14). According to an estimate of the Ministry of Interior around US$50 billion could be leaving Russia illegally and untaxed.

Foreign individuals and enterprises doing business in Russia are subject to more or less the same taxes as Russian individuals and entities. The Value Added Tax (VAT) is levied on turnover of goods and services. VAT for intermediary deals is calculated according to the mean between purchase and sale of goods. While goods imported into Russia are subject to VAT all exported goods are exempt. The basic rate for VAT is 20 per cent but effectively hovers around 23 per cent since an additional Special Tax for Support of Major Industries at a 3 per cent rate is levied on the same basis as VAT. A number of priority goods benefit from either reduction of, or exemption from VAT. Excise tax is levied on some goods of domestic production, imported luxury goods, oil and gas condensates and natural gas. Commercial transactions can also be subject to the Tax on Securities Transactions and some local taxes.

Russians and foreigners residing in Russia for more than 183 days a year are subject to the Personal Income Tax. It is levied on total income during the calendar year but requires tax declaration only over a certain level of income (5 million roubles for 1994). Money earned outside Russia should be included but taxes paid elsewhere are offset. The calculation of income for foreigners resident in Russia follows special rules. Foreigners who are not residents but work in Russia are also subject to income taxation including a tax on what they earn in Russia and a basic rate of 20 per cent at source on other incomes.

All Russian and foreign legal entities and international organizations pay tax on profit. Both hard currency and rouble revenues are taxed and growth in the dollar exchange rate is added to the taxable profit. Revenues are calculated against the gross profit by adding labour costs in excess of the minimum wage (set on a quarterly basis by the government) and subtracting abatements and special tax privileges. The rates for taxes vary enormously according to the type of activity. Enterprises are usually taxed at a rate of 30 per cent to which an extra 12 per cent is added for the federal budget while financial institutions are taxed at 25 per cent (plus 12 per cent). Dividends and interests on securities are taxed at source 15 per cent. Equally, revenues from participation in other enterprises in Russia are taxed 15 per cent at source. Profits from intermediary transactions are taxed at 45 per cent, revenues from mass entertainment at 50 per cent, video rents and salons at 70 per cent, casinos and gambling at 90 per cent. Privileges and abatements can be obtained for oil and coal, small enterprises, industrial conversion, reinvestments in production, technical re-equipment, development and agriculture. A tax on enterprise property on fixed and intangible assets is levied at a rate between 0.5 per cent and 2 per cent.

Business and the labour market

The Soviet system was characterized by full employment and frequent labour shortages. The five-year plan system, whereby targets of production were raised by the central administration, induced enterprises to hoard labour against a possible future rise in the levels of output. Very often the labour force was not used to its full potential or even not at all. Enterprises would keep employees on their payroll, even if they were not actually working, in order to have a surplus labour army. The other characteristic of this system was the social contract. In the years of economic stagnation the government effectively bought the political and social acquiescence of the population by offering benefits (stable prices, housing, health-care, basic goods, education and so on) through the workplace. Nominal full employment and an extensive pension system ensured that the majority of the population was included in this pact. Real productivity rates were increasingly ignored by the authorities.

Economic crisis and the transition process have severely undermined this state of affairs. For the first time unemployment, open and hidden, hit the country. As inefficient and unproductive enterprises started to have to fend for themselves many of them could no longer support their labour force on the basis of the social contract. Numerous enterprises are currently surviving on the basis of state subsidies which the government, even when it subscribed to shock therapy, could not afford to withdraw. State subsidies get redistributed in the form of very low wages and thus mass unemployment, with its possible consequence of social unrest, is avoided. Nevertheless, a substantial section of the Russian population are experiencing a dramatic fall in living standards. Official figures for people living below the poverty line, calculated as a basket of minimum subsistence goods, indicated that around 33 per cent of the total population in 1993 were affected (Russian Economic Trends).

Labour relations, in theory are regulated by the Labour Code even though the latter is very flexible and can be made void by the employment contract. Foreigners can work in the Russian Federation provided they obtain a working/business visa. Employers are responsible for paying employees' Personal Income Tax and also for Social Insurance Contributions on the basis of the total payroll. Social charges, paid to the centralized state fund, amount to 40 per cent of the payroll and include 5.4 per cent for State Social Insurance, 28 per cent for Pension Funds, 2 per cent for the Employment Fund, 3.6 per cent for the Compulsory Health Insurance Fund, and 1 per cent for Transport Tax.

Written contracts should be used to regulate employment but foreign firms frequently do not use them for their Russian employees. Dismissal is in theory quite hard to implement (except for cases of theft, intoxication, unjustified absences and similar circumstances) but in practice employees have very little protection against contract termination. The average working week is of five days for a total of 40 hours and overtime should be paid in excess of the basic salary.

Informal practices, corruption and the importance of having a 'roof'

Soviet society in the 1970s and 1980s was characterized by an ever-widening split between, on the one side, official ideology and formal procedures in all aspects of public life from work to health and consumption and, on the other, by the informal practices and unofficial networks based on the private sphere which people widely used to 'get things done'. The public, official sector was a highly inefficient one, a quicksand system that people tried to circumvent by using 'insider' systems of personal favours, bribery and private connections and entries. The political and social balance between the state and its citizens and between the public and the private spheres of everyday life was maintained through a phenomenon which became known as the social contract. As long as people helped the state to keep up all the appearances and forms of politically orthodox system by paying lip-service to official ideology and maintaining social acquiescence, the state would, on the one hand, ensure basic standards of living, employment and welfare services to everyone and, on the other, would tolerate the spread of 'insider' practices and unofficial networks. This phenomenon is best exemplified by a catch-phrase popular amongst workers throughout the Soviet Union and Eastern Europe which declared that 'We pretend to work and they pretend to pay us'.

One of the most extreme manifestations of this highly complex and extensive social phenomenon can be found in the development of the black and grey market economy, tolerated by the state to ease the pressure from its own duty to provide an adequate system of supplies of goods and services. Contemporary Russian society presents many elements of continuity with the Soviet second economy, which ranged from phenomena such as widespread petty corruption to violent and criminal Mafia-type activities. Organized crime has grown rapidly with the liberalization of the economy and the political transformations of recent years and has become a highly stratified phenomenon encompassing many different forms of activities, 'gangs', groupings and also different ethnic groupings. The so-called 'Russian *mafyia*' is a highly criminal and generally very successful network of informal organizations, covering most of the national territory, sometimes working together or often in conflict with each other; it is also the tip of an iceberg. Feeding directly into it is a political culture widespread at all levels of society, permeated by corruption and double standards. The business culture is heavily characterized by a prevalence of informal practices and the reliance on insider networks. For example, firms tend to employ people only if they know them through personal contacts and are in general very hostile to consider candidates, albeit with the right qualifications, 'from the street' (*iz ulitsi*). Another significant aspect of this culture of informal practices is the need for any business to 'have a roof' (*krysha*); i.e. to be under the umbrella of some larger organization (usually a state one) that will guarantee protection and ease the formal and legal aspects of a business. Often the '*gosudarstvenny krysha*', the state roof, will be sufficient to shield businesses from having to deal with organized crime. On the other hand, the borderline between the so-called state mafia (*gosudarstvennaya mafyia*) and other mafia-type organizations is very hazy. What is clear is that most businesses, whether Russian or foreign, have to deal, even if in reduced measure, with some aspect of the unofficial system.

Demographic trends

The Russian Federation has a population of 148.6 million. In 1993 the total employed numbered 71 million while pensioners were roughly 36 million. Birth-rates vary according to ethnic composition and still reflect the trends present in the Soviet Union when Central Asian titular populations had higher birth-rates (37 per 1000 in Uzbekistan in 1986) than ethnic Russians and than the Baltic republics (16 per 1000 in Estonia in 1986). The impact of economic crisis and the uncertainties of transition have produced a sharp drop in birth-rates in recent years but this trend may well revert with progressive social and economic stabilization. Death rates have been on the increase since the 1980s, due to the ageing of the population, rising infant mortality and higher death-rates for males caused by declining living standards and increased alcoholism. Violent deaths amongst the male population have also increased in recent years.

Employment and unemployment

The labour market in Russia is very much half way along the path of transition with old and new characteristics presenting a hybrid and constantly changing formation. When shock therapy was first launched, one of the bigger concerns was that of the wave of mass unemployment that was expected to hit Russian workers. Mass unemployment did not happen in the initial phases of transition because the state continued to support apparently bankrupt enterprises very much as before, essentially out of a fear of the political and social consequences of unemployment. Official figures for people out of work are thus still very low. By trying to analyse this phenomenon much can be understood about the peculiarities of the Russian labour market in the transitional phase.

The first element that needs underlining is that Russian unemployment statistics are not very reliable. While recently ILO standards have started being applied to the collection of data regarding unemployment, the problem is more one of definition. Unemployment is a relatively new cultural category for Russians since the Soviet regime had eliminated it (also as an ideological category) by implementing full employment. Thus 'being unemployed' is a very ambiguous cultural category and an unfamiliar one to many people.

Unemployment was measured by Goskomstat at 4.8 per cent in 1992 and 5.5 per cent in 1993 and around 6 per cent in 1994. Those receiving unemployment benefits were 1.3 per cent of the labour force in 1994. Total employment was measured at 71 million in 1993, with the largest sectors being industry with 20.8 million, agriculture with 9.6 million and construction with 8 million workers. While these official figures may give a rough indication of the sectoral distribution of the labour market, they fail to reveal some of the structural trends that characterize it. This

Table 5.1 *Employment (millions)*

	1991	1992	1993
Total employment	73.8	72.0	71.0
Industry	22.4	21.5	20.8
Agriculture	10.0	9.5	9.6
Transport and communication	5.8	5.7	5.2
Construction	8.5	8.3	8.0
Trade and catering	5.6	5.7	
Services	3.2	3.1	3.2
Health, sport, social security	4.3	4.3	4.4
Education, culture, art	7.3	7.5	7.7
Science	3.1	2.6	2.4
Credit and state insurance	0.4	0.7	
Public administration	2.0	2.2	2.4

Source: Russian Economic Trends (1994) Vol. 3, No.1.

apparently high level of employment, especially for a transitional economy, is merely nominal. In 1994 an ILO report suggested that one-third of industrial workers were *de facto* unemployed. Most enterprise managers have actively resisted making their employees redundant, resorting to a number of stratagems. Some workers are placed on extended unpaid leave, others have their total amount of working hours drastically reduced, others are made to take frequent unpaid holidays, pregnant women are put on long maternity leave. All these devices entail at best severe reductions in real wages but in many cases a temporary or permanent non-payment of salaries. Enterprises pay taxes on the basis of the average wage paid to workers and therefore another money-saving device is that of downgrading the functions of their workers.

It is estimated that between 40 and 60 per cent of the workers in the light, electro-chemical and machine-building industries are either on mandatory leave or work a short week (Morvant, 1995, page 47). Workers accept this state of affairs against the greater threat of redundancy because being officially registered as employed still gives them access to a number of benefits, such as health-care and social security, that they would otherwise lose. Most workers are obliged to look for second jobs or additional economic activities in order to survive.

Wages

The majority of the Russian population has experienced a dramatic fall in real wages over the last few years. Real wages in 1994 were estimated to be at 63 per cent the 1991 levels. In theory, the government imposes a minimum wage which is indexed every quarter to keep up with inflation. Unfortunately, most enterprises in those sectors which have suffered most from a decline in production, as well as the public and civil services, are often plagued by substantial wage arrears. Thus, by the time employees receive their wages the real value of monthly salaries has declined even further. The wages that have suffered the sharpest decline are those of people employed in the education and health-care sectors. Agricultural wages are also very low but at least are slightly compensated by widespread use of garden plots and small scale agricultural production, which helps people in the countryside to survive.

On the other side of the coin a small group of Russians, commonly known as the *Novye Russkie* (New Russians) are becoming very rich, mostly through entrepreneurial activities. In general, people employed in the service sector, especially connected with foreign firms and activities, are earning increasingly higher wages and forming the new Russian upper middle class. Even though this group is consistently growing, it is a tiny minority when compared to the overall population.

Gender and generational issues

Segmentation according to age and gender is a very prominent characteristic of the Russian labour market. While Soviet ideology had made one of its sources of pride the fact that women and men had achieved equality in all walks of life but foremost in employment, Soviet society presented a very different picture. Women had been forced into the labour market through policies of full employment but they were hardly on an equal footing with men in terms of job hierarchy. Overall they earned considerably less than men and they were mostly confined to specific sectors of economic activities. Predictably, the so-called 'caring' sectors like health and education were heavily feminized except for the top positions which were usually filled by men. Furthermore, Russian and Soviet society was very traditional and patriarchal in terms of gender roles and women found themselves with the added responsibilities of domestic and work responsibilities, a phenomenon usually known as the double burden.

The sectors of the labour market that were heavily feminized were the ones to suffer the most from restructuring and transition. It is widely recognized that women in Russia have paid much higher costs, both on the employment front and on that of public services and welfare as a result of political and economic transformation. In addition, social and cultural change translates itself in a return to traditional values whereby women's ideal role would be that of wives and mothers not engaged in full-time employment, relying on a male able to provide a wage for the whole family. This return to traditional models of gender relations and division of labour is, for the majority of the Russian population, in the realm of aspirations more than realistic possibilities since the harshness of economic conditions has produced widespread patterns of feminization of poverty both in urban areas and in the countryside.

The labour market is also marked by generational characteristics. Older people, especially women, are finding it harder to adjust and cope with the new economic conditions. While older men, thanks to the fact that they covered a greater number of positions of responsibility under the old system, are now using their networks to cope with the market, older women in particular, have to rely on different forms of survival strategies, cottage industry and multiple jobs in order to make ends meet.

Despite this generally negative situation there is one sector of the economy that seems to offer some opportunities to women. The service sector, albeit at the lower levels, is heavily feminized. In particular, foreign firms that work in Russia seem to prefer employing Russian women who are generally perceived as more reliable and organized than Russian men. Most jobs in the service sector, such as secretarial, lower management, clerks and shop assistants, match the traditional gender stereotypes and, given that Russia is still a very traditional society, are covered by women.

The social safety net and the welfare system

The dramatic fall in real incomes has been accompanied by a severe worsening of the social safety net. The Soviet state, albeit characterized by aspects of hidden inequality, had a highly-subsidized and widespread welfare system. While nominally still in place, most services and benefits have severely deteriorated and/or been curtailed under the current economic restructuring. The standards in public sector health-care have worsened considerably, with many doctors and health structures moving to the private sector. The same has happened to education, where most of the 'better' schools and universities have started charging fees. While kindergartens and schools have often gone completely private, universities and technical colleges usually take a smaller group of non-paying students according to merit while offering the rest of the places to people who can pay fees.

The widening gap between the quality of public and private sector services corresponds to the increasing stratifications in earnings and income distribution. As may be expected, the categories most at risk are the unemployed, old-age pensioners and families with many children. Patterns of unemployment have been analysed in the previous section. Pensioners also represent a significant section of the population. In 1994 they represented about 16.4 per cent of the total population, at an estimated 36 million. Pension levels are well below the average wage (at around 34 per cent) and even though they are indexed quarterly, they have been seriously eroded in recent years. Family and child-benefits, which used to be a significant aspect of the Soviet safety net, nominally still exist but are, in reality, completely insignificant in terms of easing inequalities and poverty. The shrinking of public sector welfare services mentioned above, further contributes to the polarization of society and the increase of poverty.

Trade unions

In Soviet times, trade unions were invested with great importance and operated as the link between the political elite (i.e. the party) and the rest of the population. They played a fundamental role in the social contract of the Brezhnev era, as distributors of goods, housing and other facilities. At the same time they controlled and regulated the labour force through a powerful and extensive network. Much of this powerful organization lost its clout with the demise of the Soviet Union since it was seen as being heavily compromised by the old political regime. Nevertheless, trade union membership is still quite high even though the real power of different organizations is highly uneven. The majority of trade unions seem to have very little clout and are characterized by their political passivity. On the other hand the coal-miners' union was very powerful in 1991 and contributed with its protracted strike action to Gorbachev's loss of power. Ever since then it has retained considerable importance and has the ability to pose serious threats to the government. Other independent unions have also emerged in recent years. Amongst the most powerful are the pilots and other transport groups. At national level the new emerging organization is the Federation of Russian Labour Unions, even though it lacks a unitary and precise political orientation, with many of its components forging alliances with very different political groupings. On the whole, trade unions do not represent a major political force in Russian political life even though they might be re-activated if unemployment carries on growing and social guarantees carry on being eroded at such a fast pace.

Business, education and training

Traditionally, education was a very strong sector in the Soviet Union. Much stress was put on the importance of mass literacy and rates of literacy, as well as on rates of secondary and higher education, which were extremely high. To a certain extent education was a vehicle for state ideology, but it also determined patterns of upward social mobility and therefore was an integral value in Soviet society at large. On the whole Russians are very thoroughly educated even though the system was never open to new ideas and modernization. Higher education institutions presented a definite hierarchy. Education was a vehicle for privilege and therefore stratified. In general the best universities and colleges, both in sciences and humanities, were in Moscow and Leningrad, with decreasing standards of quality the more peripheral they were. Larger cities in the regions could have some very good universities and technical schools. The most prestigious research body was the Academy of Sciences, which was purely devoted to research and some very limited post-graduate teaching at the highest levels. During the cold war, research in the military-industrial sector was highly developed and in constant competition with the United States. Despite this cutting edge, on the whole technological skills in Russia are of average standard since the Soviet system was a world apart and did not open up to international technology transfer and know-how.

As analysed above, in the section on the social safety net, the current situation presents many problems. Many able researchers and academics have been forced out of their jobs since there is very little money being put into education. Wages are very low and often are paid with several months delay. As a result, many of the most skilled academics have emigrated to the west while the remaining ones often look for jobs in the private sector. The quality of teaching has suffered severely in the public sector. In order to survive and pay their workers, most institutions (from primary to higher) are charging hefty fees which most students cannot afford. The fees are often comparable to what a student would have to pay to study abroad, so many of those who can afford to study, prefer to do so in the UK or in the USA. New curricula for 'capitalist' subjects (which did not previously exist) such as business, management, accounting and auditing are being developed in numerous institutions since there is growing demand for disciplines geared to market environments.

Business and the environment

Environmental conditions in the Russian Federation are, as elsewhere in the former Soviet Union, particularly bad. Years of industrialization coupled with a distinct lack of concern for ecological issues under Soviet management have left a very negative and difficult legacy. Whilst there is a consistent degree of concern amongst the Russian public for environmental issues, there is little political and financial commitment on the part of the leadership to look seriously at blatant cases of major environmental damage in the territory of the Russian Federation. Since *glasnost*, more information about environmental disasters has reached public knowledge but possibly just as many cases are still covered by military/industrial secret. Some politicians, especially those with strong nationalist inclinations, have paid more attention to environmental damage, often linking it to nationalistic discourses on the Russian heritage and identity. This was the case for the successful campaign to stop the Siberian rivers diversion project which was led in very nationalistic tones by the writer Valentin Rasputin.

On the other hand, the current leadership, even though formally it pays some attention to the environment, has done little seriously to address any of the causes and problems. The constant and mostly uncontrolled pilfering of natural resources for export purposes is usually ignored; equally the disastrous state of Russia's nuclear energy sector. Financial considerations usually come first. On the one hand Russia thinks it cannot invest in more rational and sustainable resources management at this moment because of the need for foreign currency. On the other, environmental issues are seen as something that can wait to be dealt with, given the mass of supposedly more pressing socio-economic problems that the country is currently facing. Recently the Russian leadership admitted to not having enough money to dispose of waste from nuclear submarines and power stations or to guarantee their safety. In an act of political blackmail it appealed to the west to provide the money to tackle these problems since a nuclear disaster in Russia would also affect the rest of the world.

Smaller-scale environmental issues are also a problem. Health and safety standards in a number of fields, from food production to waste disposal or worker protection, have completely broken down. Lack of information and adequate education on these issues do not improve the general situation. Furthermore, in a country where standards of living have been worsening for the vast majority of the population, most of these concerns have become luxuries rather than immediate concerns. While some businesses are concerned with the environment, they are a tiny minority and their concerns stem mainly from good will than from any attempt to respect a legislative framework of standards and regulations.

Conclusion

The Russian Federation has survived the collapse of communism and the Soviet Union and remains the key economic and political player in Eastern Europe. Its inherited political power remains substantial and is still backed up by a military capacity unmatched by any former Soviet Republic or former communist neighbour. Its economic structure continues to benefit from the particular 'hub and spoke' supply-chain development encouraged under communism, which placed the Russian economy at the centre of development and which has now left most critical industries in Russian hands and surrounding states having to rely on Russian markets and supplies in order to function even at vastly reduced levels.

Russia's major comparative advantage undoubtedly lies in its raw material resources which currently account for the bulk of its exports. This offers the potential to recycle the proceeds into economic development and the modernization of the enterprise sector, and there is some evidence that this scenario is actually occurring. But there is also the danger that this particular economic potential will not be capable of sustaining and revitalizing an entire economic base the size of Russia's. Unfortunately, there is more evidence to support this scenario than the previous one: output has declined consistently and massively since 1991 and the rate of de-industrialization in Russia has increased alarmingly over the past five years, coming on top of an already declining industrial and technological base prior to the collapse of communism in 1991. Recent studies of industry, technology and innovation in the Russian Federation make depressing reading because they highlight the decline in domestic technology, and the very worrying trend of enterprises vacating production and technology sectors to move into the more lucrative trade and export-import activities.[4] The charge of 'Kuwaitization' levelled at this scenario becomes increasingly appropriate as the Russians appear likely to be left with an economic base highly dependent upon oil and gas and the export of natural resources.

Finally, in terms of the emergence of a business culture, it seems to be the case that the Russian Federation, perhaps more than other Eastern European economies, is now characterized by the emergence of two overlapping business cultures. On the one hand there is an inheritance of the old communist system in the shape of a bureaucratic-administrative culture which has taken root within newly privatized as well as the old state-owned enterprises and has become a powerful influence. This business culture is essentially concerned with the ideas of stability, gradual change and continued support from the state, and is principally espoused by the old directors and managers of state enterprises who were able to retain control of their old enterprises after the demise of central planning. There is still some debate as to whether the resulting reluctance to see rapid and major change has undermined the transition in Russia: some consider the lack of rapid change to have hampered the process of privatization and creation of efficient management structures within Russian enterprises and thus Russia's successful incorporation into the world market economy, whereas others consider it to have contributed towards defending a selection of the manufacturing interests upon which Russian economic success will inevitably depend in future.

---

[4] See, for example, the OECD report, *Science, Technology and Innovation Policies: Federation of Russia* (1994) Vols I and II, OECD, Paris.

On the other hand, we have the rise of the new entrepreneurial class in Russia. This new class, and the business culture which it has spawned and legitimized, has created almost as many problems as it appears to have solved. Without question the new private entrepreneurial sector has contributed significantly to the supply of basic consumer goods and services within Russia and provides employment and incomes for many millions of people escaping the declining pay and conditions in the state sector. New dynamic business sectors are changing the face of Russian business, especially in the major cities. But this development is restricted to those large cities, with the non-urban areas having seen relatively little change. It also carries a heavy price in the sense that this new business class is simultaneously associated with the enormous rise in the level of corruption, criminality and violence as well as the legal but very extravagant patterns of consumption and lifestyles. Only time will tell whether these new business classes and elites will have enough dynamism and flexibility to lead Russia into widespread and even economic recovery or whether they will remain the sole beneficiaries of transition.

Acknowledgements

I would like to dedicate this chapter to Michael Levett who first introduced me to the business culture in Russia.

References and suggestions for further reading

Bim, A., Jones, D. and Weisskopf, T. (1994) Privatization in the Former Soviet Union and the New Russia, in S. Estrin (ed.) *Privatization in Central and Eastern Europe.* Longman, New York.

Campbell, R.W. (ed.) (1994) *The Post-Communist Economic Transformation. Essays in Honour of Gregory Grossman.* Westview Press, Denver, Colorado.

Clarke, S., Fairbrother, P., Burawoy, M. and Krotov, P. (1993) *What about the Workers? Workers and the Transition to Capitalism in Russia.* Verso, London.

EBRD (1994) *Transition report.* EBRD, London.

EBRD (1995) *Transition report.* EBRD, London.

Gelb, A. (1988) *Oil windfalls: blessing or curse?* Oxford University Press, New York.

Gregory, P, and Stuart, R. (1994) *Soviet and Post-Soviet Economic Structure and Performance.* Harper Collins College Publishers, New York.

Goldman, M. (1994) *Lost Opportunity: Why economic reforms in Russia have not worked.* W. W. Norton and Company, New York.

Lane, D. (ed.) (1992) *Russia in Flux. The Political and Social Consequences of Reform.* Edward Elgar, Aldershot.

Morvant, P. (1995) Unemployment: a Growing Problem. *Transition*, 28 April, pp. 46–50.

Morris-Cotterill, N. (1994) Basic Business Law for Investors in Russia. *Foreign Trade and Investment Review*, Vol. 3, pp. 115–122.

Nove, A. (1990) *An Economic History of the USSR*. Penguin, Harmondsworth.

Russian Economic Trends 1994, Volume 3, Whurr Publishers, London.

Rutland, P. (1995) A Twisted Path Toward a Market Economy. *Transition*, 15 February, pp. 12–20.

6 The business culture in Kazakhstan

Martin Taylor

Introduction

Kazakhstan reluctantly declared independence on 16 December 1991, in a move forced by declarations of independence made by the other countries of the former Soviet Union. The republic rapidly gained a reputation amongst western observers and investors as a 'future Kuwait' with huge natural resources of oil and gas, but this has already given way to some pessimism. Politically, the republic's reputation has been tarnished by the dismissal of parliament in March 1995, reports of electoral malpractice, and the president's accumulation of power during the parliamentary interregnum.

The most important tasks still facing the president and government are to stabilize the economy and to implement the reform programme. Independence in 1991 saw the start of a continuous yearly decline in GDP of around 12–13 per cent, except for 1994 when a sharp fall of 25 per cent was registered. Although the rate of decline has started to slow up in late 1995 and early 1996, it is estimated that production will not begin to rise before 1997. The government, with the support of international agencies including the IMF and World Bank, and of foreign governments including the EU and US, has made privatization the central pillar of the reform programme. Although a range of small, medium and large enterprises have been transferred to private ownership, restructuring has scarcely begun. The development of new small and medium sized business has been strongly encouraged, but the unstable macroeconomic conditions and unwieldy bureaucracy (which appears to be growing rather than contracting) combined with rising corruption have not provided ideal business conditions. The government has registered some success starting in the summer of 1995 when it stabilized the national currency and finally brought monthly inflation down to around 3 per cent. However much remains to be achieved in the spheres of legislation and banking before stable business conditions will exist.

In the meantime entrepreneurs continue to prefer to invest time and money in commercial trading ventures rather than to take the risks of establishing manufacturing concerns. President Nazarbaev has encouraged foreign involvement in the oil, gas and mineral extraction industries as the quickest method to reap the benefits and stabilize the state budget. These efforts continue to stumble on political, economic and bureaucratic obstacles which have dampened investment. Many observers believe that if the republic can create a more favourable investment environment, stabilize the economy and keep the lid on fermenting ethnic tensions and social unrest in the short term, the republic can look forward to an extremely healthy economy in the next century, based upon its mineral reserves and near agricultural self-sustainability. The 'if' is great but the republic's record to date can allow some optimism, but not complacency.

Business and government

In the four years since declaring independence Kazakhstan witnessed the dismissal of one government, one presidential election, the dissolution of two parliaments, two parliamentary elections and a referendum on the extension of the president's term of office to December 2001. In 1993 the republic was being praised by western governments and investors for maintaining political stability. But within two years reports of malpractice in the March 1994 and December 1995 general elections and the March 1995 dissolution of parliament have tarnished the republic's democratic reputation. President Nazarbaev's position, meanwhile, was strengthened by the 95.4 per cent 'yes' vote at the April 1995 referendum on the extension of his term of office until 2001 and further by the referendum on the Constitution, held in August 1995. Despite this apparent political instability, there are threads of continuity in the government's approach to the task of transforming an ailing, centralized economy into a more efficient, market economy.

The president, in conjunction with the government, sets the republic's policies (with the latter assuming responsibility for its implementation – and blame for any failures). The constitutional weakness of the elected legislature could have long-term implications in the fight against corruption, the development of a firm legislative basis to underpin economic reform and the development of a stable, democratic political system.

The government of Sergei Tereshenko, prime minister from independence until autumn 1994, developed a reform programme using privatization, marketization, foreign investment and the encouragement of entrepreneurs to reduce industry's dependence on state subsidies and to promote trade. Tereshenko's government set the republic on the course of reform but ultimately failed to implement it. Pressure on Tereshenko, the scapegoat for economic failure, mounted with the September 1994 dismissal of the Economy Minister Mr Urkumbaev, and Interior Minister Mr Shumov, because of accusations of bribery and obstruction of justice. In October 1994 the whole government was dismissed. The main achievements of Tereshenko's government were:

- setting the direction for the reform of the republic's economy;
- presiding over the liberalization of many, if not the most crucial, consumer prices;
- re-negotiating and concluding Chevron's Tengizchevroil joint-venture;
- planning and launching one of the former Soviet Union's most sweeping mass privatization programmes;
- introducing the national currency, the *tenge;*
- bringing inflation down to more manageable monthly levels.

Against these achievements has to be set a series of negative developments:

- a rapid decline in production – approximately 28 per cent in 1994, above the CIS average;
- a reduction in GDP of 25 per cent in 1994;
- a fall in the standard of living;
- rising crime and corruption;
- rising unemployment.

The appointment of Akezhan Kazhegeldin as prime minister in October 1994 saw a Kazakh businessman replace Tereshenko, the Slav career bureaucrat/politician. The new premier immediately showed his determination to accelerate the reform process with his decision to liberalize bread prices, indicating his willingness to maintain stricter economic and fiscal policies. However the new cabinet was largely drawn from former deputy ministers and some ministers.

Regional structures and administration

Kazakhstan is divided into nineteen regional administrative units (*oblast*), each led by a head of oblast who is appointed by the president. The oblast administration is similar to the republican executive branch of power, including departments responsible for a wide range of policy areas, including health, education, social security, foreign economic relations and taxation. Each oblast also has its own local parliament of deputies (*maslikhat*). This collection of administrative and legislative offices is rapidly growing in importance as the process of de-centralization (sanctioned and unsanctioned) continues.

The head of the oblast occupies a powerful position and has the authority to negotiate with foreign companies over the development of joint ventures and the privatization of enterprises. Foreign companies wishing to register in Kazakhstan must register both with the National Agency for Foreign Investment, the oblast administration and the local taxation department. Each oblast sets its levels of taxation and is responsible for its collection and redistribution according to government guidelines. The central government irons out regional income differentials between oblasts, although some economists are now calling for this system to be abandoned.

Relations with Russia

Nazarbaev was a fervent supporter of Gorbachev's failed attempts to establish the Union Treaty (a re-formulation of the former USSR as a union of independent republics) in 1991 and has been an ardent proponent of greater CIS integration and the development of a Eurasian security system. He has maintained the belief that international umbrella security arrangements can benefit Kazakhstan, which is sandwiched between the two mighty powers of Russia and China, and has a sizeable ethnic Russian population within its borders. Russia continues to be Kazakhstan's most important trading partner and a growing awareness of the inevitability of this fact has led Kazakhstan's leadership to develop a more pro-Russian policy, despite the opposition of some Kazakh nationalists. Russia's importance rests on five main factors:

- Russia is Kazakhstan's single most important trading partner, in 1994 accounting for 44.5 per cent of Kazakhstan's exports.
- The industries of the two countries are integrated so that Kazakhstan is dependent on Russia for many manufactured goods and as a market for its natural resources.
- Kazakhstan's landlocked position makes transportation through Russia vital, especially for oil and gas (see below).
- The large ethnic Russian population (approximately 38 per cent of the total population) living in Kazakhstan (mostly in the northern oblasts near the border with Russia) are essential to the country's economic development but a potential threat to its sovereignty (see below).
- The security of Kazakhstan rests to a certain extent in the hands of Russia as the (internationally recognized) major power in the region (see below).

The introduction, in November 1993, of the Kazakhstani national currency, the *tenge*, allowed the government to take full control of fiscal and economic policies. As prime minister, Sergei Tereshenko had been handicapped in his dealings with Russia by virtue of his being an ethnic

Table 6.1 *Kazakhstan's external trade in 1994 (as per cent of total)*

Country	Export	Import
China	4.6	2
Germany	2.3	8.4
Great Britain	2	1.9
Holland	7.7	0.9
Kyrghyzstan	1.9	2.6
Russia	44.5	36.1
Switzerland	4	1.9
Turkmenistan	0.8	7.5
Turkey	1.5	2.5
Ukraine	3.6	7.7
USA	2.3	3.1
Uzbekistan	4.0	3.4

Source: Goskomstat, 1995.

Slav open to accusations of betrayal from Kazakh nationalists. Kazhe-geldin, however, is in a stronger position to compromise, and has pursued a highly-pragmatic policy towards the northern neighbour focused around the need to attract Russian investment to the economy, enter a free trade area with Russia and Belarus and resolve the twin issues of oil pipelines and sovereignty in the Caspian Sea.

Geo-politically the country is concerned by its uncomfortable position wedged between the two powers of Russia and China, and also by the threat of Tadjikistan's civil war spreading northwards. Kazakhstan's response has been to propose a Eurasian Union to enable collective security arrangements to preserve its territorial integrity. This would also calm the fears of the ethnic Russian population, thus preserving internal and external security for the republic. The failure of the CIS to implement many of its decisions and the thus-far lukewarm reactions to the idea of a Eurasian Union indicate that at present Kazakhstan cannot realize this goal.

A Central Asian single market?

The idea of a single, Central Asian market has been voiced by various politicians and officials in the region, but to date nothing concrete has been enacted. Greater economic co-operation between Kazakhstan, Kyrghyzstan, Uzbekistan, Tadjikistan and Turkmenistan is probable because of ethnic proximity and the similarity of economic problems, but it is unlikely that a formal single market will emerge in the near future. From Kazakhstan's point of view this is for four main reasons:

- The government of Akezhan Kazhegeldin has set a course for further economic co-operation with Russia, aiming in particular to increase Russian investment in Kazakhstan and to harmonize tax regimes.
- Russia and the European states of the CIS are more important as trading partners and as sources of investment.
- The rivalry between Nazarbaev and President Karimov of Uzbekistan (albeit masked in friendship and co-operation) to be the 'leader' of Central Asia hinders integration.
- It is not certain that the development of a single Central Asian market will help Kazakhstan through the difficult transition period.

The benefits of closer Central Asian integration would be to reduce the region's economic dependence on Russia, though Russia's military might, geography and traditional economic dominance will clearly maintain its influence in the region. However there is no doubt that the new Trans-Asian railway from Tehran to Beijing via Mashad, Ashkhabad, Samarkand, Tashkent, Almaty, Druzhba and Urumchi will open vast trading possibilities from Iran, through Central Asia to China. The development of the Economic Co-operation Organization will lead to the development of a large Asian market including India, Pakistan, Iran, Afghanistan and Turkey.

Business and the reform programme

President Nazarbaev's commitment to economic reform, high on the republic's agenda before independence, has not diminished. His vision of the development of Kazakhstan (modelled on South Korea and Singapore) is based upon a strong state which 'guards' a free market economy. Kazakhstan needs reform to address:

- the collapse of economic ties with other CIS states;
- declining production in almost all sectors of the economy and the inefficiency of many enterprises reliant on subsidies;
- shortages of basic foodstuffs and consumer goods;
- continuing inflation;
- the lack of adequately-trained personnel to fulfil the new leadership roles of both business and government;
- a growing need to improve the provision of adequate social security during the transition period as living standards decline and unemployment rises.

In addition it also faces the specific problems of:

- nation-state building in a country where the titular majority do not constitute an overall majority of the population;
- its geopolitical position due to the large number of ethnic Russians living in northern Kazakhstan.

Kazakhstan has gone further than most of the former Soviet republics in introducing new laws to stabilize the economy and transform it into one based on market relations. The government's strategy to transform the economy is founded on a number of fundamental policies:

- privatization of state-owned enterprises, transferring ownership to encourage restructuring;
- price liberalization and marketization;
- encouragement of foreign investment to provide technical expertise, equipment and capital to exploit Kazakhstan's natural resources and develop the manufacturing sector;
- encouragement of entrepreneurs and the development of small and medium-size businesses;
- maintainance of a stable tenge exchange rate;
- cutting inflation and interest rates.

Privatization

Some small-scale privatization began in 1991 with the disposal of 380 small enterprises. This was widely dubbed 'nomenklatura privatization' because the beneficiaries of the sell-off were mainly (former) communist party officials who acquired enterprises at bargain prices. By the end of 1992 almost 6000 enterprises – mainly in the spheres of agriculture, commerce and public services – had been transferred to private ownership. In some cities, such as Almaty[1], housing privatization coupons which had been issued in 1991 could be used to buy small businesses (for instance shops and restaurants) at auctions where 50 per cent of the value had to be paid for with these coupons. An unofficial 'coupon' market developed because the unexpectedly high prices soon led to a shortage of coupons.

Following advice from international agencies, (potential) foreign investors, foreign economic advisors and local entrepreneurs in March 1993 Kazakhstan embarked upon one of the most ambitious mass privatization programmes so far attempted in the former Soviet Union. The transfer of state-owned enterprises to private ownership was

[1] This is the new name for Alma Ata. A number of other city names inherited from the Soviet period have also been changed.

regarded as the lynch-pin for allowing enterprise restructuring. In 1994 the government initiated the second stage of its privatization programme. This amounted to disposing of 3500 enterprises accounting for 30 per cent of the Kazakhstani economy. The four pillars of this programme were:

- small-scale state-owned enterprises (less than 200 employees);
- mass privatization of state owned enterprises (between 200 and 5,000 employees);
- case-by-case privatization of large (more than 5000 employees or unique) state-owned enterprises;
- agricultural privatization.

By the end of 1994 almost 14,000 state-owned enterprises, consisting mainly of consumer services, commerce and agriculture, had been transferred to private ownership. While some have begun to operate profitably, many are still awaiting investment for restructuring. The mass privatization programme has not been an unqualified success, with many people expressing discontent and disillusionment about their Privatization Investment Coupons because they cannot yet be traded (see below for other problems).

Foreign investment

The attraction of foreign capital and technology to enable Kazakhstan to exploit its huge natural resources potential is central to reform measures. Foreign involvement has been encouraged in various forms: the establishment of joint ventures, representative offices, subsidiaries and through the case-by-case privatization of large state-owned enterprises. The first few years after independence saw Kazakhstan attract great interest but in late 1994 and early 1995 a downturn in investor confidence occured as a result of increasing bureaucratic obstacles, corruption amongst high-level officials and doubts about the republic's long-term political stability. Uzbekistan, formerly viewed as anti-democratic, suddenly became more attractive to investors who found less red tape and more stability.

Foreign investment was first courted before independence when Moscow began negotiations with Chevron over the exploitation of the Tengiz oil fields. After independence Kazakhstan insisted on re-negotiating the terms to protect its interests. The progress of the Tengizchevroil joint venture, concluded in April 1993, has become the benchmark for evaluating investor confidence. The republic now has to prove that it can honour international contracts, which requires good relations with Russia. Russia's claim that it should profit from international oil deals like the Tengizchevroil project (because of Soviet investment in the initial exploitation and development of the reserves) and its control of the sole pipeline to foreign (western European) markets are proving a decisive nuisance to the government of Kazakhstan.

In March 1994 the government announced that it would allow foreign firms to participate in the privatization of thirty-eight enterprises, including many of the republic's leading mining, mineral extraction and processing plants. The acquisition by Philip Morris of a 97 per cent share in the Almaty tobacco factory in September 1993 was the first enterprise to be transferred to private ownership as part of the case-by-case privatization plan.

Business and the economy

The Kazakhstani economy, which developed as a part of the integrated Soviet economy, was primarily a supplier of raw materials and an importer of manufactured goods. Production was directed from Moscow, via Alma-Ata, and organized with quotas to be fulfilled. As a result the economy suffers from the inefficiency typical of post-Soviet enterprises, and the nature of industrial development renders agriculture, energy, mineral and metals extraction important while the manufacturing sector is weak. The decline in output and GDP from 1991 onwards (see Table 6.2) has hit all sectors, with the hardest-hit being construction and transport. Energy, fuel, minerals and metallurgy will be central to the transformation of the economy.

The industry sector is dominated by machine building and metal working enterprises which in 1994 accounted for about 25 per cent of industrial production. The government has recognized the need to support the manufacture of household and consumer goods. Many joint ventures have been established, especially with Japanese and Korean partners, to

Table 6.2   *Change in GDP (1991–94)*

	Rate of change of GDP
1989	−0.4
1990	−0.4
1991	−13
1992	−13
1993	−12
1994	−25
1995	−12[a]

[a] Projection

Source: EBRD.

produce household electrical goods for the Central Asian market. Simultaneously the restructuring and transforming of the defence complex has begun, but is hindered by a lack of investment funds, out-of-date machinery and a workforce with highly specific non-transferable skills.

Fuel and energy

The extraction and exploitation of hydrocarbon reserves accounted for almost 25 per cent of the republic's industrial production in 1994, a proportion that is set to increase given the international interest shown in some of the world's largest potential hydrocarbon reserves. Research conducted by the World Bank has shown that discovered hydrocarbon reserves stand at 2.1 billion tonnes of oil, 0.7 billion tonnes of gas condensates and 1.7 billion tonnes of natural gas. Estimates of undiscovered reserves (including the Caspian Sea) total 4–5 billion tonnes of oil, 1.6 billion tonnes of gas condensates and 5.9 trillion cubic metres of natural gas. Kazakhstan therefore has the sixth-largest reserves in the world.

The development of Kazakhstan's hydrocarbon reserves is central to the government's plans to bring investment to the country, with large international companies like Chevron, British Gas, BP and others involved in exploratory and extraction projects both on mainland Kazakhstan and in the Caspian Sea. The Kazakhstancaspishelf Consortium of Mobil, British Petroleum, British Gas, Total, Agip and Royal Dutch Shell has been established to explore the potential around the Caspian Sea shelf.

Oil extraction in Kazakhstan rose significantly in the 1960s, rising to present extraction levels of 460,000 barrels of crude oil per day and 8 billion cubic metres of natural gas annually. The further development of the industry's capacity is linked to four main issues:

- Russian control over the only pipeline to external (western markets) and demands for greater shares in profits;
- Russian attempts (backed by Iran) to have the Caspian Sea renamed a lake. This, under international law, would prevent Kazakhstan developing Caspian hydrocarbon reserves without the permission and profit of the other countries bordering the sea;
- Kazakhstan has only three refineries, linked to Siberian oil, thus limiting the manufacture of refined petroleum products. A Japanese consortium is due to begin construction of a new refinery in 1996;
- lack of capital and technology to develop the industry without foreign investment.

Transporting oil and gas to western markets along the existing pipeline through Russia is problematic because of the particularly high sulphur-content oil from Kazakhstan and because the pipeline cannot accommodate increased production. Russia is using its position to try to influence the routes of proposed new pipelines, most of which pass through Russian territory or the politically unpalatable alternatives of Iran, and the ever volatile Caucases. Some experts now believe that a pipeline eastwards to China is not out of the question. Despite the extraordinary length and cost of such a venture, connecting to the Chinese system brings the oil to the growing Chinese, Japanese and South East Asian markets. There already exist joint Japanese-Uzbekistani plans to build a pipeline linking Uzbekistan to the Pacific coast.

Coal is another extremely important resource to Kazakhstan, mostly from the large basins at Karaganda and Ekibastuz, which produce about 103 million tonnes per annum. This coal fuels twenty electric power facilities supplying much of Kazakhstan's industrial and domestic power needs, with the remainder exported to Siberia and the southern Urals. The inter-enterprise payment problem has hit the coal industry (see below), but with annual output over 100,000 tonnes per year, coal will remain crucial to the country's energy policy.

Minerals and metals

The ferrous and non-ferrous metallurgical branches of industry account for approximately 25 per cent of industrial production. The republic possesses 60 per cent of the former Soviet Union's mineral reserves, particularly gold, copper, iron, uranium, chromium and nickel. Production has not declined as much as in other sectors and since 1990 the sector has accounted for a growing percentage of the republic's exports, while the valuable gold output of 12.6 tons in 1993 contributed significantly to the ability of the Kazakhstan National Bank to build up reserves to support its national currency. The 1994 case-by-case privatization programme included sixteen large mining, smelting or refining plants including gold, zinc, bauxite, copper, iron and lead. These embraced some of the largest extraction and refining enterprises in the world: the Balkhashmed copper ore mining, concentrating smelting and production plant, the Donskov chrome mining and concentrating plant and the Ust-Kamenogorsk titanium and magnesium plant. Kazakhstan, however, does not make the most of its reserves. Inefficient separation and purification techniques lead to considerable wastage. So rich are those waste deposits that some foreign companies consider them worth investing in.

Agriculture

Kazakhstan is self-sufficient in a large number of agricultural products, including grain, fresh produce and meat. It exports grain to the CIS, mostly to Russia. Despite its potential, the sector is in desperate need of restructuring if Kazakhstan is not to become a net agricultural importer. This is due to five main problems:

- ecological damage caused by the over-cultivation of the 1950s' virgin lands campaign has rendered much land exhausted and facing desertification;
- the poor condition of farming equipment, the high cost of repairs and the difficulty of acquiring spare parts;
- the scarcity and high cost of seeds and fertilizers because of the decline in inter-state trade and inter-enterprise payments;
- the organization of production around fulfilling targets rather than profitability;
- the wastage caused by inefficient farming practices, storage and the distribution system, linked to the absence of wholesale markets.

Agricultural production dropped by 17 per cent in 1994, and attempts to reform the sector are yet to reap significant results. The transfer of farms to private ownership has been ambiguous because full land privatization has not occurred. This blurred ownership reduces the incentives privatization gives to improve the efficiency and profitability of production. Small privately-owned plots have become more important, but wholescale production has yet to be transformed from the 'at-any-cost' rationale where quotas have to be filled. Many farmers are struggling to identify their potential markets and plan their production on the basis of what can profitably be produced. The system for exporting produce also needs to be simplified. Presently export licences are sold to producers by the state within the framework of inter-governmental CIS agreements and obligations which does not promote the identification of profitable markets and discourages restructuring.

Business and the law

The legislative framework for business activity in Kazakhstan is loose, despite the enactment of a series of laws governing banking, foreign investment, currency operations, bankruptcy and taxation. Many laws are enacted with a view to supporting the short-term needs of an economy in transition, thus frequent changes deny potential investors the stability they require. The law on foreign investment, for instance, now exists in its third form in five years. Second, despite the work of the Union of Entrepreneurs in drafting new business legislation, parliament has been notoriously slow in approving it. Many spheres of activity, therefore, are covered by decrees issued by the president and the Cabinet of Ministers, or remain governed by former Soviet laws.

The Constitution, enacted on 28 January 1993 (and revised following 89 per cent approval at the national referendum of 30 August 1995) is the foundation of the country's legislation. But it too is subject to change. Following the referendum a pliant Constitutional Council has replaced the Constitutional Court, thus consolidating Nazarbaev's power. The government has begun to simplify the many laws and decrees which it has promulgated, including, for example, the latest, more manageable taxation code. However, some crucial issues have still not been tackled, including the right to own land, which has been opposed by Kazakhstan's socialist parties and Kazakh nationalists.

Companies can be registered in Kazakhstan in the form of joint ventures, sole ownership and as limited liability joint-stock companies. Further legislative changes can be expected in order to accommodate various forms of ownership and registration by local and foreign businesses. The ability of law enforcement agencies to uphold the law has been seriously questioned because of rising corruption at all levels of business and government. Good connections are often vital to negotiate the bureaucracy for registration, licensing, transport, taxation and, of course, protection. It is likely that the next few years will see many new legislative changes and that more will be heard about corruption and the 'mafia structures'.

Business and finance

The creation of a firm banking system has long been seen as critical to the establishment of a free market economy. The construction of a professionally-run and reliable institutional structure will reduce reliance on the state, promote privatization, attract foreign investment and develop a securities market to underpin the restructuring of privatized, state-owned enterprises. The republic has seen the emergence of over 200 commercial banks since independence, but few are strong enough to provide investment funds. Instead they compete for credit from the National Bank of the Republic of Kazakhstan (NBRK). Foreign investment and credit are the main sources of investment funds because of the absence of equity and the prohibitively high local rates of interest. Foreign banks have begun to enter the local market, attracted by the expanding oil and gas industry, export and project finance and for specialized commercial ventures.

The National Bank of the Republic of Kazakhstan (NBRK)

The NBRK is in the process of being transformed from a bank subsidizing the economy into an independent central bank. The March 1995 Decree on the Kazakhstan National Bank defines its primary roles as:

- maintaining stability in currency exchange rates;
- keeping inflation low;
- overseeing, licensing and regulating the commercial banks.

The bank has been given the authority to determine monetary policies but must co-ordinate its activities with the Ministry of Finance. The NBRK is central to the present reform of the banking system where its position as semi-independent from state organs will be confirmed. The national bank is ceasing to give subsidies to unprofitable enterprises and the Ministry of Finance has taken sole responsibility for the state budget. The bank and the government will however still consult on decisions concerning monetary and other policies.

Since independence the bank and the government have had to deal with two major tasks. First they have had to grapple with the hyper-inflation of the early 1990s and second, with the problems of introducing a national currency, the tenge. Inflation first appeared in 1991 initiated by consumer price liberalization, but a shortage of consumer goods, continuing large state subsidies and Russia's expansionist monetary policies, caused underlying inflationary pressures to rise dramatically. As a result inflation exploded, reaching monthly levels over 30 per cent through 1992–1994 before declining markedly from 1995 onwards.

The problems caused by the inflationary pressures of the reform programme and the economic legacy of the former Soviet Union were compounded in the summer of 1993 when Russia unilaterally decided to

Table 6.3   *Changes in retail price level (annual average)*

	Retail price level
1990	4.2
1991	90.9
1992	1381
1993	1662
1994	1880
1995	180 [a]

[a] Projection

Source: EBRD.

stop accepting pre-1990 rouble bank notes. An influx of old notes, valued at between 0.5 and 1.5 trillion roubles, ensued. The Russian decision effectively ended the rouble zone and Prime Minister Tereshenko and the NBRK finalized plans to introduce the new national currency, enabling the republic to take full control of its own fiscal and monetary policies. The tenge was introduced on 15 November 1993 at a rate of 4 tenge 68 teen to the US dollar, backed by $1.5 billion of IMF and World Bank support. The tenge immediately began to fall despite strict control of exchange rates. But Almaty's new financial autonomy enabled it to combat inflationary pressures, so that by September 1994 the rate of fall of the tenge had declined. By spring 1995 the exchange rate had remained fairly constant for several months, buoyed by the success of the NBRK in increasing its gold and foreign currency reserves to above US$1 billion, of which less than 25 per cent was foreign credit. Tereshenko's government then reduced monthly levels of inflation to 10 per cent by September 1994. Kazhegeldin's government pursued tighter monetarist policies and by early 1995 monthly inflation had fallen to under 5 per cent despite continuing price liberalization.

Kazhegeldin has also used the reduction of the budget deficit and tighter control of the money supply in the fight to keep inflation low, but further inflationary pressures can be expected when the government concludes price liberalization, especially of domestic fuel prices. The government has cut the budget deficit drastically by halting subsidies to inefficient enterprises and privatizing others. However, there will still be pressure on the government to support many enterprises, in particular to resolve the problem of inter-enterprise settlements which continues to plague many enterprises. The state still employs about 65 per cent of the population and has not allowed high public-sector pay rises. Many state employees frequently do not receive their salaries for several months, thus giving a misleading impression of a balanced budget at the end of 1994. These underlying inflationary pressures will become apparent, sooner or later, possibly due to social pressures (see below).

Commercial banks

Since independence over 200 commercial banks have been founded, ranging from large banks with overseas correspondence relationships to small banks specializing in one sector of the economy. The majority are private local banks or joint-ventures for specialized investment, but in general the commercial banking sector remains weak and the loans extended to enterprises are re-financed by the NBRK through a mechanism whereby the banks bid for credit at frequent auctions. Commercial bank activities are defined by the April 1993 Law on Commercial Banks and the NBRK's authority to regulate and issue various licences has been reinforced in the March 1995 Decree on the Kazakhstan National Bank.

By 1993, twenty-two banks had licences for foreign exchange transactions and one, Alem Bank, also operates as the receiver for hard currency which the state enforces enterprises to exchange into tenge (50 per cent of all hard currency profits). Alem Bank, along with Agroprombank and TuranBank are the three most successful commercial banks. Along with the state Sperbank they account for more than three-quarters of assets held.

Privatization Investment Funds (PIFs)

PIFs have a role somewhat akin to western fund managers who handle portfolios on behalf of clients. The public has a choice of 169 PIFs with which to deposit their Privatization Investment Coupons (PIKs). A PIF uses these to acquire shares in state-owned enterprises. PIFs can purchase up to a 20 per cent stake in a state-owned enterprise at auctions organized by the State Committee for Privatization, as long as the invesment exceeds no more than 5 per cent of the PIFs total capital (investment points). Therefore the PIFs will be forced to co-operate with each other in the restructuring of enterprises. Their importance will grow when restructuring of the economy accelerates and some will clearly become influential financial organizations in the future.

There are plans for a stock market to be established, but until that time western institutions cannot buy into the mass privatization programme, and shares are presently non-transferable. The mass privatization programme has been organized so that Kazakh financial institutions cannot establish investment funds, preventing the commercial banks from becoming owners or share traders, and thus keeping the ownership of, and trade in, securities separate from the debt-side of industries.

Foreign banks

Foreign banks have been moving into the Kazakhstani market providing a range of project and export finance, particularly in the hydrocarbon and mineral extraction industries. The leader is ABN Amro with a large Almaty office, while others include Barclays Bank, Deutsche Bank, National Westminster, Morgan Grenfell and Citibank. The majority of foreign banks operating in Kazakhstan are Turkish and Chinese joint ventures financing projects in specific sectors with the concomitant high risk. The legislative basis for foreign banks has improved with various new laws, including one on bankruptcy, providing a more comprehensive framework. The risks are still high, however, but the possibility of Kazakhstan becoming a capital exporter within twenty-five years continues to be attractive.

Business and the labour market

The Soviet Union used to guarantee full employment, encourage women to work (although few made it to senior roles) and kept a check on internal migration through the 'propiska' system whereby permits were required to live and work in different cities. Like the other former Soviet republics, Kazakhstan is now beginning to experience rising unemployment, a growing non-state sector and urbanization. It also faces the possibility of ethnic tension between the Kazakhs (approximately 42 per cent of the total) and the Russian population (approximately 38 per cent). The latter is largely concentrated in northern regions of the republic, contiguous with the Russian border. Since independence emigration by the Russian-speaking and German populations has increased rapidly due to fears of economic and political discrimination and a belief that a better standard of living can be attained in Russia, the Ukraine and Germany. Simultaneously immigration of Kazakhs, mostly from Mongolia, has risen, but not enough to prevent the total population declining.

Industry remains an important source of employment in Kazakhstan, as Table 6.4 indicates, though it is expected to continue to decline as the opening up to market competition and the reduction in state support eventually force the worst performers into bankruptcy. One of the main problems in this process are the sixty or so 'company towns' – towns where one large enterprise is effectively the sole employer. Most studies conclude that they can be helped through extensive assistance, particularly with regard to the development of small enterprises, but the fact remains many of these towns will inevitably succumb to market forces.

Agriculture is the other major sector in Kazakhstan and, unfortunately, it too has suffered as a result of the moves towards a market economy and problems in the industrial sector. The major agro-chemical and agro-machinery enterprises in Kazakhstan are no longer able to offer credit

Table 6.4 *Employment by sector in 1993 (percentage of total)*

Sector	Percentage
Industry and construction	27.8
Agriculture	25.4
Transport and communications	8.4
Trade	7.0
Health/education, etc.	19.4
Administration and state offices	2.7
Others	9.3

Source: Goskomstat, 1995.

terms to state or private farms which has meant a lack of fertilizers and pesticides, and farming machinery lying idle for lack of spare parts and the need for repair. It is not surprising that agricultural output has, as a consequence of these and other factors, declined substantially since 1991. One bright point, however, has been the rapid increase in agro-businesses being formed alongside newly-privatized state farms and small-holdings.

Demographic trends

The total population had grown steadily, reaching a peak in 1992 of 16.986 million, but since then has begun to decline because of the emigration of Russian speakers and the rising death rate. The birth rate reached a peak in 1987 of 25.7 per 1000 of the population, but by 1993 had declined to 18.6. The rising death rate (particularly amongst middle-aged/elderly men) and falling birth rate mirror trends in other former Soviet republics. Furthermore there is a long-term trend of urbanization.

Emigration by Germans and Russian speakers is possibly the single most important factor influencing the labour market because recent government figures show that between 1989 and 1994 more than 30 per cent of the German population and 7 per cent of the Russian speaking population have emigrated. These people are usually highly-skilled engineers, administrators and semi-professionals whose continuing departure is having adverse affects on economic performance as well as raising doubts about how genuine Kazakhstan's claims to be a demo-cratic multi-ethnic state really are. Russia and Germany are keen to stem the flow of émigrés because of the costs of resettlement, while President Nazarbaev has openly called for more Kazakhs to be trained in these professional and semi-professional roles to redress the traditional imbalance within the labour market.

Table 6.5　*Migration in 1993*

Nationality	Immigration	Emigration	Total
All nationalities	461,393	683,494	−222,101
Kazakhs	252,575	229,085	23,490
Russian	128,181	251,958	−123,777
Ukranian	21,570	38,150	−16,580
German	17,082	101,205	−84,123
Belarus	4,034	7,882	−3,848
Tartar	8,347	13,676	−5,329
Uzbek	3,350	4,921	−1,571

Source: UNDP.

Table 6.6 *Ethnic composition in January 1994*

Ethnic group	Total (thousands)	Percentage
All	16,870	100
Kazakh	7,474	44
Russian	6,041	36
Ukrainian	857	5
German	614	4
Belarus	178	1
Tartar	330	2
Azerbaidjani	102	1
Uzbek	372	2
Others	902	5

Source: Goskomstat, 1994.

The re-settlement of Kazakhs from the diaspora, mostly from Mongolia, has furthered the process of 'Kazakhification'. In 1993 252,575 Kazakhs were settled in Kazakhstan, many in the Russian dominated regions. In general these Kazakhs are not highly qualified or well trained and some have complained that they are being treated as second class citizens. Other demographic factors leading to the Kazakh proportion of the total population growing also include two longer-term trends in the republic; the high birth rate amongst Kazakhs and a lower birth rate amongst Russian speakers. One final factor of importance in the ethnicity of the workforce is that the present constitution holds that Kazakh is the state language and Russian the language of inter-ethnic communication. A ten-year transition period with both languages operating in parallel postpones, but does not solve, the problem that a large percentage of the population will not be able to speak the state language. It is estimated that less than 5 per cent of the Russian population can speak Kazakh. There are also similar moves to make Kazakh the language of state education, phasing out Russian and potentially leaving the population with a linguistically fractured labour force.

Unemployment

The rapid decline of the economy has led to the emergence of unemployment and the transitional restructuring period will keep the rate rising. There is no doubt that the potential for serious unemployment exists in Kazakhstan if stricter financial conditions were imposed on enterprises who would then be forced to cut back on employment in a big way. However, as in the other transition economies, the government has drawn back from such drastic measures in order to minimize the serious social and political pressures which would otherwise have been evident.

Estimates of unemployment in Kazakhstan have to be treated with care because of the unemployment registration system, the prevalence of hidden employment (and unemployment) and the large numbers of people who are on forced extended leave from bankrupt enterprises. Official state estimates at the end of 1993, however, put the figure at between 39,800 and 80,000 people, although in December 1994 the Ministry of Labour maintained that 66,700 people were registered unemployed. The official unemployment figure is artificially low because the Ministry of Labour employs a narrow definition of 'unemployed' and there is a strict unemployment registration procedure. Furthermore the high costs of severance pay discourages redundancies and the low value of unemployment benefits do not encourage people to register. Perhaps more reliably the EBRD estimated real unemployment to be running at 9.3 per cent for 1993 and 11 per cent for 1994. The regions with the highest levels of unemployment, on any measure, are the Semipalatinsk, South Kazakhstan and Atyrau oblasts.

In an effort to tackle rising unemployment and to further the restructuring of the labour market in line with the republic's economic reforms, the government established the Public Employment Service (PES) in July 1991 to provide training, job-creation programmes and a system of unemployment benefits. With offices and staff throughout the country, the PES matches the registered unemployed with vacancies, registers the newly-unemployed, organizes and co-ordinates training schemes, and administers the system of severance and unemployment benefits.

The training schemes have had mixed results, with full-time training programmes in 1993 registering 68.7 per cent of participants placed in jobs after completion, while only 12.3 per cent of people on subsidized, short-term, public works projects who left the scheme in the first half of 1993 found employment. The contraction of the Kazakhstani economy and the limited funds available for such schemes restricts their success. However the aim is to prevent some of the long-term unemployed feeling a sense of alienation, provide a natural step for some into the labour market, and provide a benefit to the community that, although expensive in the short term, will be cost effective. International agencies like the World Bank have recognized the growing social consequences of the economic reform programme.

The informal sector

The informal economy and black markets were prevalant in Kazakhstan under the old regime, as in other parts of the former USSR, because of the general scarcity of goods and services. Since the late 1980s Kazakhstan has experienced a rise in the number of people who find employment outside the state sector. In 1985 the state employed 96 per cent of the working population with the remainder working in co-operatives, but by 1992 the state accounted for only 71.4 per cent and the private sector had risen to 15.2 per cent. These figures show a trend which will continue, but nevertheless are probably not a true reflection because of the huge growth in unofficial and unregistered work performed by both public and private sector employees. It is extremely difficult to estimate the growth of the informal sector, and perhaps more importantly the value of its contribution to people's incomes. It is increasingly becoming clear that in urban centres a growing percentage of the population hold a state job which no longer provides the majority of their income and that this constitutes a very powerful 'push' factor leading to the increasing prevalence of informal sector activities. Also important, however, are 'pull' factors associated with the influx of foreigners and the growth of wealthy individuals who require the development of a service sector.

Business and trade unions

Traditionally trade unions in Kazakhstan were another branch of the command-administrative system. The transition to a market economy requires new trade unions as Kazakhstan begins to experience unemployment, low wages, long arrears in wage payment and the marketization of industrial relations. Disputes to date have focused on single issues, for example the 1995 miners' strike over wage arrears, and have not become politicized to the extent of demanding a change of government. However with social inequality rising and standards of living falling it is probable that there will be many more disputes in the republic which may threaten the economic reform process, the fragile ethnic peace and the government's tight fiscal policies. The absence of an effective arbitration mechanism raises this possibility, although to date only the miners have mobilized effectively.

Legislation

In 1993 Kazakhstan enacted a Labour Code which guaranteed workers the rights to organize, strike and have freedom to join a union of their choice. However there has not been much of a shift from the state-organized unions to the new independent unions under the umbrella of the National Independent Trade Union Centre. The unions levy a 1 per cent charge on workers' pay at source which the workers can choose to have transferred to an independent union. The state-organized unions also control the workers' pension funds (30 per cent of salaries deducted) and disability allowances.

Under the labour code unions can bargain on behalf of their members with the management over contracts, and should an agreement not be reached, then arbitration ensues with a panel representing the management, the union and independent experts. The efficiency of this system is hard to determine, but it is unlikely that any unions other than the miners have such strong bargaining positions to take into negotiations. Rising unemployment and extended leave as a result of inefficient enterprises closing down have seriously undermined the position of workers.

Disagreements

Kazakhstan's coal miners' unions are the most militant and have a bargaining position which derives from the fact that Kazakhstani coal fuels most of the republic's electricity generation supplying industry and domestic consumers not only in Kazakhstan but also in Siberia and the southern Urals. In January 1995, the independent miners' unions of two companies in Karaganda and Ekibastuz (both Russian-dominated regions) began indefinite strikes having rejected a government proposal which did not meet their principal demand of payment for the four months' owed wages. Ninety-eight per cent support led to the cessation of all work at the mines, deliveries stopped and the government became involved in arbitration between the unions and enterprise managers. The strike then spread to other mines in the Kazakh-dominated south of the country where some miners occupied their mines for several weeks.

Business, education and training

The education system in Kazakhstan, as inherited from the Soviet Union, is considered to be well developed, but rapid reform is required if the country is to have enough educated young people to take on the challenge of the transition to a market economy. A deep crisis in morale has set in because of funding cuts and teachers have realized that their salaries are shrinking in comparison with other professions. Those who have marketable skills, especially foreign languages, seek work outside the education system giving rise to a brain drain, especially from universities. Students also find it extremely difficult to live on their stipends and many have begun to doubt the value of a university education because of the inability of the state to guarantee work. Moreover they witness daily the success of many young people who have highly-paid business jobs. The present crisis aside however, one of the prime benefits of the Soviet era was the development of a strong education system which brought literacy to the masses and used to offer prestige to successful academics.

The education system

Over 3 million pupils between the ages of 6 and 17 attend schools every year while a further million under 6 attend kindergartens. During secondary education some schools provide an all-round education supplemented by specialization in one subject. Before reforms began Kazakhstan had two universities, fifty-nine higher education institutes, 243 specialist secondary institutes and 482 vocational and technical institutes which trained and educated about 1 million students with the skills required for the republic's economy. Many students from Kazakhstan also studied in other republics, particularly at more prestigious universities in Moscow and Leningrad. The collapse of links has generated higher demand for places in Kazakhstani institutions, which has led to polytechnics and institutes becoming specialized universities conferring diplomas after six years study. While the names of institutions have changed, and contact and exchanges with foreign institutions are now frequent, the development of new curricula in line with the republic's needs has barely begun.

One of the most pressing problems the republic faces is the shortage of highly-trained managers and administrators. While some managers, administrators, politicians and bureaucrats of the former system display admirable enthusiasm for reform, they are, it is believed, simply unable to implement it and responsibility ought to be handed down to the growing generation of young educated entrepreneurs. The development of business courses is lucrative and a target for foreign donors in an attempt to educate the managers and entrepreneurs of the future. The Kazakhstan Institute for Management and Economics is the leading institute, supported by President Nazarbaev and western donors, which provides MBA courses in English to over 100 students each year.

Business and the environment

Kazakhstan has four key areas of environmental concern, which the government recognizes require both domestic and international attention. However, the harsh economic transition period precludes the government from embarking on any major ecological programmes by itself. The Ministry of Ecology and Bio-resources plays an active role in introducing environmental projects into contracts with major international investors and is also developing international programmes, largely with other Central Asian states. The preservation, conservation and rehabilitation of the environment are not yet highly attractive commercially but given the republic's high levels of pollution and potential future wealth it is only a matter of time. Until then businesses are facing ever-increasing government demands for environmental protection in new contracts and projects. There is a law which requires companies to take responsibility for the pollution they cause, but the limited resources for monitoring make enforcement infrequent, if at all. The four key problem areas are:

• the rapidly shrinking Aral Sea, whose area has decreased by half, exposing three million hectares of land this century;
• desertification as a result of intensive agricultural practices on the arid steppe land in the centre and north of the republic;
• pollution from enterprises. Soviet enterprises were structured along a production at all costs basis which entailed little or no regard for water, air and land pollution from large metallurgical and other industrial plants;
• fallout from nuclear testing near the Semipalatinsk testing site.

Aral Sea

Kazakhstan, Turkmenistan and Uzbekistan have agreed to co-operate in addressing the irrigation problems concerning the Aral Sea. A three-year programme was developed in August 1994 under the aegis of the World Bank and UN agencies which aimed to tackle the environmental problems around the Aral Sea at an estimated cost of US$220 million. However the three states have been slow to invest the money required to implement the plan.

Desertification

The problem of desertification is linked to the shrinking Aral Sea, but covers a wider area, largely due to the means used to implement the virgin lands agricultural campaigns (1954 to 1960). The campaigns brought millions of hectares under cultivation, requiring miles of irrigation systems that denied water to the rivers feeding the Aral Sea and surrounding basin. Erosion and desertification of cultivated land due to over-intensive agricultural practices now renders much land useless for cultivation and unable to support the natural grazing environment that existed prior to the campaigns.

Pollution

Air, water and land pollution levels in some industrial regions of Kazakhstan are amongst the highest in the former Soviet Union. The oblasts of Ust-Kamenogorsk, Karaganda and Dzezkazgan have industrial enterprises and plants which extract and refine a range of metals and minerals (including heavy metals) with little concern for the environmental consequences. The health problems of employees are now being highlighted, but in some cases with enterprises located in residential areas, the options for a town dependent on the enterprise are few and bleak.

Nuclear testing

From 1949 to 1991 a total of 466 nuclear explosions took place in Semipalatinsk before President Nazarbaev halted testing after pressure from the Nevada-Semipalatinsk environmental movement. These included tests at ground, and underground level and aerial tests, such that radiation levels across a huge, populated area have reached levels sometimes reportedly higher than at Chernobyl. The area has infant mortality rates and leukaemia levels well above the national average and radiation is so widespread that the levels of some radioactive particles in milk are between 25 and 530 times above the norm. Some estimates of deaths and disfigurements due to the testing have reached millions. While the other former soviet republics were spawning independence movements, Kazakhstan's opposition focused on halting nuclear testing. As a signatory of the Nuclear Non-Proliferation Treaty, Kazakhstan relinquished any rights over the nuclear weapons on its territory as a result of the fragmentation of the Soviet Union, and its brief period as a nuclear power has ended, although it still possesses huge natural uranium reserves.

Conclusion

Kazakhstan has emerged from the dissolution of the former USSR in clearly a rather shaky position. In spite of substantial reserves of oil and gas as well as other raw materials, its economic development remains uncomfortably dependent upon the Russian Federation, which sees a continuing strategic and commercial role for itself in Kazakhstan and Central Asia as a whole. Particularly with regard to the development of the oil and gas industry, Kazakhstan has come up against Russian intransigence as Russia attempts to secure a major commercial presence in Kazakhstani industry. Moreover, the legacy of the old planning system is a continuing heavy Kazakh dependency upon Russian technology and equipment which is proving problematic in practice yet difficult for technical and financial reasons to curtail in favour of domestic or other foreign, especially western sources.

Compounding the above difficulties, Kazakhstan has only achieved moderate success in its moves towards developing a modern market economy. The privatization programme has been slow to produce tangible results in terms of any increased efficiency of privatized former state assets and demonopolization. New private-sector development has been held back by a combination of factors which include a lack of financial support, the absence of opportunities for business with the state sector and the very poor appreciation of standard business and entrepreneurial skills. The level of foreign investment has also been miserly and has not led so far to the hoped-for revitalization of the Kazakhstani business sector through the absorption of more advanced technologies and business practices and greater access to financial resources and market opportunities.

As in the other transition economies where the initial reform period has produced severe economic dislocation rather than immediate positive results, the emerging business culture in Kazakhstan appears to be characterized by a short-termist perspective, an unhealthy spread of corruption and a preference for trading activities over production. The old bureacratic-administrative business culture is becoming sidelined partly because a more entreprenuerial-style business culture is taking root throughout Kazakhstan but also because the manufacturing base from which the old business culture emerged is collapsing. The continuing problems encountered by the manufacturing sector cause particular discomfort to many Kazakhstanis since the economy is already heavily dependent upon imported manufactured goods and equipment, especially from the Russian Federation, and the level of unemployment is increasingly starting to become a serious political and social problem. And it remains a moot point whether or not the wealth likely to be generated from the oil and gas sector will be enough to compensate for this import dependence and the relative scarcity of manufacturing sector employment.

Nevertheless, in the absence of significant foreign investment and other domestic sources of economic activity, the increasing 'Kuwaitization' of the Kazakh economy remains the most immediate chance for economic progress if revenues accruing to the government coffers can be recycled into economic development and other measures which promote a healthy and competitive market economy. It must be remembered, indeed, that oil and gas propelled many desert kingdoms into the modern world in a very short space of time, so Kazakhstan does have successful models to follow. It remains the supreme test for the Kazakhstan government to ensure that such models will be followed. If the government can use expected revenues to restructure and build upon the existing economic base in Kazakhstan, then it can also facilitate the sort of business infrastructure, enterprise sector and, ultimately, business culture which will complement the gains represented by the oil and gas sector and will provide for stability and economic success in the long run.

Acknowledgements

The author would like to express his gratitude to Dr G. Andrusz for his valuable comments and suggestions on earlier drafts of this chapter.

References and suggestions for further reading

Akiner, S. (1996) *The formation of Kazakh identity.* Royal Institute of International Affairs, London.

Dixon, A. (1994) *Kazakhstan: Political reform and economic development.* Royal Institute of International Affairs, London.

Dorian, J., Zhanseitov, S. and Hartono Indriyanto, S. (1994) The Kazakh oil industry: a potential critical role in Central Asia. *Energy Policy,* **22** (8) 685–698.

EBRD (1995) *Transition report.* EBRD, London.

International Monetary Fund (1995) *IMF Economic Review: Kazakhstan.* IMF Washington DC.

World Bank (1993) *Kazakhstan: the transition to a market economy.* World Bank, Washington DC.

7 Comparative analysis of Eastern European business cultures

Milford Bateman

Introduction

The country studies presented here show that, after more than six years of the transition, the fundamentals of a market economy appear to have been successfully established throughout Eastern Europe. The earliest transition economies – Poland, Hungary and Czechoslovakia (and then the Czech Republic) – appear to have weathered an initial recessionary storm relatively intact and with the prospect of sustained growth in the near future. Slovenia, the small former Yugoslav republic on the borders of Italy and Austria, is making excellent economic progress. Its neighbour, and also former Yugoslav republic, Croatia, has suffered because of the conflict which engulfed the Balkans from 1991 to the end of 1995. But it too is beginning to make significant economic progress and it will no doubt become one of the economic success stories of southern Europe. Even the countries of the former Soviet Union, which for so long suffered under one of the most rigid and inefficient variants of communism in Eastern Europe, have made some progress in dismantling the old system and constructing its replacement.

However, though the emerging market economies of Eastern Europe may appear to be more consumer-friendly than their immediate predecessors, this apparent progress is deceptive: living standards have actually tumbled in almost all cases, in some catastrophically. The vast publicity given to the enormous increase in the availability of consumer goods, especially western branded goods, diverts attention from the fact that only a small section of society is actually able to purchase these goods regularly and that for the majority such purchases remain sporadic. Poverty has increased to unprecedented levels, unemployment has become a major worry for many and the previously generous social welfare system has been all but dismantled. Moreover, for much of the former Soviet Union, the apparent progress remains subject to abrupt reversal. Major worries still remain over the prospects for Russia and Kazakhstan. They are apparently still in economic freefall, with few signs of any significant improvement in living standards for anyone except a newly enriched business class. If this decline is not brought to a halt soon, the political consequences could be extremely damaging. Already an unsettling degree of authoritarianism is emerging in Russia and Kazakhstan, and in Russia extreme left- and right-wing parties have enjoyed significant electoral support.

Early expectations of the transition

If the communist systems throughout Eastern Europe appeared to vanish swiftly not long after the fall of the Berlin Wall, building replacements has so far proved to be much more difficult. The moves towards a market economy were supposed to produce thriving post-communist economies characterized by a high degree of integration into world markets, substantial private ownership, genuine market competition and efficient industry and agriculture. Economic improvement was seen as critical for underpinning the establishment of political democracy. And, crucially, progress was expected to be quick: once the fundamentals of the market economy had been introduced all that was required was to let the new private business sector 'get on with it'. At the start of the transition in 1989, some commentators expressed caution and stressed the need to proceed slowly. But this view was held by only a small minority, and anyway ignored by the major international funding agencies, which preferred a faster road to reform. Most commentators, from both Western and Eastern Europe, predicted a rosy future for Eastern Europe and one which would not be long in coming.

The progress made in Eastern Europe has not, however, as a rule, lived up to local expectations or academic forecasts. The rapid decommissioning of the old system of central planning was supposed to lead to major efficiency gains as enterprises and individuals were forced quickly to adapt to the market environment. But the results were immensely disappointing: every one of the transition economies experienced a major recession and severe economic dislocation. Inflation exploded everywhere, serious unemployment appeared where before there had been none, industries and enterprises shrivelled in the face of the instant surge of Western imports, investment fell dramatically and the social fabric has been seriously damaged. The incidence of poverty has increased dramatically. The ILO's 'World Employment 1995' study refers to a 'poverty explosion' in Eastern Europe, as a new class of working poor is created out of the remnants of the planned economies. The Central European economies have been hit hard, with the numbers of people below the offical poverty line increasing in both Poland and the Czech Republic in particular. A much worse situation exists in the economies of the former Soviet Union. Russia is faring very badly.

Official government estimates put over 80 per cent of the Russian population below the official poverty line. The Central Asian republics have done even worse. Five years into the transition and not one of the Eastern European economies had recovered the general level of living standards prevailing in 1988, and none are predicted to do so for at least ten years.[1]

Moreover, if we leave aside the immediate costs of the transition, it is also not readily apparent that the East European economies have established the necessary pre-conditions for sustained future growth and prosperity. The experience of the most successful regions and countries elsewhere[2] indicates that economic development appears to depend on two key features: a dense network of state and quasi-state financial and other economic development institutions, and national and local state intervention to promote capital accumulation and to facilitate longer run development objectives. Yet the East Europeans were encouraged instead to adopt radical free market policies, a central tenet of which is that an active state represents a sinister continuation of the old failed system of central control. Amsden *et al.* (1994) note that in some cases they were actually prohibited from establishing institutions used to very good effect elsewhere, as in the case of development banks.

The transition in Eastern Europe has not been a peaceful process either: it has instead precipitated some of the worst conflict and inter-ethnic bloodshed since the Second World War. The dissolution of Yugoslavia beginning in 1990 and the ensuing conflicts resulted in a humanitarian disaster of near biblical proportions. Though it appears that peace has been achieved at long last, the myriad of territorial concessions, relocations and transfers associated with the Dayton Peace Agreement, signed in December 1995, will continue to destabilize the region for some time to come. The break-up of the Soviet Union also gave rise to a number of smaller, but persistent and economically disruptive conflicts.

[1] Rollo and Stern (1992) calculate that Poland, Hungary and the Czech Republic, on optimistic assumptions, may possibly recover 1988 living standards by 2002, or 2012 on pessimistic assumptions. For the other transition economies they suggest an even longer time period. We should be careful here, however, since it is sometimes claimed that the measurement of 'living standards' under the old system perhaps favourably overstated the real position.

[2] By 'elsewhere' we mean Germany, Japan, the Scandinavian economies and the East Asian economies. We also include regions such as Emilia-Romagna (Italy), Baden-Wurttemberg (Germany) and Mondragon (Spain) (see, for example, Pyke and Sengenberger (1992) *Industrial Districts and Local Economic Regeneration*, International Institute for Labour Studies, Geneva; Whyte and Whyte (1988) *Making Mondragon*, ILR Press, Ithaca, New York).

Economic policies and progress

In this section we will consider the overall policy perspective and then detail some of the results.[3] After a decade or so of economic stagnation and falling living standards in Eastern Europe, the reform programmes after 1989 were expected to deliver prompt economic results. It was a great surprise to most people in the region (including most economists) when the Eastern European economies very quickly went into serious recession after the onset of reform, and living standards appeared to decline even further. A degree of pain was always seen as an inevitable element of the restructuring, but it was assumed that this period would be short as the benefits and opportunities created by the reforms began to kick in.

Shock therapy versus gradualism

Two basic perspectives on transition were evident at the start. The first, and the one which became the conventional wisdom, was associated with the 'shock therapy' approach, or 'big bang'. This approach stressed the need for a very rapid introduction of market forces into the Eastern European economies to pressure institutions, enterprises and individuals into making immediate changes. It was thought that enterprises would quickly improve their products, cut costs and search for new markets in order to survive without guaranteed state orders and subsidies. Individuals no longer given the security of guaranteed employment in bloated state enterprises would work harder to remain in work or, better still, take advantage of new business freedoms to go out and establish a business of their own. Underpinning such a recipe was an almost religious belief in the efficiency of markets and their ability to lead rapidly and independently to the best possible economic solution. Some pain was unavoidable, but it would be short and therefore politically manageable.

The alternative was a slower version of 'shock therapy', the 'gradualist' approach. This approach favoured a more gradual phasing in of the 'shock' in order to allow institutions, enterprises and individuals a breathing space in which to restructure, relearn and reinvest. Gradualists tended to be more sceptical of the efficiency of markets, especially when dealing with the chaotic results of a fifty- to eighty-year communist economic experiment gone wrong. It was felt that rapid change and economic destabilization would equally undermine both efficient and inefficient institutions, industries and enterprises in Eastern Europe – rather in the way that a flash-flood washes away all swimmers to their

---

[3] For a much more detailed economic analysis of the transition one should consult, for example, Gros and Steinherr (1995) *The Winds of Change: Economic Transition in Central and Eastern Europe*, Longman, London.

doom, whereas a gradual rising of the water level at least allows the swimmers to survive (and possibly to assist the non-swimmers). In addition, a more measured approach to reform was considered much less likely to precipitate a popular reaction to the reforms which could end up stopping them in their tracks, or worse, signal a return to the old system.

Poland was the first country to adopt 'shock therapy', in 1990, with the Balcerowicz Plan, named after the then Finance Minister Leszek Balcerowciz. As Blazyca points out in Chapter 3, it rapidly cut public spending, virtually eliminated all subsidies, introduced a tough incomes policy, opted for an immediate devaluation to promote exports and removed most foreign trade restrictions. The shock when it came was heavy, with GDP falling by more than 18 per cent over the two years 1990–91. Czechoslovakia also claimed to be in the 'shock therapy' camp, though the high degree of government intervention and the delay in implementing some of the measures makes this a somewhat questionable proposition. Dangerfield draws attention in Chapter 1 to the level of interventionism in the Czech Republic, particularly in the labour market. At any rate, Czechoslovakia suffered initially, in terms of high inflation and a rapid decline in GDP and industrial production. Since the break-up of Czechoslovakia there has been a marked divergence in the perceived economic prospects of the two sucessor states, with the Czech Republic seen as more prosperous. Hungary is usually considered to have been the first 'gradualist' reforming economy since, as Edwards emphasizes in Chapter 2, its post-1989 reforms were really a continuation of reforms begun in the 1960s. But its post-communist reform programme was in parts both 'gradualist' and 'shock therapy'. It was softer than those in the other transition economies in that it was implemented over a two-year period, starting in 1990. Its initial devaluation was mild (only 15 per cent compared to Poland's near 33 per cent devaluation) and price liberalization was less drastic since it built upon earlier liberalizations. However, Hungary's industrial and competition policy was increasingly harsh, with bankruptcy being enforced in practice, with rapid trade liberalization and with state support being curtailed sharply. It thus suffered in much the same way as its two early reforming partners, with unemployment increasing and GDP and industrial production slumping.

Slovenia and Croatia applied 'shock therapy' in the monetary sphere, since inflation was accelerating ahead unchecked as they left the collapsing Yugoslav Federation. Tighter monetary policy, incomes policies and a stronger currency to reduce import costs were part of the package. Industrial policy, however, was more 'gradualist', with the governments taking the decision to spin out the time intended to restructure the enterprise sector in order to avoid additional unemployment. Unlike Slovenia, however, Croatia was still dealing with the bitter conflict, substantial war damage and the need to provide humanitarian assistance on a large scale, which were associated with the break-up of Yugoslavia.

Russia and Kazakhstan started out as 'shock therapy' adherents in 1991, abandoning central planning, liberalizing the majority of prices and lifting many trade restrictions. The intention was also rapidly to reduce the enormous overhead represented by the provision of subsidies to the largest and most inefficient industrial sectors. When it became clear in Russia that such a policy would also very quickly create up to 15 million new unemployed persons,[4] it was soon moderated. Industrial policy became more 'gradualist', enterprises and industries carried on receiving assistance and the level of unemployment remained comparatively low.

A case of too much, too soon?

Despite the obvious differences in approach, and with the possible exception of Hungary, the early reform programmes were largely described as 'shock therapy'. They all implemented major changes in a very short period of time, especially the abandonment of the planning system and price and trade liberalization. Was this extreme haste the reason why the transition economies slumped so much so early in the reform process, or were there other reasons?

Some of the blame for the extreme decline in output can be attributed to external events – the principal one being the collapse of the communist trading bloc, the CMEA, and the introduction by the Soviet Union in 1991 of hard-currency payments for its exports. Trade within Eastern Europe slumped. A study by Rodrik (1993) found that these events accounted for a very large share of the early recession in Hungary and in Czechoslovakia, and to a lesser extent in Poland. The studies of these three countries in this volume all draw attention to the damage done as a result of the CMEA's collapse. The former Soviet states experienced an even greater trade slump, as they also had to contend with the collapse of the Soviet Union and the disruption caused to the trading links between them. Moreover, since the Soviet Union had also been propping up many of the republics via the extensive use of subsidies on its traded goods, especially raw materials and energy, its dissolution left the majority of the new republics with neither trade nor aid.

However, it can be argued that the policy of rapid change brought on much of the ensuing recession. More accurately, it proved highly destructive to tear down the old systems and institutions, whether very fast ('shock therapy') or at a more leisurely pace ('gradualism') before their replacements were in place and functioning as intended. Even

---

[4] The figure comes from an ILO study of the Russian economy reported in the *Moscow Times*, 7 November 1992.

though the old planning systems were themselves highly inefficient, and on the verge of collapse in some cases, they still provided essential guidance to, and communication between, those enterprises which allowed them to function. Three aspects of the overall shock therapy package were especially severe in their effects on the enterprise sector. First, almost instant price liberalization led to near hyper-inflationary conditions everywhere and, since the indexing of wages is always slow to respond, a fall in real wages. The immediate result was a collapse in consumer spending. Moreover, this occurred at precisely the moment when most enterprises were tentatively taking the first steps towards restructuring, identifying real consumer demand and formulating efficient responses. Some argued that this was necessary in order to improve the competitiveness of the Eastern European economies, and as a form of counter-inflationary demand management. The exception to this consumer-spending slump scenario was Hungary, where the effect on consumer spending was not as marked because real wages were held relatively steady.

Second, rapidly increasing inflation led everywhere to a payments crisis, since enterprises had to meet the immediate higher cost of inputs before they were able to recoup the increase from the sale of their final product. Short-of-cash enterprises took to demanding payment before delivery. Both the state and the banks were unwilling to help out with short-term credit assistance, particularly in Poland and Czechoslovakia, since restricted access to credit was a component of their shock therapy package. This had three principal effects: many enterprises cut production because payment in advance was not forthcoming; many enterprises cut production because of a lack of inputs caused by the first effect; and the rate of investment slumped as enterprises were forced into diverting available capital toward wages, which ultimately led to a cutback in demand for capital equipment. Subsequently, enterprises tried to get around the difficulties by issuing and accepting credit notes between themselves, but a lot of the damage had been done.

Third, the rapid dismantling of the planning system left many enterprises in a vacuum: they neither knew who their suppliers were nor who were their customers. They had very little knowledge of marketing, quality control, cash management, supply chain management and selling. Yet simultaneously, most East European governments undertook extensive foreign trade liberalization. This led to an influx of western competitors who took advantage of the confusion to establish themselves. They were able to knock out of the market many long-standing enterprises which were in temporary difficulty, and also to hinder the establishment of indigenous enterprises geared to changing domestic demand patterns.

It is relatively straightforward to argue that the speed and rigour of the early reform packages in the transition economies created a number of problems, such as those highlighted above. What we should also consider, however, is the extent to which such problems were likely to be as painful or, worse, be exacerbated in the event of a more gradual and relaxed reform programme being adopted. We can go on to explore this thorny question a little more by examining the main macroeconomic variables.

Employment

Given the extent of over-staffing in Eastern European industry, a widespread rise in unemployment was expected as enterprises slimmed down to levels in keeping with their counterparts in the west. Unemployment duly shot up in all the transition economies as this restructuring began.

Poland's shock therapy programme in 1990 induced a rapid increase in unemployment over the next three years. Hungary, in spite of its arguably more cautious approach, experienced a similar rise. The former Yugoslav republics of Croatia and Slovenia followed suit a little later, with Croatia registering significant unemployment by 1995, mainly because of the conflict. Czechoslovakia saw unemployment rise steeply in 1991, but for the new Czech Republic unemployment has been remarkably low. The separation from Slovakia at the end of 1992 seems to have been one possible factor. Slovakia had by far the most inefficient industrial profile, and thus the highest propensity to create unemployment, and on the dissolution of Czechoslovakia it had to support its industry without recourse to subsidies from Prague. Indeed Slovakia's unemployment figure did rise immediately on separation and had reached nearly 15 per cent by 1995 compared to the Czech Republic's 2.9 per cent (EBRD, 1996). Russia and Kazakhstan appear to have avoided serious open unemployment so far. One possible explanation of the generally low figures here may be that many people simply do not bother to register as unemployed because of the non-existence of any benefit entitlement from the state. Table 7.1 indicates the growth in unemployment in the economies in question.

The figures indicate a serious unemployment problem in Eastern Europe, except for the Czech Republic, Russia and Kazakhstan. One of the more serious aspects of this unemployment is the growing percentage of long-term unemployed. The ILO (1995) reports for Poland that of those unemployed in 1994 around 44 per cent had been unemployed for more than one year and in Hungary the bulk of the unemployed had been so for more than six months. It appears that a disproportionate number of women have become unemployed. Bruno points out in Chapter 5 that the position of women in Russia has become extremely difficult on account of the limited job opportunities but also because they are being forced back into more traditional roles as the previously emancipating social welfare

Table 7.1   *Unemployment rate (in percentage of labour force, year end)*

	1990	1991	1992	1993	1994	1995[a]
Poland	6.1	11.8	13.6	15.7	16.0	14.9
Czech Republic	0.8	4.1	2.6	3.5	3.2	2.9
Hungary	2.5	8.0	12.7	12.6	10.9	10.4
Slovenia[b]	4.7	8.2	11.6	14.4	14.4	13.8
Croatia	na	na	12.9	12.8	12.6	12.5
Russia	0	0.1	0.8	1.1	2.1	3.5
Kazakhstan	0	0	0.5	0.6	1.6	2.4

[a] estimate
[b] annual average

Source: EBRD (1996) *Transition Report Update.*

system crumbles. One final feature concerning the regional distribution of unemployment is causing much anxiety. Owing to the excessive concentration on giant enterprises throughout Eastern Europe there are far too many examples of 'one-company towns' – towns which literally have only one employer. If these employers are to go, and many are destined for drastic employment cutbacks or even closure, the social impact will be severe.

One mitigating factor pointed out is the existence of the 'grey economy'. It is certainly possible that the 'grey economy' has become a safety net for substantial numbers of the unemployed, thus reducing the possibility of serious social pressures. Blazyca suggests that this may be a factor behind the acceptance of very high unemployment in Poland. Bartlett and Bateman offer a similar conclusion in relation to the very high official unemployment in Croatia and Slovenia, and Bruno notes the widespread acceptance of the 'grey economy' and the substantial amount of unreported '*mafiya*' business activities in Russia (see Chapters 3–5).

However, the key point which emerges in the country studies is that, faced with the real prospect of mass unemployment, many of the transition economies appeared to lose their nerve and to back down on reform promises to stem the flow of subsidies to industry. This is clearly evident in the apparently much better employment performance of Russia, Kazakhstan and the Czech Republic, and in the desire of the other transition economies to avoid even higher rates of unemployment. The Czech Republic, in particular, instituted a radical and comprehensive labour market policy, in the shape of its Active Employment Policy. This was significant in containing unemployment from 1992 onwards. Jackman and Rutkowski summarize the general situation throughout Eastern Europe as being '. . . an uneasy compromise between (a) the explicit objective of ending financial support to loss-making state enterprises and (b) the political pressure to avoid mass layoffs and large-scale unemployment' (1994, page 147). For sure, internal pressure from the bureaucratic/administrative elite to renege on reform promises was very strong. But social pressure was also growing from those without work and, more importantly, those still in work but afraid of a future without work. The tardiness throughout the transition economies in establishing social safety nets, making the prospect of job loss virtually life-threatening in some cases, further exacerbated the situation.

Dangerfield points out that the Czech trade unions have so far tended to tolerate wage restraint policies in return for the government's strong anti-unemployment stance. This has involved continued, and very often unreported, support for industry in the form of a postponement of bankruptcy legislation and the discretionary use of subsidies. In Russia, Bruno comments on how the old bureaucratic/administrative culture remains very antagonistic to change and has played a part in the drive to retain much of the current capacity of Russian industry. Russian managers have set up a number of pressure groups and political parties to promote their preference for gradualism in reform. Taylor reports a similar pattern of behaviour in Kazakhstan, with managers preferring to put workers on enforced holidays and short-time working rather than make them redundant.

It is interesting to note that even in those countries experiencing high unemployment, there is evidence that elements of the old business culture act as a constraint on redundancy and closure programmes. Bartlett and Bateman show that in Croatia and Slovenia the new private sector owners and managers retained some of the cultural constraints associated with the previous worker self-management system and genuinely consider it their responsibility to avoid redundancy wherever possible.

Inflation

Like unemployment, inflation was an expected effect of the reform programmes in Eastern Europe, although in some cases, for example in Poland, it was already a major problem as a result of the increasingly soft macroeconomic policy which preceded the collapse of communism. Dismantling the system of state-controlled prices was expected to lead to instant price increases as now profit-conscious producers raised prices to market clearing levels. The key longer-term objective of this price liberalization and the subsequent price adjustments was a more rational system of relative prices which would allocate resources in a more efficient manner. For instance, one of the major distortions of the pricing system under communism was the low price of energy, which encouraged extremely wasteful production practices throughout Eastern

Europe. This was especially costly to the former Soviet Union since it provided the bulk of the energy requirements of the Eastern European countries at below world market prices during certain periods. The opportunity cost to the former Soviet Union of not directing its energy exports, especially oil and gas, more towards Western Europe was significant.

In the short term, however, governments had two major policy concerns related to the coming inflationary surge. First, there was the need to check the emergence of a potentially destructive wage-price spiral. Second, there was the problem of the 'monetary overhang' to consider. This was cash intended for everyday purchases but instead involuntarily accumulated by consumers over time because, especially by the mid-1980s, there was very little to purchase. Price liberalization, and the subsequent inflation, would obviously neutralize the so-called 'monetary overhang' – but just how much inflation was required?

The most visible and immediate effect of the initial price liberalizations was the rapid disappearance of the queues, waiting lists and other forms of non-price rationing so ubiquitous in pre-reform Eastern Europe. Less visible, though equally welcome, was the immediate neutralization in most of the transition economies of the 'monetary overhang' and much of the accumulated debts incurred in domestic currencies. But the consequences of this neutralization were also painful, as savings balances were devalued very quickly in the general absence of any protective measures. In the former Soviet Union this was particularly severe, with pensioners losing a lifetime's savings.

The general pattern in the Eastern European economies appears to have been that they all experienced an increase of inflation in the early period of reform, much higher than expected, but that inflation was brought under control several years later. The exceptions were Poland and the former Yugoslav republics, which inherited substantial inflation from the pre-reform system, though they too were to bring inflation under control. Some of the transition economies attempted to manage the increase in labour costs in order to slow down the anticipated wage-price spiral, though also with the aim of providing for a fall in real incomes in order to boost competitiveness. Incomes policies were a major feature of the Polish, Croatian and Russian reform programmes while tax-based and trade union negotiated wage restraint measures played a part in Czechoslovakia. Other counter-inflationary measures included providing for a stronger currency, thus cutting the cost of imported items and providing additional competition for domestic firms. By 1995, inflation throughout Central Europe had largely subsided, including Croatia's conflict-induced bout of hyper-inflation. Only the former Soviet economies have yet to really overcome the problem, though they have at least been successful in emerging from the hyper-inflationary phase.

Table 7.2 *Retail/consumer prices (end-year) percentage change*

	1990	1991	1992	1993	1994	1995[a]	1996[b]
Poland	249	60.4	44.3	37.6	29.4	21.6	19
Czech Republic	18.4	52	12.7	18.2	10.2	7.9	8 [c]
Hungary	33.4	32.2	21.6	21.1	21.2	28.3	22
Slovenia	104.6	247.1	92.9	22.9	18.3	8.6	6
Croatia	136	149	937	1150	−3	3.7	5
Russia	na	143.9	2318	841	203	131	45
Kazakhstan	na	49.5	1176	2169	1160	60.3	26

[a] estimate
[b] EBRD forecast
[c] annual average

Source: EBRD (1996) *Transition Report Update.*

The answer to why inflation in the states of the former Soviet Union was and is so difficult to tackle, can be found by referring back to the previous section on employment. There we pointed out the general tendency throughout the Eastern European economies for governments to avoid a more rapid increase in the rate of unemployment by agreeing to continue the provision of subsidies to industry. This became the main source of inflationary pressure in most countries. Given that taxation and other government revenues had declined substantially, by and large the only source of cash for these subsidies was simply the issue of money – the 'inflation tax'. Governments had the standard inflation–unemployment trade-off to consider and, for a variety of reasons, some of which we have alluded to above, they much preferred to experience the former rather than the latter. Inflation raged in Russia, reaching several thousand per cent on a yearly basis, as the Central Bank turned out billions of roubles: but serious unemployment has been, for the time being, averted. Even though Kazakhstan abandoned the use of the rouble in order to avoid the inflationary excesses of the Russian Central Bank and other former Soviet states still printing and using roubles, this did not curtail inflation: once it had its own currency in place it simply went on supporting its own industries through its own 'inflation tax'. But in Poland, where 'shock therapy' was applied perhaps in its purest form, inflation, after an initial 'liberalization surge', did decline dramatically; slowly, later, unemployment increased. The Polish authorities at the time were the most single-minded of all in their determination to bring inflation under control.

Trade

In creating single production centres catering for the input requirements of the entire economy, or even of the entire CMEA, the East European central planners created an extremely vulnerable system of trading arrangements. Two events related to the abandonment of communism quickly exposed the weaknesses of the system: the collapse of the Soviet and East German markets and the introduction of hard currency trade within Eastern Europe. As we noted above, the collapse of the Soviet market alone, it has been argued, accounted for a sizable part of the almost immediate collapse in output and employment in the early transition economies – Poland, Hungary and the Czech Republic. Intra-CMEA supply chains were severely disrupted as planned trade between the various countries was abandoned. Now-independent enterprises had to operate on their own and re-establish contact with suppliers and customers, all of whom now had the additional option, if they could pay, of turning to the western economies for suppliers and customers. The change to hard-currency payments exacerbated the situation with regard to imports from the Soviet Union and its successors.

For the early transition economies, this trade disruption was not meant to present too great a problem since it was assumed that they would anyway wish to reorient their trading links towards Western Europe, and the European Union in particular. The experience of other restructuring economies points to the fact that export-led growth is the primary way towards fashioning long-run economic success, as was the case in post-war Germany, Japan and the East Asian economies. And in fact

Table 7.3   *Trade balance (in US$ millions) in 1995*

	Exports	Imports	Balance
Poland[a]	16,634	17,501	−867
Czech Republic[a]	12,300	14,900	−2,600
Hungary[b]	7,273	9,957	−2,684
Slovenia[b]	5,316	6,080	−764
Croatia[b]	2,987	5,071	−2,084
Russia[c]	32,167	20,635	11,532
Kazakhstan[d]	3,300	4,100	800

[a] figures are for August 1995
[b] figures are for August 1995
[c] figures are for July 1995
[d] figures are for year end 1994

Source: Business Central Europe, January 1996; EBRD Transition Report 1995.

significant movement has been made in this direction, with sizable percentage increases in exports to the EU registered in Poland, Hungary and the Czech Republic. The EU now accounts for over half of exports and imports of the Central European transition economies, up from approximately a 10–20 per cent share prior to the collapse of the CMEA. Impetus for this increased trade came from the 'Europe Agreements' signed between the EU and the Eastern European countries at the end of 1991, and the General System of Preferences treatment offered to Eastern European countries, both of which eased entry to the EU market for a wide range of products.

Total export trade of Poland, Hungary and the Czech Republic, from mid-1994 to mid-1995 amounted to around US$15.4 bn, of which just over a half went to the EU (*Business Central Europe*, July/August 1995, page 65). It has not reached as high a level as was earlier hoped, partly because of the onset of recession in the west as the reforms got underway, and partly because the EU made fewer trade concessions to the transition economies than expected.[5] As a result, more or less since the beginning of 1993 all have experienced trade deficits. Table 7.3 shows that by late 1995 the trade balances in Poland, Hungary and the Czech Republic were all in deficit by, respectively, $0.9 bn, $2.7 bn and $2.6 bn. Thus, for the three major Central European countries, trade with the EU has been valuable, and has gone some way toward filling the gap left by the collapse of CMEA markets. However, a worrying structural imbalance is becoming more and more evident with respect to the three countries: their exports are mainly, and increasingly, low-value-added items and raw materials, while there is an increasing dependence upon imported technology and consumer goods.

Lagging a little way behind the shift to Western European markets was a movement to re-establish trade with the Soviet Union and its successor states through barter arrangements. This was especially useful to those Eastern European economies most dependent upon Soviet oil and gas. However, the large increase in barter trade between the former communist countries was only a temporary solution at best. Moreover, the increasing inflow of consumer goods into Eastern Europe was beginning to circumscribe market opportunities for local producers. Negotiations began in February 1991 to try to restart trade between the transition economies. This was to be done by setting up the Central European Free Trade Area (CEFTA), which included Hungary, Poland, the Czech Republic and Slovakia. CEFTA's first actions were in April 1993

---

[5] The Eastern European countries would have liked free trade in basic heavy industry products, such as textiles, steel, coal, chemicals and so on, where they were especially competitive relative to the EU competition. Brussels resisted, and continues to resist this, because of fears about the employment effects in the EU regions.

and involved tariff reductions between member states. It is too early to tell whether CEFTA will have an important impact on trade in Eastern Europe.[6] In view of their relative failure to penetrate western markets for manufactured goods, Eastern European producers share a strong incentive to rediscover opportunities for such trade with their CEFTA neighbours.

Croatia and Slovenia, never members of the CMEA, nevertheless suffered a CMEA-type 'shock' when the internal market collapsed along with Yugoslavia in 1991. Both were heavily dependent on raw materials and intermediate inputs from the republics to the south and their economic decline resulted partly from these supply chains being broken. Their immediate response was also similar to the countries described above, namely to turn westwards for suppliers and markets. They too have been reasonably successful in making inroads into the EU market, particularly in their neighbours Austria and Italy. This has cushioned the blow resulting from the collapse of Yugoslavia, but the previous level of interdependence will inevitably speed up the resumption of trading links with their old Yugoslav neighbours.

In Russia and Kazakhstan, the immediate situation remains bleak, although the future may be very bright. The collapse of the former Soviet Union in 1991 precipitated a collapse in exports to its neighbouring transition economies. As we noted above, the Eastern European economies were unable to get sufficient hard currency to pay for Russian imports. Second, there has been a sizable growth in the import of consumer goods in the former Soviet Union, which in part reflects the parlous state of domestic manufacturers. Even more so than in the Central European countries, Russian and Kazakh producers were quite unprepared for the influx of foreign competition and were unable to secure the necessary resources early enough in order to restructure and compete. In Russia, for instance, the share of foreign imports in consumer goods purchases went from 12 per cent in 1991 to 56 per cent in 1995, though the figure is probably very much higher if unofficial imports are taken into account (*Economist*, 13 April, 1996). Third, and generally irrespective of the need for hard currency, the traditional supply chains linking Russia with its former communist neighbours disintegrated more than in the transition economies of Central Europe. The results were severe. For instance, the oil and gas producing region of Tyumen in western Siberia traditionally obtained much of its equipment supplies from Azerbaidjan, but independence meant that it was now dealing with

---

[6] CEFTA appears to have coincided with an impressive revival of mutual trade, and the growth of the Visegrad states' trade with Slovenia, with whom they all have free trade agreements, expands the positive impact of intra-regional trade liberalization. See, for example, Dangerfield (1996) The Economic Opening of Central and Eastern Europe, *Journal of European Integration*, Vol. XIX, no 1.

a foreign country. This led to a multitude of problems – currencies, bureaucratic obstacles, tax and so forth – with the result that in 1993 an average of 30,000 oil wells were not working at any one time because of the severe shortage of spare parts and equipment.[7] Given that oil and gas is so important to Russian reform, such disruption to its oil equipment supply chain has clearly had an enormous negative impact on the Russian economy. Most supply chains are gradually being reconstituted in Russia, linking it back to its CIS neighbours, but the intervening confusion has been extremely destructive for all concerned and it will take many years before new, market-based supply chains are in place.

In the longer term, of course, Russia and Kazakhstan have enormous potential for developing further their energy exports, in particular oil and gas. Though this objective requires immediate and large-scale injections of capital, the strategic and economic importance of these assets – they are often referred to as the 'crown jewels' – means that domestic and foreign capital is becoming more widely available. For example, the biggest sums of foreign capital flowing into Russia and Kazakhstan have gone into oil and gas joint ventures. However, both countries are also wary of the 'Kuwaitization' of their economies and of the over-dependence on raw material exports. Table 7.3 indicates that Russia has a healthy trade balance, but the apparent export success is mainly because of the extent of raw material exports: exports of manufactured goods, especially engineering goods, have declined. Of course, raw material exports over the next decade or so will generate substantial revenues which could be directed towards restructuring and diversifying of the industrial base as has been done in some of the Gulf states.

Growth

In view of the unimpressive picture in regard to employment, inflation and trade, it should come as no surprise that growth rates everywhere in Eastern Europe tumbled after the onset of reform.

If we consider first the individual progress of the Eastern European economies after the reform, we can see that the three early reformers, Poland, Hungary and Czechoslovakia, all suffered a decline in GDP from 1990 onwards. Positive growth rates were achieved in 1992 for Poland and 1994 for the other two; 1995 was a year of slight growth for all; and the projections for 1996 and beyond are of improved growth rates, though less so for Hungary. Slovenia achieved positive growth in 1993 and looks set to become one of the best-performing countries in Eastern Europe. As Bartlett and Bateman point out in Chapter 4, this revival was expected. Slovenia benefits as a small country with exporting ambitions since

---

[7] *Source:* British Embassy, Moscow. The same sort of decline occurred in the large oil and gas fields in north western Kazakhstan.

Table 7.4   *Real GDP growth in Eastern Europe*

	1990	1991	1992	1993	1994	1995[a]	1996[b]
Poland	−11.6	−7.6	1.5	3.8	6.0	7.0	5.5
Czech Republic	−0.4	−14.2	−6.4	−0.9	2.6	5.2	5.5
Hungary	−3.5	−11.9	−3.0	−0.8	2.9	2.0	2.0
Slovenia	−4.7	−8.1	−5.4	1	5.5	5.1	5
Croatia	−8.6	−14.4	−9	−3	0.8	2	5
Russia	na	−13	−14.5	−8.7	−12.6	−4	3
Kazakhstan	−0.4	−13	−14	−12	−25	−8.9	1

[a] EBRD estimate
[b] EBRD projection

Source: EBRD (1996) *Transition Report Update.*

carving out a small slice of foreign markets is relatively easier than for its larger neighbours. It also has large current capacity and potential in the tourism industry. Croatia, too, has major potential in tourism, as well as in other industries, but it has been unable to realize it fully because of the regional conflict.

Recovery is underway for the Central European economies, but what still remains the subject of fierce debate is the **sustainability** of the recovery. In the previous section we pointed out that the experience of other restructuring economies seems to indicate that the primary method of achieving long-run economic growth is increasing the export of manufactured goods. Are the apparent recoveries in Eastern Europe based on this, or are we seeing a temporary recovery from a very low base? Some of the evidence was also examined in the previous section, and the issue of whether Eastern Europe can export its way to success in the EU was discussed. Moreover, the necessary infrastructure and level of state support which enabled other countries, for example in East Asia, to achieve manufactured goods export-led growth is missing in Eastern Europe.

Real problems exist, however, in the cases of Russia and Kazakhstan. The collapse in output continues and no return to positive growth is expected until perhaps the end of the century. This scale of economic contraction has very little but negative consequences. Though there may be a case for the immediate closure of some of the so-called 'value-subtractors' – enterprises which actually produce a product *less* valuable than the inputs which went into making it – very much more of the economic fabric of these countries must be retained in some form if they are to remain serious industrial powers. De-industrialization is a serious prospect in Russia and Kazakhstan.

Could export-led growth ensure a return to positive growth for Russia and Kazakhstan? The export-led model clearly has some relevance, if we refer to *all* exports, since raw material exports are increasingly the mainstay of both economies. However, the possibility of diversification and relying more upon manufactured exports is a remote one. Both countries have fallen so far behind in terms of technology, marketing, innovation and so on, that it is probably impossible to undo quickly the effects of several decades of decline, as well as several years of post-reform collapse. A further reason is the fact noted above, that the domestic market has to a large extent been captured by foreign competitors. Indigenous manufacturers will surely find it very hard to claw-back a significant domestic market share and thereby to derive economies of scale. What seems more likely, therefore, is that they will continue to be edged out of advanced technology markets by the big western economies – Germany, Japan, the USA – in spite of heroic defence conversion programmes.[8] Mass production markets will be dominated by the East Asian economies, principally South Korea and Taiwan. Already South Korean corporations have made substantial inroads into both the Russian and Kazakhstan markets for motor vehicles and consumer electronics.

Privatization

Why privatize?

From the very start, the transition economies laid great stress on the importance of privatization.[9] The dominance of state ownership and control of industry was seen as one of the fundamental sources of inefficiency in communist economies. Typically, the state was unable to manage its individual assets properly because it simply had too much to deal with and did not respond well to the need to innovate, upgrade and invest. Nor could it accept the need for a constant recombination of assets – closures and new starts, redundancies and new hiring programmes, retooling, re-equipping, retraining, and so on – which is a driving force in market economies. In short, as an owner, the state wished to maintain the

---

[8] The military-industrial complex represents a major concentration of technology which could be put to commercial use. However, little has been achieved so far. A recent OECD report (*Science, Technology and Innovation Policies: Federation of Russia* (1994) Vols I and II) noted how the best technologies were being bought up 'on the cheap' by the Americans. Just as bad, even new smaller high-technology enterprises formed relatively recently were giving up and moving over to trading activities only a few years later.

[9] For a very much more comprehensive treatment of the issues see, Estrin (1994) *Privatization in Central and Eastern Europe*. Longman.

status quo and not to complicate the planning process any more than was necessary.

The main economic goal of privatization, therefore, was simply to remove assets from state control – to 'depoliticize' them – and put them in the hands of private owners who were assumed to be more efficient and responsible. Private owners would encourage financial responsibility in the enterprise because they had their own capital tied up in its success or failure. Private owners were also considered to be more entrepreneurial than existing state enterprise managers, who were trained in the rigid and inflexible bureaucratic/administrative business culture characteristic of most of the former communist economies of Eastern Europe.

However, it is debatable whether private ownership *per se* has brought about a higher level of efficiency. Probably as much evidence supports the idea that it is the regulatory framework and market structure which determine enterprise performance. Moreover, the special conditions in Eastern Europe may require more substantial support than most private owners are willing or able to provide. All this suggests that there is a role for the state in the restructuring of the enterprise sector, as in post-war Germany and Japan and in the more recent history of the East Asian economies.

Some governments were also interested in financing various state operations out of the proceeds from privatization. Following the lead given by the Thatcher Government in the UK in the 1980s, governments almost everywhere in Eastern Europe were hoping to generate cash. Some of this would be spent on refloating social welfare programmes increasingly being passed over to the state by cash-strapped enterprises. Pensions and support for the unemployed and women with children are costly expenditure items for governments, even under more propitious circumstances. In some countries the cash was earmarked for economic development programmes and enterprise restructuring. However, such visions of wealth remained a mirage for many of the transition economies, since in reality they lacked the substantial private wealth which could have been used for widespread share purchases. This was one of the main factors, alongside the need to privatize quickly, which justified the use of vouchers in the privatization programmes of several of the transition economies, including former Czechoslovakia and Russia. If raising cash was to remain a major priority, there was a need to find foreign buyers. Many enterprises in Eastern Europe were indeed sold off to foreign, mainly multinational enterprises, and for considerable sums of money, especially in Hungary.

There was also a political reason for supporting privatization (and for making it as rapid as possible) related to the desire to entrench the movement to the market economy firmly in society. It was thought that a newly-enriched middle class would evolve out of the privatization programmes, either through the purchase or give-away of shares in formerly state-owned assets, and that this class would provide a measure of social stability. Key existing social groups to be targeted were managers and workers in large state enterprises. In many of the privatization programmes, for example in Russia, a constituency of support for the reforms was ensured by providing for substantial worker/manager shareholdings. This social change would also serve the purpose of underpinning the rapid growth of new private businesses, which have been subjected to intense criticism from those working in industry because of their high prices. Taken together, the growth in private property and the emergence of an entrepreneurial business culture is generating a middle class with a stake in the emerging market economy. Thus political support for further forward movement is created, as well as making the reforms difficult to reverse.

Sequencing – privatize then restructure, or vice versa?

The problem of 'sequencing' was a key issue at the beginning of the reform period. Two alternative privatization scenarios were proposed, based on differing conceptions of the best way to combine privatizing and restructuring. In the first scenario, the state restructures the enterprise, and only then proceeds to privatize it. In this process, the state should attempt to prioritize its limited resources in such a way as to protect and support those sectors and enterprises which have the best chance of competing on the market. Once this has been achieved, it can sell off the enterprise to new private owners. It would also have an important role in closing down those enterprises, or parts of enterprises, which have no commercial future and which are a drain on the government budget; parts of the enterprise could be spun-off into smaller-scale independent business units and sold off. The second scenario envisages the government privatizing an enterprise as it stands, and then allowing the new private owner(s) to undertake whatever restructuring and internal reorganization is necessary for success in the market economy. It is argued that the new owner(s) put up the capital, technical and managerial resources needed to restructure, and that they would show more resolve in standing up to dissatisfied employees seeking wage increases and resisting unemployment. Quick privatization will also provide less of an opportunity for existing managers to plunder state assets for their own gain.

In practice, both approaches had their drawbacks. The problem with the first was that in Eastern Europe, government officials and enterprise managements had been thoroughly discredited. Many refused to see them as being able to play any constructive role in righting the economic wrongs they were responsible for creating. After all, one argument ran, if they had had any real idea about how to promote greater efficiency in an enterprise, why did they wait until the collapse of communism to implement such ideas? In the 1980s they had actually resisted the introduction of market-based reforms, and changes within the enterprise, until the very end. Could these very same people now be relied on to manage the reform process and economic restructuring of the enterprise sector? Moreover, new non-communist governments and new enterprise managers did not want to be responsible for restructuring because the process promised to create social problems – unemployment, reduction of social services and so on: they no doubt preferred that the new private owners take the blame.

But the second approach also had a number of drawbacks. The new private owners generally wished to abandon all the previous agreements made with the workforce over pay and conditions, in order to restore competitiveness. This tended to generate resistance to change among employees probably more than had the state taken the measure to do this. More important was the resistance of the existing managers to changes proposed by the new owners, indeed they tended to resist change more than their employees. This was why many of the privatization programmes were designed to offer significant shareholdings to managers. There was also the problem of valuation. It was very difficult to calculate the market value of an un-restructured enterprise.

Privatization in practice

Two broad types of privatization were launched at the initial phase. 'Small-scale privatization' involved the sale of small-scale production units, retail and catering outlets, usually by local government. In all the transition economies, this process was rapid and encountered few real problems. Local governments were keen for the process to move quickly since they benefited from receiving some, if not all, of the cash generated by the sales. Any problems usually concerned the origin of the cash used for the purchase. So-called 'nomenklatura' cash was one of the major sources (money illegally acquired by members of the 'nomenklatura', or governing elite, by virtue of their position within the hierarchy). This caused some resentment, since it meant that the political elite was making too smooth and untroubled a transition to becoming an economic elite. Other sources of cash, as in Czechoslovakia's 'dirty money' scandal, included organized crime groups from abroad. More problems occurred, however, with the second type of privatization – 'large-scale privatization'. This involved the sale of the 'dinosaur' enterprises, over-loaded with a whole host of problems – slow, indebted, inflexible, with outdated equipment, low productivity and over-staffing. We concentrate on this type of privatization in the following pages.

Dangerfield points out in Chapter 1, that in Czechoslovakia most economic policy makers believed that the inefficiency of the communist system derived principally from the lack of effective ownership rights. If this was the case, then the remedy was clear: a very rapid transfer of state assets to the private sector. A variety of methods were used by the government to accomplish this, including public tender, direct sale and free transfer, but it was the innovation of 'voucher privatization' that attracted most attention. Books of vouchers or coupons were distributed for a nominal charge to all citizens, to be swapped for shares in newly privatized enterprises. The more valuable an enterprise, the more vouchers had to be given up in exchange for one share. At a stroke, state property had been converted into private property – by mid-1994 around 80 per cent of the economy had been placed into private hands – and the transfer appeared to have been achieved through a market auction which avoided the thorny issue of enterprise valuation.

More than in any other country, Poland's privatization programme was subject to long delays and numerous changes brought about by a succession of ministers. Initially the programme was more concerned with value for money, than with the speed of transfer to private owners. The programme to privatize individual enterprises began in mid-1990 through so-called 'capital privatization', which involved selling off successful state enterprises either through flotation on the new stock exchange or direct to large investors. This method was slow and complicated, but had the advantage of yielding considerable sums of money. In order to speed things up, however, the Polish government subsequently introduced new routes to privatization, with what was known as the 'Article 19' and 'Article 37' measures. As Blazyca makes clear in Chapter 3, these were meant to provide for rapid privatization but they were not fast enough for the Polish government, and discussion soon turned to mass privatization. As a result of political in-fighting, a mass privatization programme did not get underway until mid-1995. The chosen method consists of the transfer of state property to fifteen National Investment Funds (NIFs) via a lottery process. The NIFs will be able to restructure the newly acquired enterprises as they see fit, possibly making use of international financial assistance. At the end of 1995, the task of selling shares in the NIFs themselves to Polish citizens began.

As with Poland, Hungary initially favoured a privatization process which aimed at raising revenue for the state but also allowed enterprise managers to have substantial autonomy to undertake the privatization process within their enterprise as they saw fit. The early legislation encouraged managers to spin off part of the assets of the state-owned enterprise into smaller, more efficient, units. The results were disappointing, however, as managers were able to undervalue the assets being disposed of and purchase them through private companies in which they had a stake. Larger enterprises tended to be partially sold to a so-called 'strategic partner', usually a foreign enterprise, which at least fulfilled the revenue raising goal. Most recently, however, the Hungarian government has moved toward introducing voucher schemes similar to those used in the Czech Republic and also has put much more emphasis on Employee Share Ownership Programmes (ESOPs) similar to those in Slovenia and Croatia.

Slovenia's privatization programme (Chapter 4) reflects its past history of worker self-management: it has focused upon selling to insider groups (workers, managers), with outsiders being involved in those cases where the asset value of the enterprise was simply too great to be absorbed by the insiders. Bartlett and Bateman highlight, in particular, the operation of the Development Fund. This body received two-tenths of the shares of privatized enterprises and used these assets to assist in the restructuring of other enterprises and for the provision of soft loans. In view of the general absence of such proactive agencies in the transition economies, the operation of this body may provide a useful model for others. A broadly similar privatization plan was put into operation in Croatia, largely for the same reasons. Substantial worker shareholdings were built up through a system of discounts and by using hard currency accounts which had been frozen by the banking system at the time of the collapse of Yugoslavia. After the war had been brought to a conclusion, privatization by share-offering became a much more important mechanism in Croatia.

Finally, Russia and Kazakhstan followed the policy pioneered by Czechoslovakia (and then continued by the Czech Republic) of introducing a privatization programme based on voucher privatization. More than in the other countries discussed, it was considered that most citizens would not have the financial resources to support a general sell-off of the enterprise sector. In Chapter 5 Bruno reports on the widespread rise of worker/manager shareholdings as a result of the programme in Russia, partly as a result of managers simply declaring the enterprise to be a joint stock company and issuing shares to themselves. Regulation was weak. In several cases an investor has paid for a shareholding in a Russian enterprise only to be taken off the share register by the Russian enterprise managers at a later date when they took a dislike to outside participation in 'their' enterprise's affairs. The lack of effective regulation and legal redress has frequently been cited as one of the key reasons holding up foreign investment in Russian industries. In Chapter 6, Taylor refers to similar concerns in relation to the privatization programme in Kazakhstan, which has demonstrated a relative lack of success in attracting foreign investment. The latter has also been discouraged by Russian intransigence in negotiations over Kazakh access to Russian pipelines and other facilities.

The results of privatization

If one judges the process as one designed simply to effect ownership transfer then privatization has indeed been a major success story: the

Table 7.5 *Estimated private sector share of GDP, mid-1994*

	Percentage
Poland	55
Czech Republic	65
Hungary	55
Slovenia	30
Croatia	40
Russia	50
Kazakhstan	20

Source: EBRD (1995) *Transition Report Update.*

amount of private sector activity as a proportion of total GDP in most of the Eastern European economies has risen enormously. In many, if not most countries, the private sector now accounts for more business activity than the shrinking state sector.

One of the main expectations concerning the privatization pro-grammes, however, was that they would lead to changes in the way enterprises were operated, with private owners taking an active part in managing their newly acquired assets. This expectation underlies what is referred to as the 'corporate governance' argument for the transfer of state property to the private sector. The evidence for major changes in enterprise behaviour is mixed. In general most newly privatized enterprises are now better managed, more responsible and more entrepreneurial. It is clear that there is an enormous number of private enterprises and managers who are very successful.[10]

However, there remain many problems to deal with. The degree of change in management style has been over-estimated in many regions. Moreover, it seems that very little of the improvement which has taken place can be traced back to the change in ownership. Lamenting the lack of capital and real owners, one study termed the privatization process so far 'voodoo privatization' and a means whereby a few people can get very wealthy, very quickly.[11] The EBRD also concludes that change of ownership through mass privatization has 'so far produced only limited, primarily reactive, restructuring' (EBRD, 1995, page 128). It still remains far too easy for enterprises, both state and privately owned, simply to raise prices in order to generate profit, rather than to cut costs by

[10] Most of the business journals focusing on Eastern Europe, for example *Business Central Europe* and *Central European*, regularly feature newly privatized enter-prises now achieving notable success.

[11] *Economist* (18 November 1995) Central Europe: Survey.

becoming more efficient. Managers do not appear to share the kind of entrepreneurial business culture where making redundancies appears natural. Concerned about the likely social effects on their employees, they often try all manner of alternative remedies rather than cutting jobs. They are helped to take this soft option because of the continuing subsidizing of industry and the high degree of monopolization in some sectors. In many industries internal competition does not exist, and foreign competition has largely not materialized. Often even where foreign multinationals have invested in local capacity they have done so on condition that the host government protects them from foreign competition using tariffs and quotas.

Some industries have also retained the previous cosy state-management relationship, where enterprise managers work closely with their regional and local government counterparts, conspiring together to protect the old monopolies held by the former state enterprise. One study of the Russian economy (Hanson, 1993) describes how local and regional government officials often act as 'gate-keepers', deliberately frustrating the new entry of enterprises which would compete with existing ones with which they have a working relationship. This underlines the difficulty of overcoming the habits of the old bureaucratic/administrative elite, who continue to look for government assistance instead of developing a more entrepreneurial outlook. It also suggests that anti-monopoly measures need to be given far more prominence in the reform programmes than has hitherto been the case.

Part of the reason why the new private sector tries to keep close ties with local and central governments, especially in Russia, is that it faces a major difficulty which the privatization programmes have not properly addressed – the non-availability of capital. Just as in Western Europe after the Second World War, Eastern Europe is in need of major infusions of capital in order to restore its dilapidated infrastructure and restructure its collapsing industries. Early hopes that the East European economies would get their own 'Marshall Plan' or at any rate find significant injections of capital through privatization, international assistance and through foreign direct investment, have been disappointed: the amounts currently being provided are very small in relation to the problem at hand. The result is that the majority of enterprises have been converted into private ownership without the new owners having any real access to the fresh injections of capital necessary to restructure. In very many cases, therefore, private enterprises have been forced to return to the state for further subsidies (directly, or indirectly through the banking system), because the capital lending institutions which have been established so far remain extremely reluctant to invest in anything other than very short-term, high-payback projects. On the whole, the East Europeans are left to face the consequences, as Amsden *et al.* (1994) put it, of '. . . creating capitalism without the capital'.

A further, probably more publicized, phenomenon surrounding the privatization programmes has been the issue of corruption and favouritism. The term 'spontaneous privatization' came into being to describe the system whereby managers of state enterprises were effectively transferring public assets to themselves and their partners. Several abuses in Hungary, as Edwards notes, led to major changes in the privatization legislation (see Chapter 2). One case in particular, that of the wholesaling and retailing company Apisz, was instrumental in bringing about a radical change in approach to enterprise valuation, after the incumbent managers tried to sell it to themselves at a very favourable price indeed (EBRD and CEEPN, 1993). The Russian and Kazakhstani privatization programmes have been widely criticized because of the repeated transfer of state assets to current managers and to vested interests, with little transparency, accountability or legal procedure.

The rise in worker share ownership

Finally, a few comments about one of the most interesting, and possibly important, common features of the privatization programmes identified in the country studies – the large number of worker buy-outs and worker share-holdings.[12] In some cases, this feature was built into the programme in response to trade union pressures, as with Solidarity in Poland. As Blazyca remarks, worker-manager buy-outs became the predominant form of ownership in Poland in the 1990s. In Hungary there had been significant worker participation in enterprises prior to the post-communist reforms and workers expected to retain some stake. The new policy of the Hungarian government since 1992, as Edwards points out, has placed increased emphasis on employee share ownership programmes. In Croatia and Slovenia, Bartlett and Bateman note, the inheritance of the worker self-management system led to worker-shareholdings becoming an important feature of privatization programmes from the start. At least partly this was a desire to appear fair and equitable, since to have done otherwise would have amounted to enterprises being completely taken away from the workers who had been the nominal owners under the old system. They go on to point out that in Slovenia the end result of the privatization programme is likely to be that most enterprises will function with majority worker-ownership. In Russia and Kazakhstan too, manager-worker ownership has emerged as a significant feature of the post-privatization landscape, though here it may be mainly a consequence of the incumbent managers simply trying to

---

[12] For a comprehensive survey of the issues in Eastern Europe, see EBRD and CEEPN (1993) *Management and employee buy-outs in central and eastern Europe – an introduction.*

reduce the possibility of external shareholder power in order to further entrench their own control.

What are likely to be the economic results of these trends toward worker-ownership? Apart from obvious considerations of fairness and equity, it is likely that the main benefit from worker shareholdings will be increased motivation and productivity on the part of the workers – the enterprise is, at least partly, 'their' enterprise. Some of this motivation will come from the greater willingness to invest 'sweat equity' – that is time, insider-knowledge and effort, which is critical at times of great disruption (e.g. in a post-war period) to the building of a successful enterprise, but in most conventional enterprises goes largely unrewarded. On the other hand, worker shareholdings could act as a brake on any necessary job cuts within the enterprise, since managers and workers will be reluctant to agree to a restructuring plan which could involve their own redundancy of that of their colleagues. The new owners may attempt to raise their own wages above the market rate for the job and to eat into profit which would otherwise have been earmarked for re-investment purposes. It may also be the case that the incumbent managers are simply not up to the task of leading their enterprise into the market economy, perhaps because they were politically appointed managers rather than those most objectively qualified for the job. Worker buy-out firms may also have difficulty in raising external finance, a problem familiar to worker co-operatives in western economies.

Small-business development and entrepreneurship

The rapid establishment of completely new private businesses was considered central to the success of the reform programmes. Such a development generally exerts pressure on the large state-owned enterprises to restructure while also providing a source of employment growth to absorb the redundant workers such restructuring will inevitably generate. A study by Boeri (1994) pointed out that small enterprise creation mainly involved those making the break from the large state-owned enterprise sector in a form of 'job-to-job transition'. Ideally, of course, there should be a match between the rate of redundancies and the rate of employment creation in small enterprises, though this has not been achieved in the transition economies, as their high levels of unemployment demonstrate.

If the reform programmes have made uneven progress at the macroeconomic level, at least progress has been made in terms of small-scale private business development: the increase in small business activity throughout Eastern Europe has been substantial. This has resulted in significant job creation, income generation and increased consumer goods supplies. The larger enterprise sector has also benefited from the growth of flexible, dynamic and efficient small-scale capacity which it can integrate into its supply chain. At the same time, small enterprise development has given rise to a flourishing entrepreneurial business culture.

Several of the East European economies under consideration have demonstrated impressive growth in the small business sector. It is not surprising that Poland appears to be at the forefront. First, it had a very rich entreprenuerial culture prior to the imposition of communism. Moreover, this culture was not entirely undermined during the communist period, but instead given some freedom of expression in the form of one of the largest 'grey economies' in Eastern Europe. Second, the Polish communists retained private agriculture, where surpluses conventionally underpin the rise of small business activities.[13] Blazyca indicates that the small business sector boomed after 1989, and it was this growth that was the critical factor in the rapid transformation of the Polish economy from a state-run economy to a private-sector-led one. The rise in the share of private sector employment from only 12 per cent in 1989, at the start of Poland's transition, to more than 61 per cent by the end of 1994, is an indication of the change which has taken place. Of course, as Blazyca concedes, some of this private sector growth has been achieved through privatization and a high proportion is accounted for by small traders 'buying cheap and selling dear' and making only a very marginal contribution to economic growth. Nevertheless, the fact remains that the small business sector in Poland has emerged after fifty years to spearhead the push to a market economy.

Hungary and the Czech Republic also saw the private sector increase rapidly. These countries also had a rich entrepreneurial culture in the pre-communist period, having been within the orbit of the relatively economically developed Austro-Hungarian empire. However, in communist Czechoslovakia private sector business activities were far more regulated than just about anywhere else, and 'grey economy' activities were clamped down on severely. Thus the initial conditions were much more unfavourable in comparison to Poland. Nevertheless, Dangerfield points to a massive seven-fold expansion in small private businesses in Czechoslovakia only one year into the transition (though from a very small base).

Hungary had the advantage of having permitted small-scale private enterprise much earlier than either Poland or Czechoslovakia, especially in the reforms of the 1980s, and this may account for the impressive expansion in the small business sector in the early years of the transition.

---

[13] For example, this mechanism largely accounts for the rapid growth of small private business activities in China (see, for example, the excellent chapter on China in Goldman (1994) *Lost Opportunity: Why the reforms in Russia have not worked*, Norton, New York).

It is apparent, however, that this earlier start was not financed by substantial 'grey economy' capital, as was the case in Poland: the Hungarian economy remained more or less under firm macroeconomic control towards the end of the 1980s, whereas in Poland the accelerating inflation, price differentials and other economic distortions created a 'hot-house' atmosphere and the possibility for individual entrepreneurs to make a lot of money.[14] On the other hand, there was strong encourage-ment in Hungary for private business activity to be integrated within the state owned sector, and this had the big advantage that small enterprises were able to develop business relationships with large state-owned enterprises and gain a bedrock of demand upon which to grow, especially in the manufacturing sector.

Slovenia and Croatia have both been successful in developing the small-scale private sector, in spite of both having to endure the after-effects of the collapse of Yugoslavia – the destruction of the large internal market and the economic disruption brought on by the subsequent conflict. They share with Hungary and the Czech Republic a history under the Austro-Hungarian empire. In addition, as Bartlett and Bateman stress, Yugoslavia showed probably the most tolerance of all the East European economies for both legal private business development and for 'grey economy' activities. Since the reforms began, Slovenian small businesses have had a favourable legislative climate for development. Neighbouring Austria and Italy have proved to be exceptionally good markets for Slovenian produce. In Croatia the current high level of business taxation, some of it in the form of 'war-taxes', has perhaps had a dampening effect on official private business development, driving much economic activity into the 'grey economy'. A study by Bejakovic (1995) estimates that anywhere between 16 and 27 per cent of the Croatian population is heavily involved in the 'grey economy'. Never-theless, Bartlett and Bateman show how the sector has expanded and seems set for rapid development in the near future.

By contrast, private sector development in Russia and Kazakhstan has been patchy, especially outside the main business centres of Moscow and St Petersburg (Russia) and Almaty (Kazakhstan). Part of the problem appears to be the much higher degree of risk associated with private business activities in Russia. This risk manifests itself in the conventional sense, of losing one's initial capital stake: but also in the more sinister sense of the possibility of violence and extortion by one of the rising number of criminal groups within Russian society. The changing political environment in Russia also generates unease in those thinking of going into business. There is also an endemic shortage of

---

[14] This is the argument put forward by Johnson, S. (1994) Private Business in Eastern Europe in Blanchard, O., Froot, K. and Sachs, J. (eds) *The Transition in Eastern Europe*, Vol. 2, University of Chicago Press, Chicago.

capital for small-scale private business activities in Russia and Kazakhstan. Taylor emphasizes the many problems new businesses are having accessing financial resources to support their expansion, a factor which is severely undermining the sector as a whole. Moreover, in Bruno's description of resistance to change in the prevailing Russian bureaucratic–administrative business culture, an important aspect is the general reluctance of the larger enterprises to do business with the new small-scale private sector. These features undermine the development of a small private business sector and restrict it to areas where capital requirements are minimal, the risk is small and the customer is the consumer. Hence, perhaps more than elsewhere, most small business development in Russia and Kazakhstan has involved trade and services. The Russians call it the 'kiosk economy', a reference to the fact that private sector development in Russia has become connected in the mind of the population with the multitude of small kiosks which have sprung up. However, the principle applies, to one degree or another, to the other transition economies.

In spite of the undisputed growth in the sheer numbers of small businesses throughout the transition economies, the bulk of this initial development has been in trade and services, not in manufacturing. As we noted above, the risk factor in the transition economies is critical. Entrepreneurs are extremely reluctant to commit themselves to purchasing capital equipment when market demand is still weak and changeable, where legislation and taxation systems change overnight and where greater profits can be made in other areas. The financial support institutions, especially the new commercial banking sectors, often encourage this tendency by extracting a very high rate of profit. The banks generally offer only short-term credit (typically three to six months), at high interest rates. This underlines the vital need for appropriate financial support institutions for small business.

However, the 'kiosk economy' has an important role to play in economic development in Eastern Europe. The large surpluses which accumulate in the 'kiosk economy' form a capital pool from which the next stage of economic development can be financed. Surpluses can be recycled into more sophisticated activities, including manufacturing businesses and those incorporating a higher degree of technology and innovation. This process is a common development path throughout the world[15] and it is emerging throughout Eastern Europe: several studies point to the comparatively greater success of small business in Poland

[12] For a comprehensive survey of the issues in Eastern Europe, see EBRD and CEEPN (1993) *Management and employee buy-outs in central and eastern Europe – an introduction.*

than in Hungary thanks to the greater accumulation of capital in the very substantial Polish 'grey economy'. Polish entrepreneurs used their capital to finance their transition into an officially approved line of business. Polish entrepreneurs moved very quickly from 'kiosks' into shops and new developments. Russian entrepreneurs appear to have entered commercial banking on a large scale, using the large profits made on trading in consumer goods and, usually illegally, in raw materials. Croatian householders along the Adriatic use the money made from renting out rooms to foreigners to invest in food-processing equipment to supply the renewed growth in tourism.

One of the major challenges facing Eastern European governments is how to facilitate this process – how to encourage, say, an importer to use money earned by trading to move into producing goods rather than importing them. The importer has also to be encouraged not to use his earnings to purchase western consumer goods for his own consumption.[16] According to the conventional scenario, it should be the banking system which recycles this surplus cash, allocating it to the most promising new business opportunities. This may be a possibility at a later stage, but at the moment it is an unpromising route in Eastern Europe. Since conventional credit evaluation and screening techniques were not generally required under the communist system, the longer-term lending function of commercial banks is underdeveloped. One remedy has been to establish specialist enterprise development bodies, typically with foreign assistance and advisors, to offer direct support for new small-scale private enterprise. This usually involves the provision of financial assistance such as low-interest long-term loan arrangements, and other forms of local support, such as business premises, common services, technology transfer, high quality training and so on. There are many signs that such discriminatory policy in favour of manufacturing enterprise is being implemented, especially in Poland, Hungary and the Czech Republic, where the number of traders, middle-men and speculators has reached saturation point. Slovenian business development policy appears to be focusing on more sophisticated business ventures and Croatia is following suit. In Russia and Kazakhstan, however, such a policy response is a little premature, as these states probably still have room for more traders, distributors, importers and middle-men. First, the overall rate of new private business development seems not to have been anywhere near as high as elsewhere; and, second, these emerging market economies inherited from communism a much thinner fabric of 'grey businesses' as well as an under-developed official trading and distribution system.

---

[16] It is clear that 'grey economy' earnings were one of the main sources of cash used to fund the initial surge in demand, and the continuing appetite, for western consumer goods.

The emerging business culture in Eastern Europe

One of the most significant longer term changes in Eastern Europe will be the gradual decline of the bureaucratic–administrative business culture and its replacement by a more entrepreneurial one. The bureaucratic–administrative business culture was largely a communist creation, fostered by the sometimes uneasy alliance between national and regional government and local state enterprises. Local bureaucrats and enterprise administrators worked steadily together to undertake and fulfil the targets set in the plans they were given. They preferred to encounter the least possible diversion from their appointed task, and had little time to consider other dimensions including, unfortunately, the environment, health and safety at work and so on. Yet simultaneously they attempted to ensure that the greatest possible financial benefit accrued to their region. Joint delegations would be sent to the capital to argue for special consideration or a continued subsidy or a new investment. Personnel were very often interchangeable – regional governors became enterprise directors, and vice versa.

We have described the many problems of the central planning system in an earlier chapter and in the various country studies. One of the main handicaps was the bureaucratic–administrative culture and its resistance to innovation, flexibility and change. This was not a drawback in the early days of communism: on the contrary, the plan for rapid industrialization mainly involved the development of heavy industry, for which planning and standard technical management methods were ideally suited. However, such methods became increasingly redundant from the 1970s onwards, largely for two inter-related reasons. First, the new 'sunrise' industries emerging in the western economies – electronics, computers, mass communications and so forth – involved rapid product and process change and constantly rising R&D budgets. Second, steadily rising income levels led to consumers demanding constantly changing, differentiated and higher quality products. Both of these new trends could best be met through more flexible production processes and responsive, entrepreneurial management. As a result, from the 1970s onwards, the economic and technology gulf between Eastern Europe and the west began to grow sharply. The prevailing bureaucratic–administrative culture had become a barrier to internal progress as well as to integration into the wider world.

It is clear from the foregoing chapters that the business culture in Eastern Europe is itself in a state of transition. On the one hand, in Russia and Kazakhstan, we have witnessed the continuing power and influence of the old bureaucratic–administrative culture. The introduction of private ownership and the market economy should have supported its rapid evolution into a more entrepreneurial one. Yet the old bureaucratic–administrative culture appears to be very resistant to change, and in many industries and enterprises the most striking feature is the extent to which 'business as usual' continues. The bureaucratic–administrative elite continues to place a high value on guarding its sectional interests and preserving regional privileges. It has adapted to the need for some reform and restructuring. But it has also realized that there is as much, if not more, of an opportunity to ensure survival, or to make money, through maintaining monopolistic market structures, rather than competing through increased productivity, cost-minimization, attention to quality, and so on. Where this 'rent-seeking' avenue is not open, it accepts the wisdom of returning to the central government for financial support. Ironically, the bureaucratic–administrative elite has learned lessons from major western investors, such as General Motors in Poland and Volkswagen in the Czech Republic, who demanded from the host government the imposition of trade restraints to ensure their dominance on the domestic market. The prevailing bureaucratic–administrative culture thus continues to delay extensive reforms to the industrial sector and to seek favours and protection from government whenever possible. According to Aslund (1995), the most entrenched bureaucratic–administrative elite is in Russia, where it was responsible for throwing off course the entire reform programme of the Gaidar government, when it demanded and received subsidies which should not have been made available. Thus, though we may say that the prevailing bureaucratic–administrative culture has been forced into some changes, in general private ownership and reform has not had as much effect upon it as had been widely hoped: if anything, it has pushed managers into rationalizing and exploring new types of inefficiency and corruption.[17]

Economic reform and the growth of the new private sector *has* resulted, on the other hand, in a new entrepreneurial business culture taking shape at the grass roots level throughout the more advanced transition economies of Central Europe, including the former Yugoslav republics of Croatia and Slovenia. This new entrepreneurial business culture was strengthened by the enormous growth in small private businesses and entrepreneurial activities at the beginning of the 1990s. It was influenced in a small way by the return of the diaspora emigres from the west, as well as by foreign individuals, enterprises and institutions. The entrepreneurial class that has emerged has succeeded in defining a new business culture in Central European societies, in parallel to the bureaucratic–administrative culture. What is more important, established bureaucratic–administrative elites are yielding to the pressure for change. This process has not taken place without opposition from the bureaucratic–administrative elite, which feels threatened by the 'new way of doing

---

[17] It could be argued, of course, that such rent-seeking behaviour is actually a positive phenomenon, since it is the only way to generate the seed capital necessary to underpin the restructuring of the enterprise.

things' – a way of managing an enterprise that accepts change, flexibility, personal responsibility and corporate risk. These factors remain anathema to many.

A popular concern raised in connection with the emerging entrepreneurial culture, and sometimes used as a stick with which to beat it, is its widely perceived association with criminality and corruption. The first point to be made is that it is arguable whether the entrepreneurial sector is alone in this regard: many studies reveal widespread corruption among managers in large state-owned or private enterprises in both Eastern and Western Europe. Second, we could argue that entrepreneurial activities have been affected, much more than activities in the large enterprises, by the enormous economic dislocation and disruption in the transition economies. Most entrepreneurs were forced at first to operate on the margins of legality if they were to survive since they had few sources of finance to tap: the banks and other sources of government cash tended to remain the 'captives' of the large enterprises. Third, in the still highly distorted economies of Eastern Europe some entrepreneurs can make enormous sums of money quite legally, but they are still suspected of having done so by dubious means. However, it is true that the entrepreneurial culture has become tainted with charges of profiteering, price-gouging, fast practices, speculation, tax-evasion and, especially in Russia, with violence and criminality – the *mafiya* culture. For the vast majority of the population in East European societies, for example the industrial or blue-collar workers, who fared comparatively well under the old system, the new entrepreneurial culture represents something of a threat.

So, is the emerging entrepreneurial culture one reason for the current East European malaise, a malaise which has been accompanied in several of the countries under consideration by an upsurge of support for reformed communist parties? While corruption has indeed emerged as one of the major problems in Eastern Europe, it may well not represent the over-arching problem some consider it to be. It has been argued that while the criminalization of business activity is regrettable, it may be an inevitable stage of business development. In the United States in the mid-nineteenth century, the prevailing business culture was infused with criminality and sharp practice and consumers were forced to pay attention to the maxim *'caveat emptor'*.[18] The Chicago of the 1930s was a violent and gangster infested city, where fortunes were amassed by threat, coercion, violence and widespread corruption. It too was seen as a nightmare vision of the future.[19] However, over time the American business culture changed, becoming more sophisticated, ethical, professional and consumer-friendly, mirroring the changes taking place in American society.

[18] 'Let the buyer beware'.

[19] Moscow is often referred to as its modern-day equivalent.

Already there is evidence that the first stage in a similar evolution has begun in Eastern Europe, particularly in the Central European countries. Organizations such as chambers of private capital, entrepreneurs' associations, university business schools, multinational corporations, western consultancies and legal practices are establishing more civilized 'rules of the game', which are being taken up by indigenous businesses and entrepreneurs.

Conclusion

The preceding analysis and the individual chapters indicate that the rapid journey towards the market economy has been an uncomfortable one. However, it can be concluded that it has been a useful journey and that all the countries we have considered have made progress in constructing a market economy. One feature which has emerged strongly has been the use of both the shock therapy and gradualist approach in individual countries, rather than the exclusive use of one or the other. The most common manifestation of this in practice was the use of shock therapy in the monetary sphere and gradualism in terms of an industrial policy. Typically, the former was a quick fix against rapidly accelerating inflation, whereas the latter was seen as a more humane approach to dealing with the problems of privatization, inefficient enterprises and the possibility of closures and redundancies. Perhaps it is the case that there can be no one, straightforward policy approach to such a complicated process as moving from communism to a market economy.

Notwithstanding the progress made in the countries covered, there is much that needs to be done before the pain of the last few years can be put into perspective. The transition must now turn away from the destruction of the central planning system, and towards the creation and strengthening of market institutions and processes which have emerged so far. The emerging business culture must be encouraged to develop along the path to an understanding of entrepreneurship, and the responsibilities and rewards which flow from private ownership. It would be premature to say, however, that economic planning and government intervention have no useful role to play in future. On the contrary, we may infer from the experience of many of the most successful post-Second World War economies and regions, such as Japan, Germany, East Asia and northern Italy, that such factors still have an important role to play: the difference is that these newer forms of planning and creative intervention are of the sort which support the operation of the market, as opposed to the old systems in Eastern Europe which attempted to replace it.

The next stage of the transition in Eastern Europe will present more of an opportunity to prepare for the future, instead of having to dispose of the past. The governments of Eastern Europe will be able to choose from a wider range of options and possibilities with which to construct a modern society. After the pain associated with the collapse of communism, compounded by the disruption brought about by the subsequent rebuilding of their societies, it is to be hoped that they will be successful in their endeavours.

Acknowledgements

Thanks to Neil Malcolm, George Blazyca and Martin Dangerfield for their helpful comments on this chapter. I am grateful to the EBRD and to *Business Central Europe* for permission to use their data.

References and suggestions for further reading

Amsden, A., Kochanowicz, J. and Taylor, L. (1994) *The Market Meets its Match: Restructuring the Economies of Eastern Europe.* Harvard University Press.

Aslund, A. (1995) *How Russia became a market economy.* Brookings.

Barr, N. (ed.) (1994) *Labor markets and social policy in Central and Eastern Europe.* Oxford University Press.

Bejakovic, V. (1995) Research report. National Bureau for Macroeconomic Analysis and Forecasting, Zagreb.

Boeri, T. (1994) 'Transitional' unemployment. *Economics of Transition*, Vol. 2 (1), pp. 1–25.

EBRD (various years) *Transition Report Update.* EBRD, London.

EBRD and CEEPN (1993) *Management and employee buy-outs in central and eastern Europe – an introduction.* EBRD, London.

Gros, D. and Steinherr, A. (1995) *Winds of Change: Economic transition in Central and Eastern Europe.* Longman, London.

Hanson, P. (1993) Local power and market reform in Russia. *Communist Economies and Economic Transformation*, Vol. 5, No. 1.

International Labour Organization (1995) *World Employment 1995.* ILO, Geneva.

Jackman, R. and Rutkowski, M. (1994) Labor markets: Wages and Employment, in Barr, N. (ed.) (1994) *Labor markets and social policy in Central and Eastern Europe.* Oxford University Press.

Rodrik, D. (1993) Making sense of the Soviet trade shock in Eastern Europe: a framework and some estimates, in *Eastern Europe in Transition: from recession to growth?* M. Blejer, G. Calvo, F. Coricelli and A. Gelb, World Bank Discussion Paper, No. 196.

Rollo, J. and Stern, N. (1992) *Perspectives on trade and growth in Central and Eastern Europe.* National Economic Research Associates, London.

Williamson, J. (1994) *The Political Economy of Policy Reform.* Institute for International Economics, Washington DC.

Index